BAVARIA

£2.50

Other books by James Bentley

Albert Schweitzer
Alsace
Between Marx and Christ
The Blue Guide to Germany and Berlin
A Calendar of Saints
A Children's Bible
Dare to be Wise: A History of the Manchester Grammar School
A Guide to the Dordogne
A Guide to Tuscany
Languedoc
Life and Food in the Dordogne
The Loire
Martin Niemöller
Normandy
Oberammergau and the Passion Play
The Rhine
Ritualism and Politics in Victorian Britain
Secrets of Mount Sinai
Umbria
Weekend Cities

BAVARIA

James Bentley

AURUM PRESS

First published 1990 by Aurum Press Limited,
33 Museum Street, London WC1A 1LD
Copyright © 1990 by James Bentley

Map by Richard Natkiel Associates
Decorative illustration by Joy FitzSimmons

The author and publishers are grateful to the
following for permission to reproduce illustrations:
Colorific!, nos 4, 9 (Alan Clifton), 6, 8 (D. and J. Heaton);
Feature-Pix, no. 10; Robert Harding Picture Library, nos 1
(Nigel Blythe), 5; Spectrum Colour Library, no. 3; Zefa
Picture Library (UK) Ltd, nos 2, 7.

British Library Cataloguing in Publication Data

Bentley, James 1937–
Bavaria.
1. West Germany. Bavaria. Visitors' guides
I. Title
914.3'304878

ISBN 1 85410 103 X

Typeset by Wyvern Typesetting Ltd, Bristol
Printed in Great Britain by The Bath Press, Avon

Contents

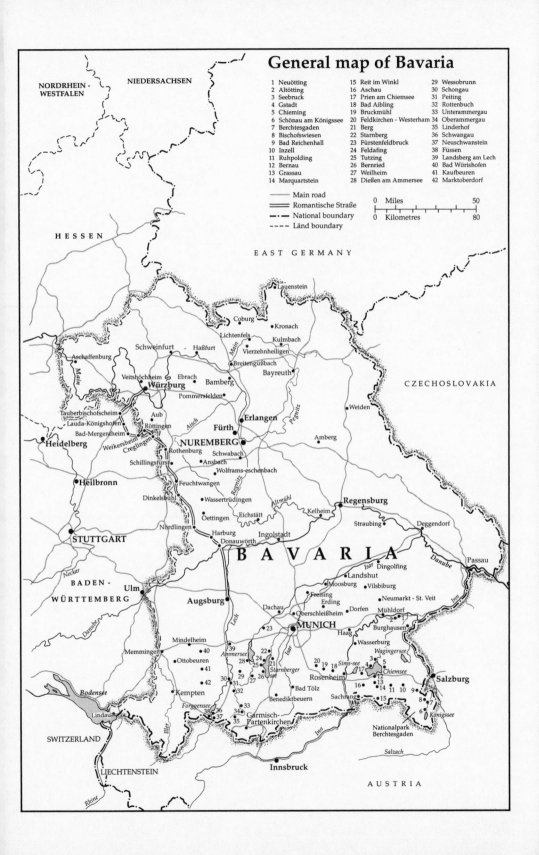

General map of Bavaria

1 Neuötting
2 Altötting
3 Seebruck
4 Gstadt
5 Chieming
6 Schönau am Königssee
7 Berchtesgaden
8 Bischofswiesen
9 Bad Reichenhall
10 Inzell
11 Ruhpolding
12 Bernau
13 Grassau
14 Marquartstein

15 Reit im Winkl
16 Aschau
17 Prien am Chiemsee
18 Bad Aibling
19 Bruckmühl
20 Feldkirchen - Westerham
21 Berg
22 Starnberg
23 Fürstenfeldbruck
24 Feldafing
25 Tutzing
26 Bernried
27 Weilheim
28 Dießen am Ammersee

29 Wessobrunn
30 Schongau
31 Peiting
32 Rottenbuch
33 Unterammergau
34 Oberammergau
35 Linderhof
36 Schwangau
37 Neuschwanstein
38 Füssen
39 Landsberg am Lech
40 Bad Wörishofen
41 Kaufbeuren
42 Marktoberdorf

—— Main road
≡≡≡ Romantische Straße
—·—· National boundary
----- Länd boundary

Miles 0 ... 50
Kilometres 0 ... 80

NORDRHEIN-WESTFALEN
NIEDERSACHSEN
HESSEN
EAST GERMANY
CZECHOSLOVAKIA

Lauenstein
Coburg
Kronach
Lichtenfels
Kulmbach
Schweinfurt
Haßfurt
Vierzehnheiligen
Breitengüßbach
Bayreuth
Aschaffenburg
Main
Veitshöchheim
Ebrach
Würzburg
Bamberg
Pommersfelden
Weiden
Tauberbischofsheim
Aub
Lauda-Königshofen
Röttingen
Erlangen
Fürth
Bad-Mergentheim
Weikersheim
Creglingen
NUREMBERG
Heidelberg
Rothenburg
Schwabach
Schillingsfürst
Ansbach
Amberg
Wolframs-eschenbach
Heilbronn
Feuchtwangen
Dinkelsbühl
Wassertrüdingen
Altmühl
Regensburg
Oettingen
Eichstätt
Kelheim
Nördlingen
Harburg
Ingolstadt
Straubing
Deggendorf
Donauwörth
STUTTGART
BAVARIA
Neckar
Danube
Passau
Isar
Dingolfing
Landshut
BADEN-WÜRTTEMBERG
Moosburg
Vilsbiburg
Ulm
Danube
Freising
Erding
Neumarkt - St. Veit
Augsburg
Dachau
Dorfen
Mühldorf
Inn
Oberschleißheim
Burghausen
Lech
23
MUNICH
Haag
Mindelheim
Wasserburg
40
39
Ammersee
22
Wagingersee
Memmingen
28
24
21
Ottobeuren
25
20 19 18
Sims-see
3 5
41
26
27
Chiemsee
42
30
29
Starnberger See
Rosenheim
12
13
Kempten
31
32
14 11 10 9
Salzburg
Bodensee
Bad Tölz
16
8
Forggensee
33
15
7
Lindau
38 36
34
Benediktbeuern
Sachrang
Königssee
37
35
Garmisch-Partenkirchen
SWITZERLAND
Nationalpark Berchtesgaden
Salzach
LIECHTENSTEIN
Innsbruck
AUSTRIA
Rhine
Iller
Isar
Pegnitz
Aisch
Regnitz
Tauber

General map of Bengal

Preface

Bavaria is so rich – in churches, history, food and drink, in great cities, small villages, magnificent scenery and the gift for merriment – that the notion of writing about it has challenged me for many years. The scenery is remarkably varied. Some of the regions of Bavaria are lush and green but never far from mountains. Rivers and lakes have scooped their way through the land. Parts of Bavaria are devoted to beer, other parts equally to wine. Its history is likewise complex. It is hard to take in the facts that Bavaria did not achieve its present size until the Napoleonic era and was not fully integrated into Germany until 1920.

In writing this book I decided to offer my readers tours. Each of my chapters bursts out into them, pausing at times for refreshment, a reflection on history and literature, or to visit museums and art galleries, but essentially pursuing routes which, in my experience, will entrance the historian, the artist and the *bon vivant* that is every tourist.

In no way do I claim to have described every hamlet in Bavaria. My more modest claim is that, having read and followed the suggestions of my book, a visitor to this magical region will recognize as an old friend any church, castle, *Winstube*, river or glass of white wine.

For help in researching this book I should particularly like to thank

Frau Agatha Suess of the German National Tourist Office at 65 Curzon Street, London W1Y 7PE, and also the director of the tourist office, Herr Günter Nischwitz.

My thanks are next due to Air Europe, which so conveniently takes one back and forth from Britain to Munich.

Frau Gabriele Tandler, of the Hotel zur Post, Altötting, was especially kind to me. So were Herr Mandeet and Frau Gabriele Cheema of the Hotel Luitpold am See, Prien. I learned much from, and enormously enjoyed, the hospitality of Herr Geiger of the Hotel Geiger in Berchtesgaden. I am also particularly grateful for the help I received from Frau Gabi Deml and Frau Sabine Kruis of the Berchtesgaden tourist office. As well as making clear what I learned from them, my book will reveal my indebtedness to Dipl. -Ing. Klaus Wiesner of the Yachthotel, Chiemsee. I have a long-standing debt to the Familie Rückert of Oberlaimbach, and I must also thank Herr Florian Schmidt, director of the Chiemgauer Hof at Inzell.

Mandy Greenfield of Aurum Press has been the extremely patient editor of this book. Finally, may I express my gratitude to Frau Berti Aschenauer of the Tourist Board of Bavaria, along with the extremely entertaining promoter of all things Bavarian, Herr Raimond Eberle, who once appeared in London in *Lederhosen* (a rare sight), gave me many tips and apologized to me for not wearing a feathered Bavarian hat.

James Bentley
SEPTEMBER 1989

Bavaria's glittering capital

I first visited Munich because a friend was jilted in love. In spite of his lack of German he had been successfully wooing a dark-haired beauty from that city. She returned home and instantly fell for an American airforce pilot. Tearfully he begged me, as a German-speaker, to come with him to win her back.

We lost her, but I much enjoyed the remarkable experience of witnessing a city resolutely pulling itself out of the colossal destruction of World War II.

My friend and I lived, appropriately enough, in the Bunker Hotel (does it still exist?). Each day he would call on his lost love and I would wander around a city consisting mostly of rubble. In the vestibule of the cathedral I saw for the first time the Devil's footprint, implanted in a slab on the floor. Legend has it that the architect of this Frauenkirche, Jörg von Halspach, wagered with Satan that he could build a windowless church. Plant your own foot in the Devil's footprint, and – so it was said – you would see not a single cathedral window. In truth, that year there were none to see. The Frauenkirche, was a bombed-out shell.

What did survive in that post-war year was the city's irrepressible vivacity. I shall never forget the pleasure I derived each evening – my poor companion forlornly beseeching his faithless lady to return to his arms – in eating white sausages, boiled in pans in the railway station restaurant, and cleansing my throat in between mouthfuls with vast quantities of beer.

The million and a half citizens of Munich relish beer as much as I do, and indeed the city is best known to foreigners for its *Oktoberfest*, when an astonishing 4 million litres of beer are downed on the Theresienwiese. At 11.00 on the last Saturday of September carriages rumble through the streets, with politicians, brewers and ample women waving from them at the crowds. The Oberbürgermeister broaches the first barrel of the *Oktoberfest* (or *Wies'n*, as the citizens themselves call it), and cannons announce that the festival has begun.

Pranksters and riflemen, brass bands and the Munich Kindl, a boy riding a horse, lead 7,000 people in a procession to the Theresienwiese, the meadow so named after Princess Therese von Sachsen-Hildburghausen, whose marriage to Crown-Prince Ludwig I of Bavaria was celebrated here in October 1810. This is the reason for the festival, which has been indulged in annually since that time, though few perhaps know the reason and fewer care. It lasts for sixteen days. In the evening each day begins again. The Ferris wheel and the roller-coaster spin, and heads spin faster. Hordes of amiably inebriated Bavarians join their foreign guests in wandering (or staggering) through the fairground and into one of thirteen massive beer tents, singing and drinking and bawling to the oom-pah-pah of brass bands until the lights go down half an hour before midnight. The quantity of sausages, chicken, salt fish and *Sauerkraut* consumed almost matches the intake of beer.

This is not in fact the only beer festival in which the citizens of Munich delight. Each March they indulge in a celebration of strong ale (the *Starkbierfest*) and in May they hold another one known as the *Maibock*. Thanks to an enlightened decree promulgated in 1516 by a Bavarian duke, Bavarian beer remains protected by a law allowing only the purest water, barley and hops to be used as its ingredients. The result is splendid beer and, during the *Oktoberfest*, amazing drunkenness.

Nor are these the sole opportunities for carnal merriment in this great city. Often such merriment is blessed by the Church. *Fasching* is one such occasion, supposedly a last moment of indulgence before Lent begins. In truth in Munich it begins on 7 January and carries on until Ash Wednesday. The principal spectacles and festivities take place on the Sunday before Lent and are held betgween Karlstor and Marienplatz. On Shrove Tuesday a similarly raucous affair, presided over by Church and State alike, takes place in the Viktualienmarkt. A *Fasching* prince is elected; he chooses his own princess; and the flying feet of their subjects dance the night away. Corpus Christi (*Fronleichnam*) brings out the churches in force, with religious processions adding their own Bavarian colour to the city, as do the celebrations in the Marienplatz on the second Sunday after Whitsun. August is the month of Munich's *Festspielzeit*, with special operas, concerts, ballet and theatre performances. And during Advent the *Christkindlmarkt* invades the Marienplatz.

All these traditions befit a capital city; but nothing in Munich is remotely as ancient as much of the rest of Bavaria. As we have seen, even the *Oktoberfest* dates only from the marriage celebrations of 1810. The first *Fasching* prince was elected only in 1894. Munich itself first appears in history only in the twelfth century, when Henry the Lion decided to fortify a monastic village here and cast a bridge over the River Isar in order to exploit the salt trade. Profits from salt attracted the Wittelsbach family, who took control of the village over a century later. Munich did not receive its town charter until Ludwig II granted one in 1253. For centuries the seat of the local bishop was not Munich but nearby Freising. Finally, in 1506 Duke Wilhelm IV made this city the capital of Bavaria. His successor, Albrecht V, founded the court library at Munich and during his twenty-nine-year reign encouraged a considerable number of foreign artists and musicians to settle here.

In 1623 Duke Maximilian I was elevated to the status of an Elector, only to be ousted by the Protestant champion King Gustavus Adolphus of Sweden nine years later. The Thirty Years War and the plagues that accompanied it were by now taking their melancholy toll. Munich did not recover her spirit until Prince Max II Emanuel acceded to the throne in 1679. Unwise enough to side with the French during the War of the Spanish Succession, he had the misfortune to lose Bavaria to the Austrians during the conflict, and the good fortune to regain it at the peace treaty. He also brought back with him a skilled artist named Joseph Effner, whose work still provides a thrill as you encounter it in Max II Emanuel's former realms.

Even so, Munich became a university city only in 1726, the last year of his reign. In consequence many of its glories are eighteenth- and nineteenth-century masterpieces, including the superb neo-classical buildings, squares and boulevards that burst out of the medieval city walls under the patronage of King Maximilian I and his successor Ludwig I. Ludwig's reign began in 1825 and ended in abdication twenty-three years later when his relationship with the Mexican dancer Lola Montez became a public scandal. Yet he is justly regarded as the second founder of the city. A new era of expansion began after the drowning of King Ludgwig II in 1886, when Prince Luitpold, regent for Ludwig's lunatic brother, patronized new architects, who created Prinzregentenstraße and built the city museum.

With its splendid metro systems and speedy tramcars, you do not really need to walk around Munich, but walking is the best way to explore this city. Since most visitors will arrive by air, taking the fast airport bus, which usually reaches the main railway station in fifteen minutes, this is probably the best place to start a tour of the inner city. It should be followed in leisurely fashion, punctuated by regular beers of the kind I have already mentioned, perhaps accompanied by the *Weißwürste* I ate so long ago on the railway station, or a *Leberkäs* – famously, neither liver nor cheese, but a blend of minced pork and beef spiced with nutmeg and marjoram. I prefer it hot.

Take Luisenstraße, which leads north-east from the main railway station, and you will plunge straight into nineteenth-century monumental architecture of a most impressive kind. Please follow me now for a tour of the city which will incorporate such masterpieces, medieval, baroque and rococo churches, cool gardens and some of the greatest art galleries in the world.

If you turn right from Luisenstraße into Karlstraße you reach almost immediately the basilica of St Bonifaz, which Georg Friedrich Ziebland built between 1835 and 1847. Its style is Romanesque because King Ludwig I had sent its architect to Italy to study early Christian architecture. Do look inside at Ludgwig's own tomb, for this was the king who did much to create the delights which are to come on our tour. Then continue up Luisenstraße, walking alongside the old botanical garden, which Ludwig von Sckell laid out in the early years of the nineteenth century. (It is called the 'old' or Alter Botanischer Garten so as to distinguish it from the later one, which is crammed with orchids, Alpine flora and rhododendrons and was laid out near the Nymphenburg Park just before World War I.) Though totally remodelled in the 1930s, the old botanical garden has kept its dinky neo-classical entrances, the work of Emanuel Josef von Herigoyen in 1812.

Beyond it is the monumental Königsplatz. The north-west end of this square is closed by the Propylaean, built for Ludwig I by Leo von Klenze between 1854 and 1862. 'Propylean' was the name of the west entrance to the Acropolis in Greece, and Ludwig's plan in copying it for Bavaria was to commemorate the fact that his second son Otto had been King of Greece since 1832. In the sculptures on the pediment you can make out the people of Greece swearing allegiance to this young Bavarian princeling who had come to rule them. Two other sides of Königsplatz are flanked by the city's museum of antiquity (the Staatliche Antikensammlung), built between 1838 and 1848, its eight Corinthian columns splendidly matched by the eight Doric columns at the entrance of the museum of antique sculpture, the Glypothek, which von Klenze designed to occupy the other side. The Antiken-sammlung is packed with magical Greek, Etruscan and Roman vases, bronzes and jewellery, and the Glypothek with major works of sculpture from the same era; but we have no time to espy them now.

Turn right here along Briennerstraße to the junction of Meiserstraße and Arcistraße, and immediately you are in the centre of a complex of superb galleries. To explore the Staatliche Graphische Sammlung at 10 Meiserstraße; the Alte Pinakothek at 27 Barerstraße, which Leo von Klenze built in the 1820s and 1830s in the shape of a Venetican classical home for the Wittelsbachs' art collection; and the Neue Pinakothek at 29 Barerstraße, commissioned by Ludwig I as a gallery of contemporary works of art, would be entrancing and would stretch this stroll through Munich to a couple of weeks.

I suggest visiting them later. Instead, walk south-west along Barerstraße to Karolinenplatz, where in 1833 Ludwig I erected an obelisk in memory of 3,000 Bavarian soldiers killed defending their country against Russia. Crossing Karolinenplatz to examine this monument more closely, I was almost killed myself by a swift, silent Munich tram.

Max-Joseph-Straße leads from here to the long, rectangular tree-shaded Maximiliansplatz. The trees keep the sun off the mute stone heads of statues of such long-forgotten worthies as someone named Pettenkofer, sculpted by the equally long-forgotten Wilhelm von Rümmer in 1909, whose statue is coldly regarded by that of a more gifted man, the chemist, agronomist and physiologist Julius Liebig.

His statue was set up here by his friends in 1883. Properly, too, here stands a statue of the creator of these gardens, Karl von Effner. If you turn left out of Max-Joseph-Straße along Maximiliansplatz, you will soon see on your left a little square surrounding the Norwenbrunnen, a fountain created by Hubert Netzner in 1907. Here on two successive hot days I once saw a lady bathing her grateful dog in one of the three pools, and the next day a coach party of football fans draw up and for some reason drop one of the party in the water.

At the far end of the park you find a romantic-looking statue of Schiller, sculpted by Ferdinand Miller, who was commissioned by Ludwig II in 1863. The poet and dramatist looks out across Briennerstraße, on the other side of which rises the elegant façade of the Almeida-Palais, built in the classical style by Métivier in 1824.

The shady Maximiliansplatz should tempt you to stroll back as far as Max-Joseph-Straße to find, immediately opposite across the park, an ornamental classical gateway which leads into Prannerstraße. Among its luxuriously expensive antique shops is the Palais Gise (No. 17 on the right-hand side), elaborately pink and white and created around 1760 by Karl Albert von Lespilliez. Close by stands the Palais Sensheim, with a sinuous rococo façade by an architect whose name has been forgotten.

Munich continually threads its elegant shops and its baroque and rococo palaces with modern and equally enticing treats. One of these is the Siemens museum, standing on the opposite side of Prannerstraße from the Palais Gies and the Palais Sensheim. It opens from 09.00 to 16.00 on weekdays and from 10.00 to 14.00 at weekends, to reveal a treasure store of ancient and modern technology. Siemens & Co. is today an immensely profitable energy, communications and electrical engineering company with branches in over 120 countries. Almost half of its business comes from outside the German Federal Republic. This excellently mounted exhibition traces the company's history from the beginning under Werner von Siemens, whose first patent – for a method of galvanized gold-leafing – was acquired in 1842, to the present day. Ancient and modern telephones, electric trams, the electric telegraph, beautifully appointed old motor cars in pristine condition, galvanometers of today and yesterday, evocative photographs of factories and happy workers, the steamer *Faraday* laying the first transatlantic cable from Ireland to North America in 1874, today's satellite stations: after seeing all these intriguing exhibits

I reeled out almost believing in progress.

Then come two more lovely glimpses of the achievements of the past, for on the same side of Prannerstraße rises the rococo Palais Preysing, which François Cuvilliés the elder built in the eighteenth century, followed (just round the corner on the right in Kardinal-Faulhaber-Straße) by the Palais Porcia, commissioned in the 1690s from Enrico Zucalli by the Fuggers, the greatest merchants of the late Middle Ages. You could be forgiven for supposing that Zucalli had somehow anticipated the rococo of Cuvilliés, but the truth is that the façade is a later addition, by Cuvilliés himself. The name Porcia derives from the married name of a countess whom Elector Karl Albrecht had taken as mistress and installed in the former palace of the Fuggers.

Walk back along Kardinal-Faulhaber-Straße to spot the house where the archbishops of Munich have lived since 1818, its rich Cuvilliés façade made even richer by my second favourite architect, Johann Baptist Zimmermann. At the end of Kardinal-Faulhaber-Straße you now see the unmistakable six-storey, late-Gothic spire of the Salvatorkirche. This dark-red brick church was built in 1494 by Lukas Rottaler, the Munich city architect, as a cemetery chapel attached to the cathedral. Greek Orthodox Christians have worshipped here since 1829. On a Sunday, even if you are not Greek Orthodox, it is worth while slipping quietly inside to hear for a while the rich voices of the priests chanting the Orthodox liturgy, to revel in their sumptuous vestments and in the icons that line the church walls and separate the people from the Holy of Holies, and to relish the savour of incense.

Make your way east from Salvatorplatz to Theatinerstraße to find the Theatinerkirche, or parish church of St Cajetan, which was built for Theatine monks as a thanks offering for the birth in 1662 of Crown-Prince Max Emanuel, heir to the throne and son of the Electress Henrietta Adelaide. Suddenly Munich surprises us. Here is a quarter inspired by Italy. The Theatinerkirche, the work of Agostino Barelli (and finished by his compatriot Enrico Zucalli, architect of the dome and the towers) was modelled on the church of S. Andrea della Valle in Rome. The marble figures on the façade (Saints Cajetan, Adelheid, Ferdinand and Maximilian) are by Antonio Boos, another Roman. The Italian stuccoist Nicolo Petri decorated the interior in the mid-1680s, and Carlo Cignani painted the 'Holy Family' for the Lady

Chapel. But the atmosphere of Bavarian rococo in the end prevails, even though François Cuvilliés, who built the rococo façade in 1765–8, was really a Walloon.

Slightly further south across Theatinerstraße, Munich becomes Italian again. The Feldherrnhalle (Hall of the Generals), built by Andreas Gärtner in the early 1840s, was inspired by the Loggia dei Lanzi in Florence. The generals in question are Count Tilly, who commanded the Bavarians during the Thirty Years War, and Prince Wrede, hero of the campaign against the French in 1814, both commemorated by bronze statues designed by Ludwig Schwanthaler. Between them is a memorial to the Bavarian dead of the Franco-Prussian War of 1870–1. To remind us that we are still in Munich rather than Florence, the rococo Palais Preysing now appears, built in the 1720s by Joseph Effner for Graf Maximilian von Preysing.

Theatinerstraße, as you stroll down it to turn right into Maffeistraße, is filled with more elegant clothes shops, shoe shops and art dealers. Beware: though pedestrianized, Maffeistraße still admits trams. It leads under the archway of the Bayerische Vereinsbank into slender Promenadeplatz. Here Ludwig I in 1839 erected the statue of the Dutch composer Orlando di Lasso. Eleven years later, as if he doubted his own patriotism, he set up the statue of another composer, this time the German Christoph Willibald von Gluck. Finally, in 1861, musicians were abandoned altogether, and between the two composers now stands the statue of Max Emanuel, Kurfürst von Bayern, and liberator of Belgrade, looking very much like Errol Flynn playing one of the Three Musketeers. He faces the delicious pale-yellow Gunetzrhainerhaus, a home which the court architect J. B. Gunetzrhainer built for himself in 1733.

From Promenadeplatz, Pacellistraße leads to Bavaria's oldest baroque church, the mid-seventeenth-century Carmelite church (which is now deconsecrated, turned into a library and hence difficult to visit and enjoy). The Italianate Dreifaltigkeitskirche (or Holy Trinity Church) just across Pacellistraße is adequate compensation, an Italian baroque masterpiece designed by Giovanni Antonio Viscardi and built by his followers in 1718. A genius named Cosmos Damian Asam frescoed the dome. In the gable is a triumphant statue of St Michael. Look out also for the fine tabernacle on the high altar, the work of Johann Baptist Straub; and note, too, the influence here of a Spanish saint, Teresa of Avila, who repeatedly appears in the decoration of this lovely church (for this is also a Carmelite church and she is the heroine of the Carmelite order).

If you continue west along Pacellistraße, you reach Lembachplatz and turn south-west to reach the heart of the city, which begins at Karlsplatz, although no one in Munich calls this square by that name. Even the underground dubs its station the 'Stachus' as well as Karlsplatz. The nickname indicates the perennial influence of beer and hunting lodges in Munich, for 'Stachus' was what everyone called Eustachius Föderl, who ran such a lodge here in the early eighteenth century. His lodge then stood outside the city walls. Fifty years later Elector Karl Theodor had these walls demolished, filled in the moat and substituted a square named after himself. Stubbornly the beer-drinking successors of his subjects ignore the Elector and remember their former innkeeper.

The city courts of justice stand to the north side of the square, built in the late nineteenth century in the late Renaissance style by an architect named Friedrich Thiersch. Nearby is another delightful and tiny gateway to the former botanical gardens, set up by Emanuel Josef von Herigoyen in 1812 and leading into the quiet park. And here I always need a rest.

Elector Karl Theodor did not tear down the city gate that had stood on the south-east side of Karlsplatz since 1302, and it stands here today, though considerably re-Gothicized in subsequent rebuildings. Fronted by a powerful modern fountain, Karlstor leads into the lively and traffic-free Neuhauserstraße.

The glories of Neuhauserstraße begin with a magnificient church known as the Bürgersaal, designed by the same Viscardi responsible for the Dreifaltigskeitskirche and again built by one of his pupils (he deserves naming: Georg Ettenhofer). Since the church is dedicated to the Blessed Virgin Mary, Andreas Faistenberger was commissioned to sculpt a Madonna on a crescent moon which stands over the doorway. Faistenberger also created the higher altar, over which he set an 'Annunciation', which is marvellously asymmetrical, the angel almost overpowering the Virgin Mary in her humility. The interior is astonishingly airy, with eighteenth-century frescos by Johann Anton Gump, a baroque oratory, and under the organ angels by Ignaz Günther. Fourteen oil paintings by Franz Joachim Bleich represent Bavarian pilgrimage sites dedicated to the Virgin Mary. The mid-eighteenth-century statues by Ignaz Günther are extremely entertaining as well as elegant, that of an angel leading a little boy being justly famous. (The lad wears a woolly cap, the angel a richly tasselled golden and blue robe.)

A more sombre note is provided by the tomb of Father Rupert Mayer, military chaplain in World War I until he was invalided with an amputated leg. As a Jesuit priest in Munich, Mayer soon became the leading light in the charitable Caritas organization. In 1936 his superior, Cardinal Faulhaber, wrote, 'Wherever Father Mayer is, there the churches are full.' And, like the cardinal, Mayer was a convinced anti-Nazi. As early as 1923 he had openly proclaimed, 'No German Catholic can ever be a National Socialist.'

When the Nazis came to power he was a marked man. Banned from 'speaking', he continued to 'preach', so on 28 May 1937 he was specifically banned from preaching too. He rejected the ban. On 5 June the Gestapo arrested the priest. Release under a general amnesty was but a prelude to re-arrest as war broke out in 1939. Father Rupert Mayer was taken to Sachsenhausen concentration camp near Berlin, and although he was later moved to a cell at Ettal Abbey, his health was gradually broken, and when the war ended he returned to Munich simply to die. Pope John Paul II beatified him in 1987.

The Bürgersaal is a Jesuit church, and nearby (at No. 51 Neuhauserstraße) they built what is now known as the Alte Akademie in the late sixteenth century to serve as a school and seminary. In front of its orderly Renaissance façade stands a far from orderly fountain, devoted to the composer Richard Strauss, and in particular his opera *Salome*. Hans Wimmer, who sculpted the fountain in bas-relief in 1962, obviously relished the notoriously salacious ingredients of Strauss's masterpiece. As Arnold Bax wrote, the first performance in 1905 presented 'a quite horrifying Herod, slobbering with lust, and apparently almost decomposing before our disgusted but fascinated eyes'. At that performance the soprano playing Salome refused to perform the dance of the seven veils and a professional dancer was engaged as a lascivious stand-in. All this depravity culminates in Salome's ecstasy before the severed head of John the Baptist, crazily kissing his dead lips with her own. All this depravity, it seems to me, Hans Wimmer has sculpted on his fountain in peaceful Neuhauserstraße, Munich.

Immediately east in Neuhauserstraße stands the church of St Michael, built for the Jesuits by Duke Wilhelm in the late sixteenth century and designed by Wendel Dietrich and Wolfgang Müller. The gable carries the scene of Jesus Christ presiding over Otto's victory at the Lech in 955, with portraits of successive emperors and dukes of Bavaria, including that of the founder of the church. (The carving of Duke Wilhelm is third from the right in the second row of figures, holding a model of the church.) Between the main doors a bronze Archangel Michael slays the dragon, the work of Hubert Gerhardt in 1592. The inside of the church is roofed by a massive Renaissance barrel-vault, sheltering ten altars, including Wendel Dietrich's splendid high altar. One touching note is the 1830 memorial to Eugène de Beauharnais, Napoleon's stepson, by the Danish sculptor Bertel Thorwaldsen. No fewer than forty dead Wittelsbachs, rulers of Bavaria for over 700 years, lie in the vault.

East of St Michael's church is the former Augustinerkirche (Neuhauserstraße 53). An Augustinian monastery church was built here in the 1290s, on a site which then lay outside the city walls. Enlarged in the fourteenth, fifteenth and seventeenth centuries, it was deconsecrated in 1803. Its walls now shelter tobacconists, coffee and cake shops, the vendors of perfume and watches. It also houses the Museum of Hunting and Fishing, which opens daily between 09.30 and 17.00 from May to October. A couple of bronze denizens grace the pavement outside; a stuffed bear welcomes you inside (with a notice pinned to his chest asking you not to touch or harm him).

Augustinerstraße curves gracefully to the left into Frauenplatz, where rises the cathedral and city parish church of Our Lady, Munich's Frauenkirche, in front of which stands a fountain constructed in 1972 from blocks of granite by Bernhard Winkler. Before building its new parish church the citizens of Munich had to pull down a Romanesque church that had stood here since 1271. Duke Sigismund laid the first stone of the present, late-Gothic brick basilica in 1468. The architect was Jörg von Halspach (known as Ganghofer), replaced after his death in 1488 by Lukas Rottaler. Their church was finished within twenty years, though the cupolas on the towers were added only in 1525 and Ignaz Günther designed the five splendid doorways in 1772.

Oddly enough the twin towers, which have become Munich's symbol, are not quite the same height, one being a hundred metres high, the other ninety-nine. The cathedral itself – its three aisles all the same height – is surprisingly light inside, with exquisite yellow-painted groins holding up the ceiling, and the rest painted pure white. No arch holds back your view of the chancel from the nave, and Josef Henselmann's modern hanging crucifix scarcely interrupts the rhythm of the design. The spareness of the church has been intensified over the centuries by the loss of much of its furnishings. During the seculariz-ation brought about by Napoleon from 1800 to 1803 most of the church silver was sold, though the citizens of Munich bought back the bust of St Benno, patron saint of Bavaria, which had been created in 1601. Next the nineteenth-century Gothicists replaced the baroque additions to the cathedral with neo-Gothic furnishings, which in turn were almost all destroyed when the cathedral was savagely bombed in World War II.

Yet some masterpieces remain. A statue of St Christopher, carrying a whole tree as a staff, with the infant Jesus riding him like a jockey, dates from around 1520, as do a couple of less animated pieces, St Rasso and St George. The picture of the crucifixion over the high altar, with one of the dying thieves hideously twisted, was painted in the 1440s. An early seventeenth-century 'Ecce Homo' shows the captive Jesus leaning over a balcony, half-covered in a red cloak. Peter Candid's 1620 painting of the 'Assumption of the Blessed Virgin' has survived, along with some fine Gothic stained glass: the Astaler window of 1392; the altogether splendid five-light window by Peter Hemmel of Andlau, in the main chancery chapel, painted in 1493; windows of 1480 in the former chapel of the Blessed Sacrament, depicting contrasting Old and New Testament scenes according to the medieval tradition known as the mirror of salvation; and the seven joys of Mary illustrated in early fifteenth-century glass in the chapel of the Immaculate Conception. Do not miss a *pietà* from Salzburg (in the *pietà* chapel), carved around 1400, with the blood streaming from a vicious gash in the dead Redeemer's side as if someone had raked his flesh with a steel comb, or the earliest sculpted representation of the Ecce Homo theme, in the baptismal chapel. Above all, look for the figures of Jesus and the Apostles which Erasmus Grasser carved for the choir stalls.

Many of the former Archbishops of Munich and the Wittelsbachs (from the son of Ludwig the Bavarian to Albrecht V), as well as the last King of Bavaria, Ludwig III, lie in the crypts, which you enter from behind these choir stalls. The most imposing tomb in the cathedral, that of Emperor Ludwig the Bavarian, is not, however, here but at the west end of the southern aisle. Hans Krumper designed it in the early seventeenth century, adding the bronze figures of Albrecht V and Wilhelm IV. He left the design of the four guardians to Hubert Gerhard. Far more humble, but none the less moving, are the tombstones of the architect of the cathedral, Jörg von Halspach, and of the blind organist Konrad von Paumann, who died in 1473 – the former on the wall beneath the organ loft, the latter near the entrance.

Return from the cathedral to the Alte Akademie and cross Neuhauserstraße to take Damenstiftstraße in order to reach St Anna-Kirche, built in 1733 by the Gunetzrhainer brothers and decorated by the Asam brothers. Its interior, as by now we have come to expect, is lovely. This part of the city, known as the Altes Hackenviertel, is noted for several fine buildings. In Herzogspitalstraße (leading east from St Anna-Kirche) are the Herzogspitalkirche, housing a powerful 'Sorrowing Virgin' carved in wood in 1651 by T. Pader, and the former Gregorian seminary, built in 1574 with a façade of 1808. Brunnenstraße (further south along Damenstifststraße and then east) leads to No. 7 Hackenstraße, the home between 1827 and 1828 of the poet and satirist Heinrich Heine. Its classical façade was added by Jean-Baptist Métivier in 1817. You can also take a drink on the corner of Hackenstraße and Hotterstraße in Munich's oldest inn, 'Zur Hundskugel', which dates back to 1440 and derives its name from the six dogs playing with a ball, over the doorway of the rococo house at No. 10.

At the corner of Brunnenstraße, Damenstiftstraße becomes Kreuzstraße, on the right of which stands the Gothic Kreuzkirche. Its tower rises to over sixty metres. Built in brick, the Kreuzkirche boasts a rococo interior of 1770 and an early sixteenth-century crucifix by Hans Leinberger, as well as a late eighteenth-century tabernacle, which came from the former Carmelite church. An eighteenth-century painting over the high altar is the so-called 'Rotenhamm Madonna'. The church is now used by Czech Christians. Kreuzstraße meets Herzog-Wilhelmstraße, and here you turn left to reach the Sendlinger Tor. This brick, wide-arched gateway, flanked by a couple of stubby brick towers, derives from the 1318 fortifications of Ludwig the Bavarian.

If you want to go on to the site of the *Oktoberfest*, Nußbaumstraße leads south-west from Sendlinger Tor, passing the Protestant church of St Matthew, an ugly building designed by Gustav Grassener in the

1950s. Continue south-west across Kaiser-Ludwig-Platz and you eventually reach the Theresienwiese. The west side is flanked by the massive figure of Bavaria, a lion at her side, created by Ludwig Schwanthaler. Inside, 130 steps lead to the statue's eyes and three other lookouts, offering fine views of the city. Behind the statue is another massive mid-nineteenth-century monument that somehow avoids being ponderous: the huge Hall of Fame built in the Doric style by Leo von Klenze at the behest of Ludwig I. At the other side of the Theresienwiese stands Munich's exhibition centre (Messe), a huge complex covering 330,000 square metres and incorporating twenty halls.

If you prefer not to take such a long walk, go north-east from Sendlinger Tor along the pedestrianized Sendlingerstraße, to find one of Munich's loveliest churches. The decorator Cosmos Damian Asam and his sculptor brother Egid Quirin built St Johann-Nepomuk for themselves between 1733 and 1746, on their own land and at their own expense. Today it is thus known simply as the Asamkirche. Its baroque façade has portrait medallions of the Pope and the Bishop of Freising, and a statue of St Johann Nepomuk over the main door, which is carved with scenes from his life. Cosmos Damian and Egid sculpted the whole façade with flowers and ribbons. The rococo interior, long and narrow with red stucco marble walls, glitters with silver and undulates with life. The high altar, black and gold and marble, carries a wax model of St Johann Nepomuk in a glass sarcophagus, with twisted columns and medallions of the architects on either side. In a niche to the left of the high altar Egid set a Virgin Mary carved by himself. The only later addition consisted of two angels on the Bruderschaftsaltar in the gallery, the work of Ignaz Günther in 1767. To the right is the priest's house, and to the left a sixteenth-century house bought by Egid Quirin Asam in 1733. There he lived as a happy bachelor, adding a rich façade and a little sundial.

Turn right where Sendlingerstraße meets Dultstraße to reach Oberanger. Across the road lies the city museum, exquisitely situated in the old Zeughaus of 1526. You can get in free on Sundays, to enjoy the frequently changing displays of photographs, the puppet museum and the film institute, and above all to relish the remarkable morris-dancers, which were carved by Erasmus Grasser for the Town Hall in 1480. I cannot say why one of them is not painted and all the rest are, but all are stunningly brilliant works by a virtuoso.

Walk along Oberanger and turn right along Rosental. To your left are bookshops, to your right jewellers. Rosental leads to Munich's flower, fruit and vegetable market, the Viktualienmarkt, which happily also incorporates little cafés and sells wine, cheese, bread and meat as well as groceries. In the market square are the figures of six Munich theatre artists: Elise Aulinger, Karl Valentin and his partner Liesl Karlstadt, Weiß Ferdl, Ida Schumacher and Roider Jackl.

Heiliggeistkirche (the church of the Holy Spirit), rises unmistakably above the market, standing where Duke Otto founded a hospital in 1250. This church was rebuilt in the 1720s by Georg Ettenhofer, but its baroque form derives from the work of Cosmos and Egid Asam. Its treasures include a late-Gothic crucifix of 1501 (in the war memorial chapel), Hans Krumper's late sixteenth-century bronze memorial to Duke Ferdinand, a high altar created by Nikolaus Stuber and Antonio Matheo in the late 1720s, and the mid-fifteenth-century so-called 'Hammerthal Madonna' (on the middle altar of the north side), which came here from a monastery at Tegernsee.

To the west of this church stands the oldest parish church in Munich, St Peter, whose famous tower (built in 1386 and rebuilt in 1607) offers fine views not just of the city but also of the Alps. You can climb to its platform on weekdays between 09.00 and 17.00, and on Sundays from 10.00 to 17.00. St Peter's was first a Romanesque church, rebuilt in the late twelfth century and again (after a catastrophic fire of 1327) in 1368. Like virtually every ancient Munich church, it is packed with later treasures. They include the stone Schrenkaltar of 1407; the red marble tomb of U. Aresinger and a statue of St Peter, both by Erasmus Grasser; late-Gothic altar paintings by Jan Polack; a font of 1620 by H. Krumper; a high altar created by Nikolas Stuber in 1730; and, best of all, statues of the four doctors of the church by Egid Quirin Asam (unless you consider Ignaz Günther's Corpus-Christi and Mariahilf altars even better).

Just north of St Peter's church is Isar-Tor-Platz. Isartor, the east gate of the walls built by Ludwig the Bavarian, was restored in 1972. The fresco of Ludwig returning from the Battle of Mühldorf in 1322 was painted by Bernhard Neher in 1835. Today it looks decidedly unmedieval. The tower houses the Spielzeugmuseum, devoted to the comedian Karl Valentin, who lived from 1882 to 1948. A gangly, thin, lugubrious clown with large boots and a pointed nose, Valentin epitomized the little man harassed by bureaucrats, officials and, indeed, the normal stresses that most of us simply put up with. His museum opens on Mondays, Tuesdays and Saturdays from 11.00 to 17.30 and on Sundays from 10.00 to 17.30.

Walk through the Isartor into one of the dream squares of Bavaria: Marienplatz. It houses both the old town hall and the new town hall. At its centre is a statue of the Madonna crowned and sceptred, standing on the moon, the whole set on a column in 1638, with four armoured cherubs on the plinth slaying various mythical beasts. Jörg von Halspach built the old town hall (Altes Rathaus) between 1470 and 1480, though much of it had to be rebuilt after World War II. Its barrel-vaulted council chamber displays ninety-nine coats of arms and medallions. Next to it stands the New Town Hall (Neues Rathaus), built by Georg von Hauberisser between 1867 and 1908. The Glockenspiel in its 85-metre-high tower consists of forty-three bells and is the fourth largest in Europe. It plays each day at 11.00 (and in summer at 17.00). As it plays, mechanical figures depict the marriage of Herzog Wilhelm V and Renate von Lothringen in 1568. Other mechanical dancers celebrate the deliverance of Munich from a plague in 1517.

Burgstraße leads north to the Alter Hof. No. 5 Burgstraße is the best preserved late-Gothic house in Munich, built in the mid-sixteenth century and incorporating a courtyard and a staircase tower behind its façade. In 1781 Mozart was living at No. 6 and composing *Idomeneo*. The court architect François Cuvilliés died at No. 11 in 1768. Here too stands the Alter Hof, the court of the Wittelsbachs from 1253 until they moved to the Residenz.

Across Hofgraben is the Postamt, which was built between 1747 and 1754 by the Gunetzrhainer brothers for Count von Törring-Jettenbach. Leo von Klenze transformed it into the chief post office in the 1830s, adding the loggia on the north side. Further east along Pfisterstraße you come to the celebrated Hofbräuhaus, successively a ducal, royal and state brewery. The present building dates from the 1890s and daily hosts brass bands and beer-swillers, while souvenir-sellers briskly sell junk nearby.

Follow Orlandostraße north-east from the Hofbräuhaus into Maximilianstraße. Eastwards along Maximilianstraße stands the Max-Monument. Kaspar von Zumbusch created it in 1875 in honour of King Maximilian II, so that the people of Munich irreverently call it 'Max-Zwo'. Its allegorical figures supposedly represent the four virtues of a sovereign, and cherubs bear the coats of arms of Bavaria, Franconia, the Palatinate and Schwabia, and the Pfalz). Follow Maximilianstraße across the Maximilian bridge, with its stone statue of Pallas Athene, to reach the Renaissance Bavarian parliament and senate house. Known as the Maximilianum, it was begun by the architect Friedrich Bürklein in 1857 and finished by Gottfried Semper in 1874.

Return along Maximilianstraße to Max-Joseph-Platz. Here in 1835 Ludwig I commissioned the Berlin artist Christian David Rauch to set up a monument in honour of his father, Maximilian I Joseph. Behind it is a graceful neo-classical building, the National Theatre, completely destroyed in World War II and rebuilt at a staggering cost of 63 million Deutschmarks. It houses the Bavarian state opera and ballet. Next to the National theatre is the Residenztheater, built in the 1950s as the home of the Bavarian state theatre.

North of Max-Joseph-Platz is the Residenz itself, which owes its origin to the decision of the Wittelsbachs in 1385 to leave their Alter Hof and build a new palace. Today it consists of eight courtyards joining together seven buildings, none of them much respecting each other architecturally, but all splendid in their own particular fashion. Undoubtedly the most dazzling building is François Cuvilliés's rococo theatre. The Antiquarium was constructed under Albrecht V two centuries earlier and constitutes the oldest German museum of Greek antiques, though most of them are Roman or Renaissance copies. The Maximilianische Residenz itself, designed by Hans Krumper and Heinrich Schön, stretches its elegant Renaissance self along Residenzstraße. The early nineteenth-century royal palace (Königsbau) is modelled on the Pitti Palace in Florence. Not content with the National Theatre, under Maximilian III Joseph the city of Munich acquired the Residenztheater. Finally, the architect Leo von Klenze added a 250-metre-long Festsaal, which Ludwig Schwanthaler decorated with bronze statues.

The courtyards themselves are even lovelier than the buildings. The main one, the Königsbauhof, is dominated by a mid-seventeenth-century statue of Neptune. The arcaded Grottenhof was built in the 1580s and houses a contemporary bronze fountain. The Brunnenhof, an octagonal courtyard designed by Hans Krumper, is dominated by an early seventeenth-century fountain. Topped by a statue of Otto von Wittelsbach, the sculptures of the fountain also depict the four main Bavarian rivers, as well as numerous gods, goddesses, cherubs and beasts. The Apothekenhof, designed by Leo von Klenze in the 1830s, contains the remains of the earliest building in the Residenz, the Neufeste, which was begun in 1385 and burned down in 1750. East of this courtyard, the Apotheken wing houses the Munich academy of science.

The Residenz is also a museum, well worth visiting for its superb rooms alone, particularly the Antiquarium, the Papal Rooms designed by Agostino Barelli in the 1660s, the mid-eighteenth-century Elector's rooms, Cuvilliés's justly named Rich Rooms (Reiche Zimmer), which were enhanced by the skills of J. B. Zimmermann, and Leo von Klenze's Hall of the Nibelungs.

Escape from all this glamour into the elegantly arcaded Hofgarten, which was laid out in the French style on the north side of the Residenz by Heinrich Schön between 1613 and 1617. The way in is through a gate designed by Leo von Klenze in 1816. At the east end is the grave of Bavaria's unknown soldier. And at the north-east corner of the Hofgarten stands Munich's finest early neo-classical building. The Prinz-Carl-Palais is today the official residence of the Bavarian president. Carl von Fischer built it at the very beginning of the nineteenth century and Jean-Baptist Métivier added the west wing in 1826.

The Hofgarten is bounded on the west by Ludwigstraße, that monumental street laid out by Ludwig I's favourite architects (especially Leo von Klenze and Friedrich von Gärtner) between 1816 and 1850. Both architects were drawn from time to time to Italian models, so that, for instance, von Klenze's Leuchtenberg-Palais imitates the Palazzo Farnese in Rome, and von Gärtner's Bavarian state library, though boasting statues of Homer, Thucydides, Aristotle and Hippocrates, is patterned on the Palazzo Strozzi in Florence. Eventually you reach the Siegestor, which von Gärtner modelled on the Arch of Constantine in Rome, to honour the Bavarian soldiers killed in the Wars of Liberation against Napoleon. Its inscription reads 'Dedicated to victory – destroyed by war – an exhortation to peace'. To the west of the Siegestor stands another Italianate building, the mid-nineteenth-century academy of fine arts, this time built in the Venetian Renaissance style. Further north you reach the residential and artists' quarter called Schwabing, noted today not only for its antique shops and boutiques but also for its rather dubious night life.

No British visitor to Munich should fail to see the so-called

Englischer Garten, which you reach by walking east from the University in Ludwigstraße along Veterinärstraße. This delightful park, crisscrossed by a couple of streams, was laid out in 1789 for the Elector Karl Theodor not by an Englishman but by the American Benjamin Thompson, who was known as Count Rumford. Rumford was certainly an honorary Englishman, having lived in Britain as a young man. His patron, the Elector Karl Theodor, decreed in 1790 that he was 'kindly disposed to have the local deer pasture fashioned for the general pleasure of the city of Munich, and would no longer withhold this most beautiful natural park from the public in their leisure hours'.

This 373-hectare park, today the largest landscaped garden in Europe, was then extended and refined by the brilliant landscape gardener Ludwig von Sckell. Its incidental treats include a Chinese Tower and a Chinese Inn, both built in 1790, a classical temple (the Monopteros) by Leo von Klenze, and a restaurant (the Ökonomie-gebaude) designed by Johann Baptist Lechner in 1790. The latest addition is a Japanese Teahouse, given to the city by the Japanese after the 1972 summer Olympics.

What is more, if you are by now dusty and hot after this tour of Munich, you can speedily remedy the condition by taking off all your clothes, as the citizens of Munich so readily do in their Englischer Garten.

You can pick up from the tourist offices Munich's *Theater-Fibel* to discover what is happening in its stunningly prolific theatres. To speak of its galleries and museums is infinitely more difficult, for they are astonishingly rich. South of the English Garden, where we have just been resting, at No. 1 Prinzregentenstraße, is the Haus der Kunst, built by Paul Ludwig Troost in the monumental style typical of the Third Reich to replace a glass pavilion burnt down in 1931. The west wing houses the state gallery of modern art. Here Max Beckmann's horrifying 'Temptation' triptych puts in the shade the works of such masters as Franz Marc, Ernst Ludwig Kirchner and Paul Klee. No. 3 in the same street is the Bavarian national museum (built in the Gothic style by Gabriel von Seidl in the late 1890s), displaying some 20,000 items illustrating nine centuries of German history. The works I most adore here are the sculptures of Tilman Riemenschneider.

In Luisenstraße, at No. 33, the municipal gallery in the Lenbach-haus houses over 1,000 works by the Russian Vassily Kandinsky as well as other members of the school known as *Der Blaue Reiter*, which was founded in Munich in 1911. No. 60 Prinzregentenstraße is the Villa Stuck, an art nouveau treasure house, built at the end of the nineteenth century to designs by the artist Franz von Stuck. To tempt you inside, Stuck placed over the main doorway the bronze figure of an Amazon launching a lance.

But on my first visit to Munich, succouring my heartbroken friend, I spent most of my time in the Alte Pinakothek, the Neue Pinakothek and the Deutsches Museum, and art lovers today with limited time should do the same. Any visitor to the Alte Pinakothek, at No. 27 Barerstraße, must see François Boucher's 'Nude on a Sofa', a painting of Louis XV's fifteen-year-old mistress Louise O'Murphy, posed unnaturally on a rumpled bed. The picture hangs in room 12A on the upper floor. Room 3 on the same floor contains Albrecht Altdorfer's 'Battle of Alexander', which no less an authority than Napoleon himself dubbed the best battle painting ever created. In gilded armour, Alexander the Great pursues the equally gilded Persian King Darius. In room 28 on the upper floor is another masterpiece, a self-portrait by Albrecht Dürer, dressed in a fur coat. The artist – who was a devout Christian – has mingled his own image with the iconography of Jesus himself.

Munich's Alte Pinakothek also houses five paintings of the 'Passion of Jesus' by Rembrandt, his first major commission, done for the Calvinist Prince Frederick Henry of Orange (they are in cabinet 16 on the upper floor). I like them, but I like even more the portraits of Rubens's two wives, Isabella Brant (in room 7 on the upper floor, alongside her husband) and Helena Fourment (on the same floor in room 8), wandering in their Antwerp garden with Nicholas, the thirteen-year-old son of his first wife, who had died five years previously.

The core of the Neue Pinakothek, across the street at No. 29 Barerstraße, is a breathtaking collection of French and German Impressionists, yet I think I love best here the nineteenth-century German romantics, above all Caspar David Friedrich, whose hauntingly spellbound landscapes seem to reflect his own disordered mind.

Finally, cross Ludwigsbrücke and look for a virtually hidden little signpost on the bridge, which points right to the Deutsches Museum on the island in the River Isar. Founded in 1903 by the engineer and scientist Oskar von Miller, it constititutes the greatest museum of science and technology in the world.

When you have admired its contents, I suggest you demolish another technological masterpice – one created each day by the bakers of Munich – by slicing through the layers of icing, chocolate cream and cake that make up the celebrated *Münchner Prinzregententorte*.

The Romantische Straße

Ancient towers, medieval villages whose fortifications – necessary defences in the past – have now become picturesque; vineyards rising on western-facing slopes above meandering rivers; woodlands; evocative ruined castles; superbly stuccoed churches; baroque palaces where architects indulged their wildest fancies; castles and churches of the Teutonic knights; memories of Martin Luther and the desperate sixteenth-century wars of religion – all these fuse into the masterpiece of human ecology, Bavaria's Romantische Straße.

It begins 219 kilometres north of Munich, in the city of Würzburg whose fortress, the Marienberg, rises dramatically from a ridge above the left bank of the River Main. An annual river trade of more than 1 million tonnes passes through its port; chemical and metal works add to the city's prosperity; World War II left Würzburg horribly disfigured; yet none of this you would guess today, for industry and even the river trade are cunningly tucked away, and the destruction of war has been heroically repaired.

The first thing to do in Würzburg is to sample its wine, for the drink of Franconia is virtually the only acceptable beverage I know of in this region, other than Bavarian beer. One of the most delightful aspects of Würzburg is that the city possesses some of the finest cellars for wine-bibbers in the whole of Germany. The Bürgerspital zum Heiligen

Geist, which was founded in 1319 and whose church was built in 1371, must be the kindliest old people's home in the world, for its privileged inhabitants are offered a glass of the local vintage with every meal. The rest of us are privileged to buy the exceedingly cheering booze, either here or in the equally lovely Juliusspital, which was founded by Prince-Bishop Julius Echter von Mespelbrunn in 1576 and encloses, among other treasures, a rococo apothecary.

As you drink, prepare yourself for a trip of almost unbelievable splendour, with village after village vying with each other in medieval and Renaissance beauty along Germany's Romantische Straße. It begins and ends with two fascinating cities: Würzburg and Augsburg. At Würzburg start your tour at the Marienberg. Once the home of the prince-bishops of Würzburg, the Marienberg instantly indicates the antiquity of the city by boasting an early eighth-century chapel, the Marienkirche, the second oldest surviving church in the whole of Germany. (The oldest is Trier cathedral.) Although both Celts and Teutons had made their home on this same height, modern Würzburg effectively began when the Franks built a stronghold here, *Castellum Virteburgh*, some time in the seventh century. By the mid-eighth century the spot had become the seat of bishops, who elevated themselves under Frederick Barbarossa to Dukes of Franconia and then, in the thirteenth, to the status of prince-bishops.

The old Marienberg fortress was now deemed unworthy of these rulers, and they set about rebuilding it. In consequence, apart from the Marienkirche, the oldest parts still standing derive from the thirteenth century. In the fifteenth century Prince-Bishop Rudolf von Scherenberg added more quarters and embellished the older buildings. Then a couple of fires in the second half of the sixteenth century enabled Julius Echter von Mespelbrunn to crown his years as prince-bishop by rebuilding much of his castle in the Renaissance style. (He also founded the university, some of whose Renaissance buildings still dot Neubaustraße in Würzburg.) Of all the Renaissance additions to his Residenz the most charming, I think, is the fountain next to the Marienkirche.

The Marienberg was by now ceasing to look like a fortress, but after Gustavus Adolphus of Sweden captured it during the Thirty Years War, the prince-bishops who reoccupied it later obviously regretted that their home had proved indefensible. Under Johann Philipp von Schönborn the walls were once more fortified. None of this meant that glamour disappeared from inside them. On the contrary, the round interior of the Merovingian Marienkirche, which had been given an incongruous choir in 1603, was re-decorated in the baroque style. Its splendour gives a foretaste of the whole city.

The Marienberg fortress offers a splendid view across the river to the old city. If you look south, on the slopes of the Nikolausberg, which rises from the right bank of the Main, you spot a pretty pilgrimage chapel, known as the Käppele, built by Balthasar Neumann over an ascending way that many followed, as if imitating Jesus's last journey to Golgotha. (The stations of the cross were sculpted by Peter Wagner between 1767 and 1775.) The Käppele dedicated to the Blessed Virgin, was stuccoed by Johann Michael Feuchtmayr in 1748. To add yet more magic, Matthäus Günther and the Asam family frescoed the interior. You reach it from the Marienberg by way of the church of St Burkard, which is part Romanesque, part late-Gothic. Inside is a beautiful Madonna attributed to Tilman Riemenschneider. Walk through the Burkard gate, built in 1680, and from Mergentheimer Straße turn right along Nikolausstraße to reach the church.

The Marienberg fortress also houses the Mainfränkisches museum, which opens each day from 10.00 to either 17.00 or 16.00, depending on the season. This is the best spot to sample the works of Würzburg's greatest son, the sculptor Tilman Riemenschneider, who lived from 1460 to 1531 and became Bürgermeister of his native city. He eventually suffered for both his humanity and his services to Würzburg, for when the peasants revolted in 1525, the sympathetic Riemenschneider was one who counselled inaction instead of repression. When the revolt was put down, he was imprisoned and tortured, at the age of sixty-five, by Prince-Bishop Konrad von Thingen.

From here find your way down to the fifteenth-century bridge across the river, the Alte Mainbrücke, which is adorned with a dozen pompous statues of saints, added in the eighteenth century. The statues include St Johann Nepomuk, recognizable by his halo, which allegedly appeared on his head as he rose in the waters of the Danube for the third and last time when King Wenceslas of Bohemia had him martyred by drowning. The baroque fountain by the bridge dates from 1765 and the old town hall from the thirteenth century.

Domstraße leads from the bridge to the cathedral square and the magnificent Dom of St Kilian, one of Germany's largest Romanesque churches. Building began in 1040, but in succeeding centuries few could resist adding to the cathedral in their own preferred styles. Thanks to this foible we can admire both a fifteenth-century Gothic cloister and also Balthasar Neumann's delicious chapel of the Prince-Bishops von Schönborn. I relish Neumann, but every discerning connoisseur relishes even more Tilman Riemenschneider. Three pillars he carved for the cathedral vie in beauty with the tomb-portrait of the aged Rudolf von Scherenberg, which he also sculpted.

Walk a few yards north from the cathedral to find the Neumünster, founded in the Romanesque age, built over the grave of St Kilian, and transformed into a rococo masterpiece by the brothers Zimmermann. Its façade is baroque, designed by the brilliant Johann Dientzenhofer. An architect named Joseph Greising added the rotunda and its cupola, and Nikolaus Stuber painted it. St Kilian lies in the crypt beneath. Once again Riemenschneider and his pupils have left us their unmatched works in this church. A tiny garden adjoins the north side of this house of God, in which you should seek out the tomb of the eleventh- and early twelfth-century troubadour Walther von der Vogelweide.

Balthasar Neumann himself lies entombed in the fourteenth- and fifteenth-century Marienkapelle north from here in the Marktplatz, though the finest tomb in this chapel is the one Riemenschneider created in 1499 for Conrad von Schaumberg. This is the sole church in Würzburg to have preserved its pure Gothic aspect. It stands on the exact spot of the former synagogue of the town. The Jews were disgracefully blamed for a plague which raged throughout Europe between 1347 and 1352. Their synagogue was razed and replaced by the Marienkapelle. On the south wall of the nave is the 'schöne Madonna', a majestic statue carved around 1430.

In the same exquisite square stands the Haus zum Falken, built in 1765, easily recognizable by its rococo façade. It serves as the city tourist office. Make your way due east to find Würzburg's most impressive building, the Residenz. Balthasar Neumann built the Residenz between 1719 and 1744 for two nepotic prince-bishops, Johann Philipp Franz and Friedrich Karl von Schönborn. Had this palace been destroyed by Allied bombs it would have been irreplaceable, for the valut of its stairway, a breathtaking construction by Balthasar Neumann thirty metres long and eighteen metres wide, was magnificently painted in 1752 by the Venetian Giovanni Battista

Tiepolo. This is the largest fresco in the world, lauding the far from meek Christian, Prince-Bishop Karl Friedrich von Greiffenklau. Fortunately, one of those legendarily intelligent American officers knew of its repute and prevented its obliteration. Today we can still exult at Tiepolo's allegorical depiction of the four continents (people counted only four in those days). Tiepolo also painted the imperial hall (the Kaisersaal), depicting the marriage of Frederick Barbarossa and Béatrice of Burgundy, as well as the investiture of the Bishop Würzburg as Duke of Franconia.

The Residenz is the annual venue of a Mozart festival. Neumann must also be thanked for its church (the Hofkirche), which contains two more paintings by Tiepolo and splendid decoration by Johann Lukas von Hildebrandt. The garden (or Hofgarten) is equally entrancing, laid out in the second half of the eighteenth century and guarded by ornate rococo, wrought-iron gateways. Johann Georg Ogg, who made them, is properly celebrated in statue close by.

As always in Bavaria I seek out as many Riemenscheider masterpieces as I can, and Würzburg is the best place to find them: in the church of St Burkard and the early Gothic Franciscan church for which he created a touching *pietà*. Every other architect seems to pale beside Neumann, but Antonio Petrini, who was appointed court architect to the prince-bishops in the late-seventeenth century, has left us a fine Carmelite church in Sandestraße, and the church of the Stift Haug in Hauger Pfarrgasse. The second, built between 1670 and 1691, arrogantly displays a double-towered façade, which lours eight-five metres above you. It houses a powerful crucifixion, designed by Jacopo Tintoretto in the middle of the sixteenth century. Petrini also built the colourful university church in Neubaustraße.

The easiest way to follow the Romantische Straße from Würzburg is to cross the Alte Brücke and make for the B27. Thirty-two kilometres south-west you reach Tauberbischofsheim, lying amid succulent vineyards and dominating the Tauber valley just outside Bavaria. Its four ancient towers are all that remain from the thirteenth-century castle. Cross the bridge over the River Tauber and continue along the Hauptstraße to the utterly entrancing Marktplatz, which houses the Rathaus and the baroque church of St Lioba. The saint, who was a relative of the missionary bishop Boniface, founded a monastery here in the eighth century. The town itself, however, derives its name not from Lioba but from her episcopal relative. The name of the River

Tauber was added to the word 'Bischofsheim' only in 1806.

The Marktplatz of Tauberbischofsheim not only boasts the Rathaus and the church of St Lioba but is also surrounded by well-restored half-timbered houses, of which the baroque Haus Mackert, built for a rich wine merchant in 1744, and the Sternapotheke opposite are the loveliest. Some of them are carved with mermaids, allegorizing the importance of the river to Tauberbishofsheim. Occasionally the river can be less than friendly, as you can see from the metal plaques indicating the level to which the waters rose when they flooded the town in 1985. If you walk along the traffic-free Hauptstraße from the Marktplatz to Sonnenplatz you see ahead the Gothic church of St Martin, built in the second decade of this century but housing treasures from the fourteenth and fifteenth centuries. They say that Tilman Riemenschneider had a hand in carving its Marienaltar. Once the church had its own charnel house, but this has been transformed into the chapel of St Sebastian and displays a 'Last Judgment' over its door, painted in 1476.

To the south of this pedestrianized area is laid out the pleasingly irregular Schloßplatz. Its name derives from what is certainly a far from oppressive Schloß, built between the fourteenth and sixteenth centuries – though the stumpy, round watchtower (the Türmersturm) is older. Today this Schloß serves as the local history museum. I have in my time been bored beyond all reason in local history museums, but unlike many, this one is well worth calling on, to see some pretty Gothic paintings and above all woodcarvings of the school of Riemenschneider. (It opens from Easter until mid-October, from Tuesday to Saturday between 14.30 and 16.30 and on Sundays and holidays in the mornings as well.)

The Romantische Straße now follows the B290 and the right bank of the river to pass under the Heilbronn–Würzburg motorway and reach Distelhausen, where there is a baroque parish church dating from the 1730s and built, some say, by Balthasar Neumann. Catholic monasticism has flourished greatly in this region, and our next stop, Gerlachsheim, boasts a former monastery church richly stuccoed in the first half of the eighteenh century. Its rococo pulpit dates from 1788. The mid-eighteenth-century statue of Mary comforting the distressed in the centre of the town was restored in 1878.

Since my own view is that not a single masterpiece by Riemensch-neider should be missed, make a brief diversion from here to

Grünsfeld, whose parish church of Saints Peter and Paul, built over four centuries (beginning in the fourteenth) contains a number of his intricately carved tombs. The best is that of Countess Dorothea von Rieneck, who died in 1503. Another treat at Grünsfeld is the town's late-sixteenth-century, half-timbered town hall. Virtually any excursion in this part of Germany produces delight after delight, and this trip is no exception. If you travel a little further north-east, at Grünsfeldhausen you will find a remarkable twelfth-century Romanesque chapel, eight-sided and attached to a second, smaller eight-sided chapel with a nineteenth-century tower. Go inside the chapel, which is dedicated to St Achatius, and you will be delighted to find twelfth-century frescos.

The Germans call this region both the country of the Lord God (Hergottsland) and the country of Our Lady (Madonnasland) and the roadside is dotted with little shrines and crucifixes. Drive on to Ilmspan to look at the rococo church, again richly stuccoed and this time designed by Johann Michael Fischer in 1768. Finish this detour from the Romantische Straße by driving as far as Oberwittighausen. Just outside the little town is another Romanesque, eight-sided chapel. Which came first, this one or that at Grünsfeldhausen? The one outside Oberwittighausen is capped by a Gothic bell tower.

Now drive back to the Romantic Road by way of Zimmern, to admire the church there which Johann Michael Fischer built, again in 1768. South of Gerlachsheim and on the other side of the river, which you traverse by a bridge thrown across it in the early sixteenth century, lies Lauda (as distinct from the nearby sizeable new town of Lauda-Königshofen). Rising from the river are Lauda's reputed vineyards, producing a pleasingly sharp white wine. No. 25 Rathausstraße is a restored mid-sixteenth-century farmhouse now serving as a museum of wine history. The rest of Lauda is exquisite, with a town hall dating from 1591, half-timbered seventeenth- and eighteenth-century houses (some of them painted with images of the Virgin Mary) and the early eighteenth-century church of St Jakob.

In 1826 a magnesium sulphate spring was discovered at our next stop, Bad Mergentheim, which since then has flourished on those who flock to be cured of kidney, liver and gall-bladder diseases by its medicinal waters. 'Mergentheim' derives from the name of a medieval duchess, 'Marigund', who ruled her son's realm when he was a minor. The word 'Bad' was added to its name only in 1926. Medicinal fountains and a pump room were first constructed here in 1829, and the town today attracts thousands to its Kursanatorium.

Before the discovery of the healing spring, Bad Mergentheim had prospered as the seat of the Catholic branch of the Teutonic knights, an order founded in the Holy Land in 1128. In 1330 they fortified the town. When they lost their Prussian lands in 1525, Bad Mergentheim became one of their chief strongholds. The grand master of the order had his seat here from that year until 1809, when Napoleon dispossessed the knights. Their Schloß, with spiral staircases in its Renaissance towers, still stands on the east side of the town. Built between 1568 and 1628, the Schloß is grand enough to be used for concerts and *son et lumière* displays. Today it is also a museum of the Teutonic order. It oddly incorporates a tower from an earlier moated thirteenth-century Schloß. You can visit the Schloß from March to October on weekdays, except Mondays, between 14.30 and 17.30, and on Sundays and during the rest of the year from 10.00 to 12.00, to admire not only stern portraits of the Teutonic knights and their robes of office, but also some dolls' houses and peasant costumes. Sculpted over its doorway is the knights' coat of arms. Inevitably, the tombs of the Teutonic knights have invaded the early eighteenth-century church of Bad Mergentheim, which was built partly by Balthasar Neumann and partly by the Walloon architect François Cuvilliés .

Wilhelm Schutzbar was the knight who brought the order to Bad Mergentheim, and the fountain in the Marktplatz bears his statue. You reach this square by following Burgstraße from the Schloß, discovering there its noble patrician and half-timbered houses, as well as the town hall dating from 1564. From here you can see the tower of the parish church of St Johannes, built around 1300 and containing the tomb of the Marquardt von Eck, commander of the Teutonic knights, who died in 1610. This is not, however, the richest of Bad Mergentheim's churches. To the south of the Marktplatz rises the fourteenth-century Marienkirche, built by Dominican monks. Inside is a splendid bronze memorial, which Hans Vischer of Nuremberg created in 1543 for Grand Master Walther von Cronberg. In the Lady Chapel are frescos said to date back as far as the early fourteenth century. The poet Eduard Mörike came to Bad Mergentheim in 1844. He married a girl of the town and stayed for the rest of his life. I cannot understand why Nos 2–4 Burgstraße, connecting the Marktplatz and the Schloß, house an automobile museum, but they do.

We are now fifty kilometres south of Würzburg and here the
Romantische Straße begins to be signposted with green signs, lettered
in yellow. They point us eleven kilometres south-west to Stuppach and
to one of the artistic marvels of all Germany. The Stuppach Madonna
hangs in a chapel of the late-Gothic church. Only in the early years of
this century did experts recognize that this is a masterpiece painted
around 1520 by Mathias Grünewald. A priest named Balthasar
Blumhofer had bought it after it reached Stuppach in 1812. How it got
there is hard to say, for the panel had previously served as the main
part of a triptych on the Maria-Schnee altar in the hospice church of
Aschaffenburg. It had been overpainted to resemble the work of
Rubens. The temperament and style of the two artists are light-years
apart. Grünewald's world has been described as 'hard, cruel and
merciless'. Here, however, he has created a Virgin and child seated
amid lush plenty. She wears a blue fur coat, and figs await her grasp,
while roses and lilies symbolize the purity of the humble mother and
her divine (though in this painting decidedly crinkly) child. What a
rich skirt she wears, its red making the couple of pink roses look
miserably pale.

Drive the short distance back from Stuppach to Bad Mergentheim
and then travel eleven kilometres east to reach what was for centuries
the seat of the counts of Hohenlohe, Weikersheim. The little town is
dominated by their moated Renaissance Schloß, curiously triangular
in plan and built between the sixteenth and the eighteenth centuries.
The counts were enlightened enough not to demolish the twelfth-
century keep when they built their new Schloß. They were also
enormously fond of the chase, as you surmise from the patterned
ceiling of the knights' hall (Rittersaal) inside the Schloß. Full-scale
plaster sculptures of emperors and empresses line its wall. The
banqueting hall is even more splendid, with a coffered ceiling measur-
ing thirty-five metres by twelve metres, designed by E. Gunzenhaüser
and painted with hunting scenes by B. Katzenberger. The superb,
formal park, which dates from 1710, luxuriously stretches in baroque
curves as far as an orangery of 1719, taking in mythological statues
and a gallery of dwarfs along the moat.

Weikersheim also rejoices in a graceful, semi-circular Marktplatz,
sheltered by the late-Gothic parish church of 1518 and cooled by a
Neptune fountain set up in 1768. You reach it from the Schloß by
passing through what are known as the Zirkelhäusern (compass

houses), built in 1720. Four kilometres south-east you reach the little town of Weikersheim-Laudenbach. In the crypt of its late-fifteenth-century church Field Marshal Melchior von Hatzfeld lies in a mid-seventeenth-century alabaster tomb.

We are now approaching the mecca of all lovers of Tilman Riemenschneider, for the Romantische Straße continues east from here through rolling countryside to Röttingen, with its medieval town walls, and then turns south to reach Bieberehren. Just north-east of Bieberehren is Aub, where without delay you should make your way to the parish church and the crucifixion group Riemenschneider carved around 1500. Then enjoy the Rathaus, built in 1482, whose square is adorned with a baroque pillar topped by a gilded statue of the Virgin Mary.

Whenever I drive through this spot my pulse rate increases as I anticipate seeing a yet greater work by the master of limewood sculptors, for south of Aub lies Creglingen, and two kilometres outside this town is the Herrgottskirche. Built by the Hohenlohe family in 1380, it houses Riemenschneider's superb, seven-metre-high Marienaltar. He and his pupils carved it in 1505. The wings of the altar depict the life of the Virgin. The centre represents her assumption (this piece certainly by the master himself). The church (which opens from April to October between 08.00 and 18.00 and otherwise, except on Mondays, between 10.00 and 12.00 and between 13.00 and 16.00) was built to celebrate the discovery of a sacred Host by a ploughman in the fourteenth century. The high altar was constructed around 1510, the side altars around 1460. Opposite the church (can one believe this?) is a museum of thimbles. The town of Creglingen itself boasts fine houses and a Riemenschneider crucifix in its parish church.

The Romantische Straße now runs eighteen kilometres south-east to the acknowledged gem of medievel Germany, Rothenburg ob der Tauber. On the way it passes Detwang, whose Romanesque parish church possesses an early sixteenth-century crucifixion altar carved in part by Riemenschneider.

Almost completely unspoilt, surrounded by two and a half kilometres of medieval walls, Rothenburg ob der Tauber rises for some 100 metres over the right bank of the River Tauber. German tourist authorities are never slow to exploit such a situation and have decreed that here the 'Romantische Straße' crosses the 'Burgenstraße' (castle route) between Nuremberg and Heidelberg. They have also managed to attract an annual total of 5 million tourists, so that Rothenburg ob der Tauber is in my view undoubtedly best visited out of season.

The red castle over the Tauber, from which the town takes its name, has long disappeared, but the strategic importance of the town remains clear. For centuries the site, which overlooks a meander of the river, has been prized. First the Celts built a fortress here. Then the Franks made this fortress the capital of the Duchy of Franconia. In 1115 the emperor gave the Rothenburg to his nephew, Conrad von Hohenstaufen, who became Emperor Conrad III in 1138. By the mid-twelfth century the Hohenstaufens owned two castles here. In 1356 an earthquake destroyed them both, though the twelfth-century Markus Tower and the White Tower still stand, solitary remnants of the powerful burgs.

In the second half of the thirteenth century Rothenburg ob der Tauber became a free imperial city. At the Reformation she turned Protestant. Blood ran down the Schmiedgasse in 1525 when seventeen rebels were executed in the Marktplatz during the peasants' revolt. During the Thirty Years War the town sided with Gustavus Adolphus, Protestant King of Sweden. As a result, in 1631 the Catholic General Tilly threatened to raze Rothenburg. The Bürgermeister of the town persuaded Tilly not to destroy Rothenburg by accepting and winning a challenge to drink at one gulp a huge draught of wine. Each Whitsuntide the citizens of Rothenburg ob der Tauber re-enact the *Meistertrunk*, in homage to this great alcoholic. The throng of tourists bears mute testimony to his courage in saving a marvellous fifteenth- and sixteenth-century relic.

At the end of the Thirty Years War the Peace of Westphalia confirmed the free status of Rothenburg ob der Tauber. Apart from its incoporation into Bavaria in 1802, the town dozed during the next three centuries, to become a magnet for nineteenth-century German Romantics. Fortunately, during World War II an American general named Devers also spotted the glamour of Rothenburg ob der Tauber. Some lovely buildings had already been bombed, but after an unfortunate delay Devers ordered the US air force to spare the rest.

The best place to begin a tour of Rothenburg is the Marktplatz. Here is situated the arcaded town hall, half of which was built in the Gothic style in the mid-thirteenth century, the other, Renaissance half added in 1578, built by a genius named Leonhard Weidemann. Its fifty-five-metre-high tower dates from the sixteenth century, and in 1681 the citizens added a pretty balcony. An open-air staircase leads into the Renaissance wing and the imperial hall, a superb room with Renaissance benches and finely chiselled bas-reliefs. If you climb to the top of the staircase tower you discover that Weidemann was proud enough not only to carve the German eagle, the coats of arms of the Electors and of Rothenburg itself, but also his own monogram. Then descend to the dungeons and the torture chamber.

To the right of the town hall is the Ratstrinkstube of 1446. Daily on the hour windows open in its baroque gable end (the one with two clocks and a sundial) for puppets to appear and reconstruct a stiffly boring representation of General Tilly and Mayor Nusch eternally re-enacting the *Meistertrunk*. Far more graceful is the fountain of St Georg opposite, set up in 1446 and rebuilt in the Renaissance style in 1608.

Follow Obere Schmiedgasse south from the Marktplatz. I greatly admire its noble patrician houses, which include, at No. 21, the Roter Hahn, the home of the same Bürgermeister Nusch who saved the town from Tilly's wrath in 1631. Next to Nusch's house is the church of St Johannes, built in the thirteenth and fifteenth centuries and enhanced in the early seventeenth century. No. 3 Obere Schmiedgasse is the Baumeisterhaus, a Renaissance building with a sandstone façade, designed by Leonhard Weidemann and built at the very end of the sixteenth century. On the first storey its statues represent the seven cardinal virtues. On the second they depict the seven deadly sins. Today this house is a comfortable, slightly expensive restaurant. Next door stands the Gasthof zum Greifen, once the home of Bürgermeister Heinrich Toppler, who led Rothenburg to its greatest prosperity in the fourteenth century. He was, alas, a crook and died in the town gaol. The house on the other side of the Baumeisterhaus is romantically painted with coats of arms and dates from 1388.

Walk west from here along the Burggasse, to find at No. 3 an enticingly vicious criminals' museum and torture chamber, the Kriminal und Folermuseum. It opens daily from April to October between 09.00 and 18.00 and at other times between 14.00 and 16.00. How long will we have to wait before some ardent feminist sets alight the 'neck violins', long ago used to deter quarrelsome women? From here, if you follow Burggasse as far as Herrngasse, you find the fourteenth-century Gothic Franciscan church. Spare a moment to go inside, if only to see the late-Gothic rood screen, carved in wood, decorated with scenes of Christ's pasison. St Francis himself has an altar here, whose fifteenth-century statue depicts him with the stigmata of Jesus on his own hands, side and feet. One of the many tombs in the church shelters the body of Dietrich von Berlichingen, grandfather of the more famous Götz, the knight one of whose adventures cost him his right hand, who fought on the side of the peasants in 1525 and fathered a celebrated expletive (*Leck mich am Arsch*) in a play written about him by Goethe. The name of this street derives from the gentry (*Herren*) who were once privileged to hold a cattle and horse market in the wide area between its rich patrician houses. Jutting out from their gables you can still see the beams that were once used for hoisting up merchandise. Look inside Nos 11 and 15 at the charming courtyards, and do not miss the Staudtisches Hauss across the street, where once lodged Kaisers Charles V and Ferdinand I, as well as Gustavus Adolphus's wife Eleanor. Its galleries are quite perfect. The Herrn fountain dates from 1575, and the end of the street is closed by the thirteenth-century burg gate, cold and haughty, humanized by the sixteenth-century guardhouse at the front. Close by is Rothenburg's puppet theatre.

Beyond this gate you find the Burg garden, which houses the chapel of St Blasius. Built at the beginning of the thirteenth century and decorated with wall paintings two centuries later, this is all that remains of the old burg. Today it serves as a war memorial. From the Burggarten you can see across the mills of the valley as far as Detwang. The strange white castle opposite is the Toppler Schloß, built for Bürgermeister Heinrich Toppler in 1389.

I like to rest a while in this garden, before returning to the church of St Johann and walking south to the much photographed corner known as Plönlein. Two streets lead from Plönlein, each one ending in a fortified gateway. In consequence you can choose to walk either right along Kobolzellertsteig to the Kobolzeller gate, or left along Untere Schmiedgasse to the late fourteenth-century Siebers Tower, built in 1385. The second route takes you through the late thirteenth-century hospice quarter. A century later the people of Rothenburg ob der Tauber built the Heiliggeistkirche here (it houses a couple of lovely fourteenth-century statues). Then in 1591 they added to this quarter the turretted horse-breaker's house (the Hegereiterhaus), another creation of Leonhard Weidemann.

From the Hegereiterhaus you should stroll back to the Marktplatz, passing between the town hall and the Ratstrinkstube to reach the Grünen Markt and then the Kirchplatz. Here is another religious treat, the late fourteenth-century basilica of St Jakob, slender and tall, its west end sporting two square towers with crocketed spires. Legend has it that the master mason responsible for the work designed the south tower, and his apprentice designed the yet more graceful north tower, at which the master mason flung himself to his death from the south one. This church, which you enter by way of the beautifully decorated 'bride's portal', proudly houses a carving of Our Lady in stone, done in the mid-fourteenth century, some delicious fourteenth-century stained glass, and an early fifteenth-century aumbry. But the best surprise here is the mid-fifteenth-century high altar, the altar of the twelve apostles, sculpted by H. Waidenlich. The painted panels are by Friedrich Herlin and represent the miraculous life of St Jakob and the pilgrims who dedicated themselves to his shrine. In the picture depicting the corpse of the saint you suddenly realize that Herlin portrayed the cortège on the way to Rothenburg itself.

This is a treat; but in this church everyone rightly swoons over Tilman Riemenschneider's 'Holy Blood' altar. It depicts the Last Supper, and incorporates a crystal, which is said to contain a drop of Jesus's own blood. Riemenschneider carved it between 1501 and 1505. In the centre panel Jesus, surrounded by his disciples, is offering his betrayer Judas a morsel of bread. In the wings he prays passionately on the Mount of Olives and then goes to Jerusalem on the way to his death.

The north side of the square is bounded by a three-storeyed Renaissance former Gymnasium (or secondary school), built by Weidemann in 1581. If you walk north from the church along Klingengasse and then turn west at Feuerleinserker you will reach the museum of Rothenburg ob der Tauber, which is housed in No. 5 Klosterhof, a twelfth-century former Dominican monastery. Here one marvels over Bürgermeister Nusch's famous flagon, as well as twelve paintings of 1494, the 'Rothenburg Passion', in the early Gothic cloister. Here too is what claims to be the oldest kitchen in Germany.

No one visiting Rothenburg ob der Tauber should miss walking along its ancient walls. Through the Burg gate to the west of the town and the Burg garden, this walk crosses the early fourteenth-century 'double bridge', passing the late fifteenth-century Kobolzeller church.

Once this church was filled with treasures, but lost them when the citizens of Rothenburg ob der Tauber sided with the peasants' revolt. On Easter Monday 1525, several millers forced their way into the building, ripped out these priceless works of medieval art and flung them into the river.

West of the Kobolzeller church rises the Toppler Schloß, which we have already glimpsed from the Burggarten. Rödergasse leads from here east to the Röder gate, fronted by a couple of guardhouses, from which you stroll in a northerly direction to the Würzburger gate. Long ago the citizens of Rothenburg hanged miscreants here. Further on you reach the Klingen gate. It was built in the late sixteenth century, but its quiddity is the fortified church of St Wolfgang, built as if to strengthen the fortifications. Since St Wolfgang is the patron saint of shepherds, this is Rothenburg's 'shepherds' church', a sweet, late fifteenth-century shrine, with some unusually intricate windows and splendid altars by a contemporary local architect named Wilhelm Ziegler. Wolfgang himself is sculpted on the exterior, between the double doors.

Rothenburg ob de Tauber knows how to exploit its unique medieval beauty. Throughout the summer the town hosts a riding school. Nearby is superb hill-walking country, and the environs are lovely. Twelve kilometres away is Schillingsfürst, where you can visit an early eighteenth-century baroque Schloß. Franz Liszt lived here and his statue stands in the Schloß park. If you drive south from Rothenburg ob der Tauber along the B25, you cross the A7 motorway and, after 31 kilometres, reach Feuchtwangen.

Feuchtwangen developed in the neighbourhood of a Benedictine monastery allegedly founded by Charlemagne in the eighth century. Charlemagne, the legend insists, was led here by a dove (hence the dove fountain in the Marktplatz). On the north side of the Marktplatz rises the Romanesque monastery church. Its high altar was created by Michael Wohlgemut of Nuremberg in 1484. This Stifstkirche guards some fine tombs, one of which carries the life-size figure of the Teutonic knight S. von Ehenheim, who died in 1504, and that of Lucas Freyer, created by Loy Hering in 1523. Run your hand along the choir stalls, dating from the early sixteenth century. The west wing of the church has become a museum of local crafts, and south of the church are a calvary and Romanesque cloisters, where plays are held in summer. Nearby are a local history museum and another crafts museum, situated in the west wing of the cloister.

To the north of the Stifstkirche stands the Romanesque church of St Johann, with a fine tithe hall (the 'Kasten' of 1565) adjoining. Through the half-timbered Café am Kreuzgang you reach a Romanesque cloister, venue of an annual theatre festival from June to the end of August, which also houses a museum of handicraft. As for the local history museum at No. 19 Museumstraße, this includes a collection of firefighting equipment from the eighteenth century to the present day. Does anyone ever ask to see it? If so, by request, they can enjoy the exhibits each day between 10.00 and 12.00 and between 14.00 and 17.00.

An excursion from Feuchtwangen follows the B14 north-east for twenty-five kilometres to Ansbach. The Hohenzollerns ruled here from the thirteenth century. Then the Margraves of Brandenburg-Ansbach lorded it over the town. Today it is the capital of central Franconia. Its Italian baroque castle, the Markgrafenschloß, was built by Italian architects and dates from the first half of the eighteenth century. Part baroque, part rococo, its charms include a hall of mirrors and china, a splendid porcelain gallery, a Gobelin gallery and a Red Salon hung with portraits of the Hohenzollerns. Christian Carlone beautifully frescoed the ceiling of its double-storeyed great hall. In its park an avenue of lime trees is said to be 200 years old, and its early baroque orangery dates from 1726. If by now you are not tired of church-crawling, find here the Romanesque church of St Gumbert, whose choir is Gothic and whose nave is baroque. Inside are eleven tombs of Knights of the Swan, an order founded by the Elector of Brandenburg in 1440.

This little town of no more than 10,000 inhabitants also possesses the Gothic church of St Johann, built in 1441, and the cemetery chapel of the Heiliges Kreuz, built twenty years later. Its baroque chancellery dates from 1593 and the town hall from 1623. As if these were not enough treasures, some of the wide sreets boast eighteenth-century baroque houses. Ansbach runs an international week of Bach music at the end of each July, and a rococo festival at the beginning of the same month.

Drive south-east from Ansbach, looking for the sign leading off the B13, to find Wolframs-Eschenbach, the birthplace of Wolfram von Eschenbach, the medieval author of *Parzifal*. His romance, the first to be written in German to celebrate the mystery of the Holy Grail, recounts how a simple, humble fool became its keeper. The man whose work inspired Wagner lies buried in the thirteenth-century church here (a building remodelled in baroque in the eighteenth century). Here too the seventeenth-century Schloß of the Teutonic knights, which is surrounded by half-timbered houses, now serves as the town hall.

Travel back to Feuchtwangen and from there follow the B25 south for thirteen kilometres to a medieval town that I hold to be as fine and unspoilt as Rothenburg ob der Tauber. The romantic fortifications and twenty towers of moated Dinkelsbühl rise beside the River Wörnitz. Eight times besieged during the Thirty Years War, it was finally taken by Gustavus Adolphus. Because the town's children are said to have saved it in 1632, each year in mid-July their present-day successors perform a *Kinderzeche* in thanksgiving. The Swedish Colonel Klaus Dietrich von Sperreuth spared Dinkelsbühl because the children of the town, bearing only flowers, had marched out to his army to beg for mercy. Today the town's *Kinderzeche* includes the famous boys' band of fifty musicians, who dress in rococo uniforms to celebrate not only this reprieve but also St George's feat in slaying the dragon. My only complaint is that on the chief day of the festival the boys' band wakes everyone up at seven o'clock. Why Dinkelsbühl also hosts a festival during which men in knee-breeches balance precariously on swords, I do not know.

If you park outside Dinkelsbühl and enter by the thirteenth-century Wörnitz gate (one of four surviving from the turreted medieval fortifications), you reach the oldest part of the town, with its late twelfth-century castle, Burgus Tinkelspuhel. The road runs across to the Altrathausplatz, which is enriched with a mid-fourteenth-century former town hall and a lion fountain. Beyond this square you reach the Marktplatz. Nearby, in the direction of the Rothenburg gate, stands the altogether splendid half-timbered Deutsches Haus of 1449, which is now both a hotel and a restaurant. Above its entrance is a late seventeenth-century statue of the Virgin Mary. The east side of the Marktplatz is sheltered by the fifteenth-century parish church of St Georg. The architect of this church clearly revelled in tricks of scale, for its three aisles, each twenty-two and a half metres high, match the width of the church and virtually match its seventy-seven metres in length. The slender pillars and fan vaulting of the interior are sumptuous late Gothic, and the ciborium in the chancel dates from

1480. Three fifteenth-century statues (of St Bartholomew, the Virgin Mary and St George) decorate the pillars of the apse. Although its portal is Romanesque, the rest of this masterpiece of religious architecture is almost entirely the work of Nikolaus Eseler and his son Nikolaus.

Walk past the present town hall along Föhrenberggasse to reach the eighteenth-century Schloß of the Teutonic knights (the Palais des Deutschen Ordens). As you walk on along Martin-Luther-Straße towards the Rothenburger gate, passing the Deutsches Haus, you come to the former cornhouse, built around 1600, and the town's former hospice, today a local history museum – though it still houses a few elderly residents. The Rothenburger gate was built around 1380, and from here Obere Schmiedgasse leads to the town walls. Kapuzinerweg runs around them as far as the former Capuchin monastery church, built in the seventeenth century. Close by is a granary (Kornhaus) of 1378. Soon you find the Segringer gate, which was rebuilt in 1655. Then you reach the mid-sixteenth-century chapel of the Magi, which now serves as a war memorial.

Everyone wandering around the medieval walls of a Bavarian town will indulge his own romantic fantasies. Oberer Mauerweg at Dinkelsbühl follows the town wall from the Segringer gate to the late fifteenth-century Nördlinger gate. Outside this is the late fifteenth-century town mill. Beside the Nördlinger Tor is another ancient fortified town mill. And to walk outside these walls is also exceedingly rewarding. To the west they overlook parks and a large sports centre.

Drive east from here through Gerolfingen to Wassertrüdingen, whose remaining medieval walls are lovely but pale in comparison with those of Dinkelsbühl. The former Benedictine monastery church at Wassertrüdingen has a Renaissance tabernacle of 1512 by Loy Hering and an altar by Hans Schäufelin of around the same date. Further south you come upon Oettingen, which retains part of the chapel of its former Schloß and its 'new' seventeenth-century Schloß (which has profited from some early nineteenth-century restoration). Here too is the parish church of St Jakob, with stucco work by Matthias Schmuzer. And at Whitsuntide the citizens devote eight days to a merry folk festival.

To the south-west is one of the most quaintly situated towns in Europe. Medieval Nördlingen lies 430 metres above sea level at the heart of a crater excavated by a huge meteorite, which smashed into the earth some 15 million years ago. After Rothenburg ob der Tauber and Dinkelsbühl, it is the third of the free imperial cities on the Romantische Straße, and you can see how it developed outwards from its medieval core to the sixteenth- and seventeenth-century buildings which ring this gem. The architects of the late-Gothic church of St Georg, built between 1427 and 1519 on the south side of the Marktplatz, must surely have conceived its eighty-nine-metre-high tower (which was finished in 1539 when the Renaissance copper dome known as 'Daniel' was added) not just for the glory of God but also to offer a remarkable view of the crater in the midst of which the town nestles. At any rate, climb its 365 steps to exult in the panorama. Then descend and relish the pulpit of 1499, the sandstone tabernacle of 1525, the baroque organ gallery of 1610, the funerary motifs on the walls, which date from the sixteenth to the eighteenth century, and above all the magnificent baroque high altar, which incorporates five Gothic statues: the crucified Jesus, his mother, St John and two angels. On either side are statues of St George and St Mary Magdalen.

To explore the Spital zum Heligen Geist at Nördlingen is to enter a thirteenth-century community, with its own mill and farm as well as its church (which is decorated with fourteenth-century wall-paintings). This is now the town's museum. The Marktplatz houses the fourteenth-century town hall, to which the citizens in a flurry of exhibitionism added an external staircase in 1618. Across the square is a mid-fifteenth-century dance house. And among the finest buildings in Nördlingen are the nine-storeyed 'Hohes Haus' of 1444 and the Klosterle, a former monastery built some twenty years earlier. Another pleasure at Nördlingen is simply to wander around its completely preserved, mostly medieval walls, with their five gates and eleven towers.

Nördlingen never seems to pause between festivals. Every June a fair and festival commemorate Nördlingen's right to hold a Whitsun market, granted in 1219. The town boasts an open-air theatre in July and August, which conflicts with its celebrated steeplechases (the Scharlachrennen, held in September, is Germany's oldest). Even in the winter months the town remains active, hosting concerts and theatrical events.

If you leave Nördlingen by the Reimlinger gate and follow Augsburger Straße to take the B25 south-east, after seventeen kilometres you reach Harburg, a town dominated by the most massive

surviving Schloß in Bavaria, the Felsenburg. The princes of Oettingen
built it between the twelfth and sixteenth centuries. Except from
January to mid-March, you are guided through its collection of fine art
and impressive rooms, and along its ramparts and beside its keep. The
museum houses works by Riemenschneider and his skilled prede-
cessor Veit Stoss, as well as tapestries and carved ivory from Normandy. The Schloß church, basically Romanesque, was extended in
the fourteenth century and houses a fine carved Madonna of 1480 and
a statue of St Michael of 1510, which is nearly as fine. Harburg hosts
an annual *Bockfest* in June. Leisure pursuits here include fishing in the
Wörnitz and relaxing in the saunas of the Ozon-Hallenbad.

Twenty-five kilometres further on you reach Donauwörth, where
the River Wörnitz, which washes Harburg, joins the Danube. Rightly
the citizens of Donauwörth are pround of their exquisite Reichsstraße,
which culminates in the parish church of the town, its tower rising at a
curiously charming angle from the thrust of the street. Dedicated to
Our Lady in her Assumption, it was built in the mid-fifteenth-century
and contains a fine tabernacle created in 1503 by Gregor Ehrhart (a
sculptor from Augsburg), as well as fifteenth-century wall-paintings
and stained glass. Its belfry supports the heaviest bell in Schwabia, the
6.55-tonne 'Pummerin'. In Reichsstraße you can also see a fountain set
up in 1977. I sat beside it, fell into conversation with a local man, told
him I did not much like the new fountain, and he grew extremely
upset.

Two of the medieval gateways of Donauwörth have survived the
centuries, as has its fourteenth-century Rathaus, its early-seventeenth-
century Spitalkirche and its classical house of the Teutonic knights,
built in the second half of the eighteenth century. Less fortunate was
the late medieval Tanzhaus, destroyed in World War II but well
reconstructed in 1974 and now the town's concert hall and archaeological museum. Seek out also in this town Heilig-Kreuz-Straße and the
church of the Holy Cross, once a Benedictine monastic church and
succulently decorated in the eighteenth century. Franz Xaver Schmuzer
of Wessobrunn created its high altar in 1724. The monastic buildings,
also dating from the eighteenth century, are now a school. Here too
stands the Renaissance Fuggerhaus, built by the rich merchant Anton
Fugger in the 1530s, readily recognizable by its grandiose portico.

Augsburg lies thirty-six kilometres south of Donauwörth along the
B2. The charm of the city is enhanced both by its geographical position

in the foothills of the Alps and at the confluence of the Lech and the Wertach, and by its historical redolence. Its name derives from Augustus Caesar, who founded the city in 15 BC. Emperors called parliaments here, and in the late thirteenth century, under Rudolph von Habsburg, Augsburg became a free imperial city. Great merchant families – the Fuggers, the Welsers, the Höchstetters – were soon trading from Augsburg with the whole known world and became immensely rich. Artists, such as Hans Holbein the Elder and his equally celebrated son, were born and nurtured here. Dürer, Titian and Altdorfer painted, and music, theatre and poetry flourished in this city. Augsburg was the birthplace of Leopold Mozart, who at the age of twenty decided to devote his life to music, moved to Salzburg and married Anna Maria Walburga Perti, who bore him a prodigy baptized Wolfgang Amadeus. Bertolt Brecht was born here in 1898, though I find the poems he wrote at Augsburg little better than doggerel. He would have been pleased to see the city's annual open-air theatre festival, today held from mid-July until early September and partly housed in a spectacular arena by the medieval Rotes Tor (or red gate), which seats 2,500 spectators.

Today the capital of Bavarian Schwabia is an industrial city with 250,000 inhabitants. Rudolf Diesel produced his revolutionary internal combustion engine here in the 1890s (having been nearly killed by its prototype, which exploded), and diesel engines as well as the manufacture of aircraft and electrical machinery contribute to its prosperity.

But the city has not forgotten its past. If I had to choose twenty-five years in which to have lived at Augsburg they would begin in 1530, when the Protestant Reformer Martin Luther and his ally Melanchthon drew up a profession of faith, which their followers presented here to the Holy Roman Emperor Charles V. My twenty-five years would stretch through 1548, when theologians on both sides of the religious struggles of the time drew up a peace proposal. Alas, to the emperor's sorrow, this compromise document, the Interim of Augsburg, failed to produce peace in his realms. The struggles would end in 1555, when his successor Ferdinand I presided over an imperial Diet here, which did produce some fifty years of peace in Germany. The Diet agreed that each prince should decide whether the religion of his own territory was to be Catholic or Lutheran (though the latter were slightly disadvantaged by the fact that any prince who turned

Protestant was required to cede his land and revenue).

Because of this history a tour of Augsburg should, I suggest, start not at one of the great showpieces of the city – the Dom, or the Fuggerei – but at the Lutheran Heilig-Kreuz-Kirche, a neglected treasure built in 1653 on the site of a twelfth-century chapel, by a pupil of the master Elias Holl named Johann Jakob Krauß. Easily reached, from the Kennedyplatz (where Augsburg's modern theatre, seating 1,000 spectators, is sited), the church was beautifully restored in 1981. When Luther sought refuge in Augsburg it was the church of an Augustinian monastery, and as an Augustinian monk he naturally stayed here. If the Reformation started, as historians will tell you, in Worms, in Wittemberg or the Wartburg, I think this too is where one of the greatest cataclysms of Christianity began. The great, flat open span of the wooden roof is bordered on the west and south sides by lovely classical galleries. The organ, set over the altar, dates from the restoration of 1981, although one could hardly guess this, for the design of 1730–1 has been immaculately reproduced.

Everywhere in this church artists have glorified the great reformer and his allies. In the Große Sakristei an unknown master has depicted both a fat-chopped Luther and a scrawny Philipp Melanchthon. The same sacristy houses a splendid triptych of 1515, in whose centre panel naked little angels worship a naked Christchild. In the Kleine Sakristei, pictures of 1730 by Johann August Corvinus display in almost cartoon form Luther's dangerous life and the presentation of the Confession of Augsburg to Charles V in 1530. But most of the works of art in this church relate to the life of Jesus. On the west wall hang Johann Heinrich Schönfeld's vision of Jesus preaching from a boat, painted in 1670, and Johann Georg Bergmüller's 1730 portrayal of God the Father and the Holy Spirit. On this same wall hangs an 'Annunciation' by Johann Heiss, painted at the end of the seventeenth century, as well as Friedrich Sustris's 'Adoration of the Shepherds', dating from around 1570 (the chubby infant Jesus seems to be about to clap his hands).

The north wall is equally rich in paintings, including two from *circa* 1660 by Johann Heinrich Schönfeld depicting a pathetically suffering Jesus, falling under the weight of his cross, and a 'Deposition'. Ernst Philipp von Hagelstein's painting of Jesus using a little child as an example of Christian humility also hangs here, painted in 1712. I cannot help surmising that the child's mother energetically plastered down the boy's hair before letting him into the painter's studio as a model. Hagelstein also executed a less good picture of the marriage feast at Cana, which hangs on the north wall. But every picture here pales beside the vivacious baptism of Jesus by John the Baptist, said to be by Jacopo Tintoretto and painted around 1570.

No. 4 Heilig-Kreuz-Straße was the surprisingly humble home of Kaiser Maximilian I from 1504 to 1519. To see the elegant house where the father of Wolfgang Amadeus Mozart was born on 14 November 1719 you have to turn north from the church to reach No. 30 Frauentorstraße. Retrace your steps and Frauentorstraße will lead you towards the twin copper spires of Augsburg cathedral, which rise above ancient brick and stone towers. Its foundations were laid in the tenth century, and the crypt is still low and lovely. The Gothic choir was built between 1326 and 1431. Naturally Hans Holbein the Elder contributed to the treasures of this cathedral, in his case by painting scenes from the life of the Madonna, which adorn the pillars of the nave. But the greatest treasures are the five stained-glass panels in the south clerestory, Germany's oldest – the sea-water greens as clear as when they were fired in the twelfth century. In the south aisle windows there is less good old glass. I wonder how anyone had the nerve to put in the twentieth-century rubbish that passes for religious stained glass in the rest of the church and feebly imitates the faces of the ancient glass in the clerestory.

The bishop's throne here dates from 1100. The south transept bears a huge late fifteenth-century painting of St Christopher carrying Jesus across a stream. Walk around the cloister, with its endless tombs, and then make sure you look at the bronze panelled door in the south wall, the one protected by a grille. Every time I stand entranced outside this eleventh-century masterpiece I wonder why I am alone. Does no one appreciate its naïve brilliance, the half-reliefs of men gingerly avoiding a snake bite, others putting out their tongues at a lion, Samson killing another extremely weedy lion, and centaurs armed with bows and arrows?

Leave the south side of the cathedral by way of Karolinenstraße to reach the massive Rathausplatz, where people sit under umbrellas sipping beers. Rathausplatz derives its name and its glamour from an onion-domed, seven-storey town hall built by Elias Holl between 1615 and 1620, from the Romanesque Perlach watchtower which flanks one side, and from a splendid late sixteenth-century fountain whose statues represent four of the region's rivers.

The west side of the Rathausplatz is sheltered by the twelfth-century church of St Peter. And just by the town hall you see a notice pointing along Am Pelachberg towards both the Fuggerei and the house of Bert Brecht. The Fuggerei is an amazing example of generosity. By 1519, when he built it, the fortune of Jakob Fugger the Elder was greater even than that of the Medici in Florence. The centre of his coat of arms was a pine cone, and as you walk past the town hall towards the Fuggerei, you notice it crowning Elias Holl's Rathaus. The Fuggerei comprises four gateways, which enclose eight streets passing between sixty-six picturesquely gabled homes and a church. Jakob Fugger decreed that here should live virtually rent-free worthy citizens who had fallen on hard times. Such worthy citizens still do.

The Fuggers also gave to Augsburg one of the gems of Italian Renaissance architecture, their funeral chapel, which you will find in the former Carmelite church of St Anna. Locate it by crossing the Rathausplatz from the town hall and entering the traffic-free shopping area of Anna Straße. St Anna is yet another church that gave shelter to Martin Luther, and its superb Gothic patterns are marvellously complemented by the rococo frescos and stucco. Entranced by the Fugger chapel, which was decorated by Dürer (or maybe his pupils) and Lukas Cranach the Elder, you must not miss the fine Gothic goldsmiths' chapel on the north side of the chancel.

Augsburg boasts many other delights. Seek out, above all, two of them. In the Schaezler Palais, which now serves as the city art gallery, is a baroque banqueting hall which K. A. von Lespilliez built in the 1760s. And Augsburg surprises one by having a second cathedral, the Catholic Münster of Saints Ulrich and Afra. Emperor Maximilian I founded it in the fifteenth century. The architect of the present late fifteenth-century church was a citizen of Augsburg named Burkhard Engelberg. Inevitably many Fuggers are buried here in splendid tombs, and here too are three baroque altars. But one feature of the church of Saints Ulrich and Afra is particularly important. Around 1600 someone decided that its asymmetrical tower should be topped with an onion dome. It started a fashion that has continued throughout Bavaria to the present day.

The glamour of baroque and rococo

The owner of the Yachthotel, Chiemsee, is an architect as well as an hotelier, who designed his own establishment to fit with perfect harmony into the local environment. (Planning permission alone, he told me, took seven years to obtain, with no fewer than five government bureaucracies to contend with!) As well as running his hotel he specializes in restoring churches, which immediately endeared him to me. One evening we talked for so long, happily tucked into one of his bars, that the kitchen closed before I sat down to eat and I had to manage on the so-called *Kleinkarte*. In consequence I fed myself on a powerful, spicy goulash soup followed by one of the most massive *salades niçoise* that I have ever eaten, all washed down with a beer from the 'Herzogliches Brauhaus Tegernsee'.

As I ate I meditated over what I had learned. My host, Dipl-Ing Wiesner, loves taking guests on little runs into the countryside – maybe to a farmhouse or an artist's studio – taking along, of course, the kitchen staff to fill these fortunate guests to bursting point. 'What then was, in his opinion, the finest church in the neighbourhood?' I asked. Instantly he answered, 'Sachrang.'

So I went to Sachrang, which turns out to be the last place in this part of Germany, situated just before the Austrian border. Its whole ensemble is delightful. In summer its citizens, well aware of their tourist potential, run Friday evening folk dances, as well as leading their visitors on treks through the spectacular mountains. Its late seventeenth-century church is indeed a gem, unusually Italianate, created by Lorenzo Sciasca.

Is it as fine as the church a few hundred yards from Herr Wiesner's hotel at Prien? Hesitating to differ from my host, I still think not. The parish church of Maria Himmelfahrt at Prien am Chiemsee was first built in the late-Gothic style, to be half-demolished and then enlarged and sumptuously refurbished in the mid-eighteenth century. The architect was Johann Steinpeiß from Wasserburg. To walk into the late-baroque nave is a breathtaking experience – tall windows shedding light on the high altar, whose proportions are matched by two blue-canopied side altars. The canopies turn out to be exquisitely cunning stucco work by Johann Baptist Zimmermann. What makes the church outstanding are the frescos by this same genius and his son Joseph. For the presbytery they painted the Trinity in its glory, surveying the earth from its heavenly seat. On the main ceiling they depicted the Battle of Lepanto, when Spanish and Venetian galleys destroyed the Turkish fleet in the Mediterranean in 1571.

> Don John pounding from the slaughter-painted poop,
> Purpling all the oceans like a bloody pirate's sloop,
> Scarlet running over on the silvers and the golds,
> Breaking of the hatches up and bursting of the holds,
> Thronging of the thousands up that labour under sea
> White for bliss and blind for sun and stunned for liberty.
> *Vivat Hispania!*
> *Domino gloria!*
> Don John of Austria
> Has set his people free!,

as G. K. Chesterton wrote to celebrate this famous Christian victory over the Moors. In the fresco at Prien, ships reeling under attack, Turkish prisoners, liberated Christians, Pope Pius V who launched the Catholic fleet and Don John of Austria who commanded it, can all be made out, along with the legend (under the group of naval commanders) *Joh. Zimmermann pinxit anno 1738.*

As you leave the church of Maria Himmelfahrt a further treat is to glimpse its wildly twisting baroque organ, exactly contemporary with Johann Baptist Zimmermann's frescos and built by a citizen of Prien named Sebastian Mayr.

Bavarian baroque and rococo has invested the churches with such splendour that any visitor should find time to explore them. One way would be to start at Prien am Chiemsee and drive to see a dozen or more. Nearly all of them are set in unbelievably romantic villages and towns. If I were to suggest such a tour, it should begin by following the road from Prien am Chiemsee that runs due west through twenty-three kilometres of rolling wooded countryside to Rosenheim. Gentle peaks rise to the south, and soon the waters of the Simsee and its bathing places appear on the right. Nine kilometres before Rosenheim a signpost directs you left up Neukirchenerstraße to the pilgrimage church of Maria Stern at Neukirchen am Siemsee. The church exterior is stern, compared with that at Prien, with no indication of the riot of baroque and rococo beauty inside.

There has been a church here since the eighth century, but the present building dates basically from the mid-fifteenth century. Its domes and tower, like the baroque interior, are eighteenth-century. As on many Bavarian churches you will find chalked over the entrance the initials of the three wise men, Caspar, Melchior and Balthasar, surrounded by the date of the last feast of the epiphany, thus for example 19+C+M+B+87. Inside, stucco cherubs seem to fly around like bats. On the reredos of the high altar is a peaceful painting of the Madonna, and over her head a clock ticks away the hours. She stands between the statues of St John the Baptist (recognizable from his symbols: the lamb and the cross) and St John the Evangelist (whose symbols are the eagle and the chalice), all framed in an early rococo swirling altar of 1730. The exact image of this Madonna is repeated in the ex-voto paintings that hang on the side walls of the church, her *bambino* still dressed in swaddling clothes but already standing up on her knee. The ceiling of the nave is decorated with a *trompe-l'oeil* painting whose pillars recede into the heavens.

You return to the Rosenheim road and cross the River Inn just before entering the town. Rosenheim is a modern town and, with 52,000 inhabitants, a large one, refreshed by fine parks. Hidden among the bustle are surviving relics of earlier ages, such as the old burger's house in the pedestrianized and arcaded Max-Josef-Platz, at one end of which stands the church of St Nikolaus shading the daily fruit and vegetable market. Gothicized in the nineteenth century, St Nikolaus still retains a fifteenth-century tower, somewhat inappropriately topped by an onion dome. On the outside wall a simpering nineteenth-century mosaic depicts the Virgin Mary. The town was devastated by fire in 1641, but one medieval gate remains, the fourteenth-century Mittertor close by St Nikolaus. And running south from the church is Helig-Geist-Straße, sheltering the Heiliggeistkirche, a quaint church built in 1449 with a ladies' gallery and a couple of baroque chapels inside. A later treasure of Rosenheim is the seventeenth-century baroque Heilig-Blut-Kirche, which you find on the very edge of the town by taking Kufsteinerstraße on the way to the Munich–Salzburg motorway.

Bad Aibling, eleven kilometres further west of Rosenheim, is a sizeable health resort, its spa park spotted with a mini-golf course for the fit and convalescing, its centre washed by little streams – offshoots of the Rivers Glohn and Mangfall. The eighteenth-century church of St Sebastian (in spite of some pretty statues, especially that of the pincushion saint over the high altar) is scarcely a match for the much grander Maria Himmelfahrt, whose magnificent tower rises high above the town up Kirchzeile. Kirchzeile also houses the colourfully painted Hotel Ratskeller, embellished with pretty oriel windows. As I entered the church just beyond the hotel I was delighted to find someone practising on the organ, whose loft supports a couple of carved musical cherubs, one doubling up on the horn and the double bass, the other playing a celestial trombone.

Our Lady in her Assumption seems to have a head start into heaven on this hill. Above the first pillar on the left of the nave is painted Elijah, also off to heaven without the intervention of death, and thus a precursor of Mary. (The Bible tells us that a chariot of fire and horses of fire separated him from his faithful follower Elisha, and he went up by a whirlwind into heaven.) The hill on which the church stands turns out to be of yet more interest, for it was once the site of a Celtic *oppidum*. Here in 855 Kaiser Ludwig the German built a palace – hence its name, the Hofberg. The church itself derives from Ludwig's palatine chapel. A Gothic church replaced the medieval one in 1431. Then in 1754 Johann Michael Fischer, Munich's civic architect, drew up plans to transform it into a baroque and rococo building. The work was beautifully executed by Abraham Millauer. Courtly patronage helped to enhance the church, for the court painter Martin Heigl was despatched to Bad Aibling to decorate the ceiling. Over the high altar he painted a fresco of the Blessed Virgin succouring the four corners of the earth. You can make out the date: 1755.

As for the delicate rococo stucco work, it was entrusted to a native of Bad Aibling, Thomas Schwarzenberger, helped by another stucco master named Fink who came from Erding. A grisly touch is the skeleton of St Honoratus, brought here from the catacombs and exhibited underneath a fine crucifixion group sculpted by Josef Götsch, another Bad Aibling artist.

Drive on north-west for eleven kilometres to Feldkirchen-Westerham, passing its massive classical church of St Laurentius, built in the late nineteenth and early twentieth centuries and furnished with elaborate Gothic altar pieces of a similar date. By now the distant peaks have begun to subside into wooded hills. A kilometre out of Feldkirchen-Westerham our route turns south-west. After winding for twelve more kilometres through woodlands and farming villages it reaches Holzkirchen, which, as its name implies, boasts more than one church, though neither today is built of wood. St Laurentius dates from 1711. Go inside, if only to relish on the right of the apse a statue of around 1500 depicting St Lawrence delicately holding the griddle on which he was roasted to death. Equally enchanting is the statue on the left of the apse, of roughly the same date, showing the infant Jesus springing from his mother's lap into the arms of his grandmother St Anne. Both Mary and Anne are dressed in golden robes, but whereas the Madonna also sports a golden crown her mother wears a simple homely headscarf.

As you drive on south-west along the Bundestraße 13 towards Bad Tölz, on no account miss, after twelve kilometres, a signpost directing you one kilometre off the main road to Sachsenkam and Kloster Reutberg. You park outside the old monastic buildings to be assailed by the welcoming tangy smell of hops from the Bräuerie Genoßen-schaft Reutberg, the former monastic brewery, whose produce you can sample at the nearby Bräustüberl. Thus refreshed, slip inside the church to admire the Madonna and her divine child, sculpted over the high altar and both wrapped up, it seems, in one sleeping bag. They come in fact from Loreto in Italy, brought here in 1616 to grace the monastery that had begun to be built ten years previously. Today's building dates from over a hundred years later, begun in 1729 and finished within six years. Over the clock above the entrance to the apse is a fresco depicting the miraculous transfer from Nazareth to Loreto of the house in which the Virgin Mary was born.

Bad Tölz lies just ahead, washed by the Stausee and the River Isar, its Aldstadt well marked as you approach. You reach it through a gate dated 1353, though restored in 1969. You can park on the left beside the town hall. Before exploring the Kirche, why not eat perhaps in the Gasthof Zantl or take a picnic beside the little stream running through the dark, shady and usually deserted park. (You find this park by following Am Schloßplatz left from the town hall past the Haus Schmidt and down some winding steps.) Then stroll down the pedestrianized Markstraße, which is flanked by beautiful houses with overhanging roofs and elegant façades. One of the houses sports an incongruous onion dome.

The local hero of Bad Tölz is Kaspar von Winzerer, who perished in a joust with Jörg Frondsberg of Brandenburg on 25 October 1552. When the citizens of the town set up in Marktstraße their memorial to the dead of the Franco-Prussian War they decorated it with panels showing Kaspar's unfortunate death, a happier time when he fought a tourney against Kaiser Max I at Vienna in 1515, another occasion when he and Frondberg took prisoner King François I of France at Pavia in 1515, and a contemporary scene depicting Napoleon III fleeing from Sedan in September 1870.

Halfway down Marktstraße, Schulgasse leads left to the church of Maria Himmelfahrt. The church was rebuilt in the late-Gothic style after a fire destroyed it on 4 May 1453. The stained glass of around 1500 in the aisles includes rich purples and blues, especially in the scenes depicting the birth of Jesus and the visit of the Magi. Delicate tracery in the apse announces what I find a bizarre, sub-Leonardo da Vinci 'Last Supper' adorning the high altar. Far more to my taste is the baroque Madonna which Bartholomäus Steinle carved for the arch of the choir in 1611. She rises to heaven on a white cloud, radiantly blessing the earth. Seek too the Winzererkapelle, added in the sixteenth century, its entrance frescoed with both St Sebastian and St Roch, defenders against the plague.

Marktstraße continues its gentle way, with a modern Maria fountain complementing the 1870–1 war memorial, as far as the River Isar. Young and old bathe in summer from the shingle. Rising high ahead is the Franziskanerkirche, set today in the war memorial gardens. You can read the date of the church (1735) painted on the west wall, a reminder that the Elector Maximilian I of Bavaria had summoned the reformed Franciscans into his realm fifteen years earlier. The foundation stone of this church was laid in 1724. We do not know the name of its architect. Though he built a recognizably baroque church, he deliberately kept it simple in accordance with the spirit of the order of beggars.

Beyond the church is laid out one of the three spa parks. People come to Bad Tölz to swelter in peat baths and to taste the waters of the iodine spring discovered in 1846. Both of them are reputed to improve the circulation, to cure bronchial asthma, to relieve rheumatic fever and to ameliorate spinal deficiencies. The sick bathe in the open-air swimming pool at Eichmühle and in the 'Alpamare', a pool with artificial surf waves and thermal bubble pools. Sick and healthy listen to the concerts of the Bad Tölz boys' choir, and the hale take the Blombergbahn chairlift for vigorous mountain walks in summer and ski runs in winter. On 6 November they all take part in the *Tölzer Leonhardifahrt*, when the citizens dress in traditional costume, brass bands play and horses pull decorated carts through the streets.

To reach Benediktbeuern from Bad Tölz cross the River Isar and take the B472 in the direction of Schongau. The road runs for thirteen hilly kilometres by way of Bad Heilbrunn to Bichl. There you turn left along the B11 and fing Benediktbeuern but one kilometre further on. Benediktbeuern boasts the oldest monastery in upper Bavaria, an abbey founded twelve and a half centuries ago in 789. At the crossroads in the middle of the village look for the sign Kloster-Basilika, pointing right. The twin-towered, onion-domed monastery church rises ahead of you along Don-Bosco-Straße. Its eighteenth-century buildings now house a philosophical and theology high school, an institute for young people and a youth hostel. The huge cloister is humanized with a massive copper beech, a fountain and a rose garden. From here you walk into the baroque abbey church, elaborately crammed with swags of stucco work.

Returning to the village of Benediktbeuern you can continue for six kilometres to Köchel am See, and take a right fork which will lead you after another seventeen kilometres to Murnau. This is the way to Oberammergau, to the great monastery of Ettal, and to Ludwig II's entrancing Linderhof, all of which are described on other pages of this book. But in search of the baroque and rococo I recommend retracing your steps to Bichl and taking the B472 west towards Peißenheim.

After twenty kilometres a T-junction sends you thirteen kilometres to the right to entrancing Weilheim.

The town surrounds its main church, Maria Himmelfahrt in Kirchplatz, standing on the site of an old hospice. The bulbous dome and cupola contrast with the sturdy stone tower, early Gothic in date and style and forty-five metres high. A date on one side tells you that the dome and cupola were added in 1573 (when in fact lightning had destroyed the Gothic spire). A date on the other side reveals that they were restored in 1975. Georg Praun and Bartholomäus Steinle were responsible for transforming the church into a baroque one in the 1620s, just as the woodcarvers and goldsmiths of Weilheim were becoming famous. In 1690 one of the latter, Josef Anton Kipflinger, was to supply the church with a superb monstrance, designed in the form of a tree of Jesse setting out the heavenly and earthly origin of Jesus. Jörg Schmuzer, the stucco-master from nearby Wessobrunn, enriched the rest. A typical rococo motif is found in the Anger chapel – Judith with the head of Holofernes, frescoed in 1761 by Johann Baptist Baader. Another is an extremely nonchalant St Michael sticking his lance through the neck of Lucifer – the work of Franz Xaver Schmädl. Amid these seventeenth- and eighteenth- century treasures, do not miss the font. It dates from 1547, though its base is Romanesque. Close by on the wall is what the Germans call an *Astkreuz* (or 'branch crucifix'), made in 1350, with Jesus hanging on two leafy branches of a tree.

Traffic is banned from Marienplatz on the far side of the church. On a red marble column rises a statue of the virgin, set up as a thanks offering by those spared by the plague of 1698. Marienplatz is also adorned by a stone fountain depicting rustic children at play. It happens to be a copy made in the eighteenth century of a fountain from the monastery at Steingaden. In the hot sun, umbrellas shelter men and women quaffing beers on the pavement outside the local hotel. The square is flanked by the former Rathaus, which dates from 1533. Now the Heimatmuseum, this charming small building houses a remarkable range of masterpieces – works by Hans and Adam Krumper, by Steinle, Schmädl and J. B. Zimmermann, and a terrific 'Man of Sorrows' by Hans Leinberger – as well as the requisite number of cribs that no self-respecting Heimatmuseum in his part of Germany can be without.

Walk on past the Rathaus to the end of the street and you discover a sad notice telling you that the Oberer Tor stood here from 1238 until it was smashed down in 1871. Even so, Weilheim remains unspoilt, uncolonized by tourist traps, with elegant shops selling Bavarian delicacies and clothing to the residents and nobody thinking of exploiting its charm simply in order to make money.

The tiny and famous village of Wessobrunn lies twelve kilometres from Weilheim on the tree-lined road to Landsberg. On the way, at Polling bei Weilheim, stands a fifteenth-century church formerly belonging to Augustinian canons. Its mighty tower was added by Hans Krumper in the seventeenth century. Its high altar was created by B. Steinle in 1623. It houses a lovely enthroned Madonna carved by Hans Leinberger in 1526. Notice too the *trompe-l'oeil* arches frescoed at the entrance to the sacristy, another fresco depicting the flight into Egypt, with Mary dressed like a mid-eighteenth-century Bavarian milkmaid, and an amazing fresco of Jesus's resurrection, with the skeleton of death falling defeated and a denizen of the deep scratching his head in puzzlement. The rococo artist was Johann Baptist Baader.

Wessobrunn became celebrated in the eighteenth century for producing an astonishing number of brilliant craftsmen and artists: stucco workers such as the Feuchtmayr brothers and J. G. Üblherr; Franz Xaver and Johann Schmuzer and his son Josef; and the supreme Zimmermanns. Look out as you arrive for the signpost for Kloster-Pfarrkirche, which suddenly appears on a bend pointing right. This Benedictine monastery was founded around 753 by Duke Tassilo III and three noble brothers. Tassilo is said to have dreamed that angels were ascending and descending a ladder to a holy well discovered on this spot by a huntsman named Wezzo – hence he called the site Wezzo's well (Wezzobrunnen).

Apart from the grumpy fortified belfry, built in the twelfth century, today the monastery buildings, long and low, date from the late seventeenth and early eighteenth centuries and are largely the work of the Schmuzer family. The often lavish plasterwork seems ill-befitting men supposedly devoted solely to the godly life (or to such women, for the convent was taken over by Benedictine nuns in 1913). The hunting scenes in the Hall of Tassilo are particularly opulent.

In the forerunner of this Benedictine monastery, around the year 814, the oldest document in the German tongue was composed. This document, which glowingly bespeaks deep, Christian spirituality and is known as the Wessobrunn prayer, runs thus:

Das erfragte ich unter den Menschen
als des Wissens Größtes: Daß die Erde
nicht war noch den hohe Himmel, noch
Baum noch Berg war, noch irgendetwas,
noch die Sonne schien, noch der Mond
leuchtete, noch das Meer war.
Als da nichts war von Erden und Grenzen,
da war doch den allmächtige Gott,
den Menschen ganze milde, und da waren
auch mit ihm viele gottähnliche Geisten,
und Gott war heilig.
*   Allmächtiger Gott,*
der du Himmel und Erde geschaffen und
den Menschen so manch Gutes verliehen hast,
verleihe mir in denier Gnade
rechten Glauben und guten Willen,
Weisheit und Klugheit und Kraft,
den Teuteln zu widerstehen
und das Arge zu meiden
und deinen Willen zu vollbringen.

(This I learned as the greatest thing known to men:
that the earth did not exist, nor the sky, nor tree
nor mountain nor anything at all,
neither did the sun shine nor the moon give light,
nor was there any sea.
When there were neither ends nor limits
there was one almightly God,
the mildest of men, and with him many glorious spirits,
and God was holy.
    Almighty God,
who made heaven and earth
and has showered mankind with so many gifts,
in your mercy give me true faith and good will,
wisdom and insight and strength
to withstand devils and avoid evil,
and to accomplish your will.)

Since the surviving manuscript (now in the Bavarian state library in Munich) contains eighteen pen-drawings, Wessobrunn must also be acknowledged as the source of the earliest Christian paintings in Bavaria.

A century and a half later, in 955, Huns razed the monastery, slaughtering the abbot and six monks. It was refounded in the mid-eleventh century. You can visit the monastery today only with a guided tour (on weekdays at 10.00, 15.00 and 16.00; on Sundays and festivals at 15.00 and 16.00), but the parish church is open throughout the day. From the outside the church of St Johann Baptist seem unprepossessing, the tower apparently the sole remnant of the former Romanesque building. But in the mid-eighteenth century F. X. Schmuzer transformed the interior into a rococo masterpiece. The frescos are by Johann Baptist Baader and date from 1759. That depicting the baptism of Jesus contains the artist's signature – or part of it, the legend 'Baa' on the collar of a little dog.

On the north wall of the church hangs a Romanesque gem: the Wessobrunn cross, carved in the mid-thirteenth century. If you are to believe local legend, another survivor of that era is a lime tree with a circumference of 13.17 metres, the Tassilolinde, said to be 700 years old. As for Wezzo's well, Josef Schmuzer in 1735 built a well house which still stands to the east of the church and encloses three springs.

Our journey now takes us to Dießen am Ammersee, twenty-four kilometres away and reached by turning right at Rott (six kilometres from Wessobrunn). The first half of the road is wooded, until it emerges into open countryside to give tantalizing glimpses of the lake ahead. Exquisitely situated on this lake, which is sixteen kilometres long, six kilometres wide and plied by steamers, Deißen has flourished as a holiday resort. Its Klosterkirche, which we are making for, is signposted to the right at the entrance to the village. Unlike St Johann Baptist at Wessobrunn, Maria Himmelfahrt at Dießen is instantly impressive, flanked by monastic buildings and boasting an entrancing curved and gilded baroque façade. To delay experiencing the stupendous effect of the interior, you can slake your thirst and eat a snack at the monastic Chorherrstüberl next to the church.

I think the exquisite baroque ironwork and gates separating the nave from the entrance or atrium inside the church are usually locked, but the last time I visited Dießen the lady who was cleaning the church kindly let me walk down the great building. As you advance towards the high altar, cupolas reveal themselves, seemingly in motion and extending eastwards. Gesturing extravagantly, the four doctors of the church (here depicted by J. Dietrich) flank the high altar, over which God the Father, his son and a wide-spanned flying dove welcome the ascending Virgin Mary (painted by G. B. Tiepolo) into a gilded and white heaven. Cherubs peep out on to the scene. As you pick out details, barking dogs chasing a little fleeing child appear among the great ones. Look back at the organ, which divides itself wildly in the rococo fashion.

This is the climax of the whole trip, a building designed by Johann Michel Fischer in 1739 and decorated by the Feuchtmayr brothers and François Cuvilliés the Elder. One relic of the earlier church remains: a fifteenth-century Renaissance statue of St Peter, balding but still with curly locks and a curly beard, sculpted in wood by Erasmus Grasser. He was as witty a genius as the Wessobrunn masters who decorated this church, but I think the finest joke is in the carving of St Jerome, one of the four doctors of the church on the high altar. Jerome is usually recognized by the fact that he wears a cardinal's hat and carries a skull. Here indeed is the skull, but his hat has been borrowed by a cheeky nearby putto, who is about to try it on.

If your passion for churches has not abated, look at Dießen for another, St Georg, first set up in the fifteenth century and embellished by baroque masters (particularly Matthäus Günther and F. X. Feucht-mayr) in the mid-eighteenth century. If you arrive on Ascension Day you will find that the annual Dießben pot market (*Töpfermarkt*) has brought in potters from all over the region. Otherwise, drive on to Andechs by turning right at the T-junction at the bottom of the hill from Maria Himmelfahrt and following the signs for another eleven kilometres. For centuries Kloster Andechs has been famous for its cheese and its beer, and to sit outside the Bräustüberl sampling both just below the monastery church is a treat. Needless to say, though founded in the Middle Ages on the Heiliger Berg, a holy mountain 711 metres above sea level, the church was rebuilt many times, and what we see today is a ravishing blend of mid-fifteenth-century Gothic and Johann Baptist Zimmermann's rococo. If you do find time to slip inside, inspect the Törringkapelle to see Zimmermann's 1755 charm-ing, but exceedingly effete, depiction of Duke Tassilo and his three noble friends deciding to found a monastery at Wessobrunn beside Wezzo's well.

The Wessobrunn geniuses would leave their village in early summer to create exquisite buildings throughout Bavaria, returning home as the winter drew near. By 1716, however, Domenikus Zimmermann had settled at Landsberg am Lech (which is our next stop, reached by driving north along the lakeside and then due west along the E54). When Zimmermann arrived, Landsberg was already a lovely town, as its splendid Bayertor (the fifteenth-century Bavarian gate), its surviving thirteenth-century walls and towers, the citadel built by Henry the Lion and the basilica of Maria Himmelfahrt still reveal. By this time the basilica, designed by an architect from Strasbourg named Kindlin, was being enriched inside, with stained glass from Augsburg, lavish stucco work and, above all, Hans Reichle's huge and richly detailed high altar, whose massive columns twist and writhe.

Domenikus left his own singular mark on the town's architecture. In 1730 he had been asked to decorate the lady chapel of the Heiliggeist-kirche, which had been built in the 1580s by Elias Holl. (Alas, Holl's unique genius can no longer be seen in the church, for it was rebuilt in the 1750s.) Then in 1741 Zimmerman was given the opportunity to build his own church at Landsberg, St Johannes. He revealed his triumphantly eccentric mettle by submitting and carrying through a horseshoe-shaped chancel.

In 1749 he became Bürgermeister of Landsberg, and fittingly enriched the Rathaus in the delightful Marktplatz with a new rococo façade. Yet Landsberg was not his first choice of home after Wessobrunn, and it was not his last. Already he had lived for eight years at Füssen, on the edge of the Austrian Alps. The road from Landsberg to Füssen runs south through Schongau (where Domenikus stuccoed the chancel of the parish church in Marienplatz) and, more importantly, past the monastery of Steingaden, which had grown rich on the salt trade. In the sixteenth century the monks had used part of their wealth to transform the interior of their Romanesque church. During Zimmermann's time at Landsberg, F. X. Schmuzer had been commissioned to stucco the interior and the Augsburg painter J. G. Bergmüller to add frescos.

Today Domenikus Zimmermann lies buried in the Romanesque cloisters of the monastery, whose monks had provided the funds for him and his brother Johann Baptist to create an unsurpassed rococo masterpiece, the Wieskirche. Wieskirche means 'church in a field', and that is precisely what it is, a building standing on its own in a meadow south-east of the monastery. Domenikus and Johann Baptist built it between 1746, when the first stone was laid, and 1757, when the organ was completed. When it was finished Domenikus built a house next door and there he died nine years later.

The Wieskirche is a pilgrimage church and the most astounding of the whole route. Sixteen years before the Zimmermann brothers began working here, the monks of Steingaden had carved a statue of Jesus scourged, for use in their Good Friday procession. Not long before a mystic, the Blessed Crescentia of Kaufbeuren, had persuaded many Bavarian Christians to give particular reverence to such images of Jesus; but soon after carving their statue the monks concluded that their suffering Lord was too intensely depicted. They threw the statue out. A pious farmer's wife, Maria Lory, rescued it and built a small chapel in its honour in the meadow next to her home. On 14 June 1738, as she was praying before the image, she saw that it was weeping.

In no time pilgrims were arriving in their hundreds to pray before this miraculous flagellated Jesus, and the Steingaden monks commissioned the new church because the little chapel was bursting open with the crowds. Domenikus Zimmermann designed the exterior deliberately to match the line of the hills beyond. Painted yellow and white, its muted tones only serve to emphasize the wild pink, blue, gold-leaf, red and green of the interior. Basically an oval, the nave sinuously draws you to the choir, flanked by six blue-veined columns, which lead your eyes to the four red-veined ones carrying the canopy of the high altar and the image of the scourged Christ.

Johann Baptist brilliantly contrasted this image with that of Jesus judging the world, the ceiling fresco of the nave. This Jesus is one who has atoned for the sins of the elect, not a stern condemner but the Good Shepherd gently gathering in his flock.

I love above all in this church the evidence of Domenikus Zimmermann's playfulness. When he came to design the organ he used woodwork covered with stucco to give the illusion that the arches are upside-down, by some miracle defying gravity. And at each 'corner' of his oval nave he set the four doctors of the church, each identified by his own symbol. On the pulpit he set four merry cherubs, each one mimicking the symbols of the great doctors.

If you take the Munich road from Steingaden you can compare this religious jesting with the architectural playfulness displayed by the decorations by Franz Xaver Schmädl and Balthasar Freiwiß in the mid-eighteenth-century interior which they (with the help of Josef Schmuzer and Matthäus Günther) created for the Romanesque Augustinian monastery church at Rottenbuch. The fat, trumpet blow-ing cherub atop Schädl's pulpit is delightful enough, but those playing the fiddle, flugelhorns and kettle-drums on Freiwiß's organ of 1747 are utterly charming. But for the Wieskirche and the church of Vierzehnheiligen, which I am about to describe, one might ascribe to the whole interior of this church the palm of Bavarian rococo.

At this point my tour breaks down, for the church of Vierzehnheiligen stands at virtually the opposite, north-eastern corner of Bavaria, near Lichtenfels. Vierzehnheiligen was created after another peasant had enjoyed visions similar to Maria Lory's glimpse of the tearful scourged Jesus. The name of the church means 'fourteen saints' and refers to that select number thought, in Bavaria, to be specially devoted to succouring mankind. In the mid-fifteenth century these saints, accompanied by the infant Jesus, repeatedly appeared to a pious shepherd who lived beside the River Main three kilometres south of Lichtenfels in Franconia.

His visions occurred on the opposite bank from the abbey of Banz, which retains aspects of a fortress even though the Dientzenhofer brothers added their lighter touches in the seventeenth and early eighteenth centuries. This abbey had brought to the region the architect who was to create Vierzehnheiligen, for in 1752 Balthasar Neumann had contributed a wing incorporating an elegant rococo gatehouse.

Neumann was one of those great architectural innovators who, alongside Johann Baptist Straub, Ignaz Günther and Joseph Anton Feuchtmayr progressed from elegant baroque to a rococo style whose sublimity verges on the tormented. In 1743 he and his pupil Johann Michael Küchel were commissioned to build a church on the spot where the fourteen saints (or *Nothelfer*, as the Bavarians called them) had appeared. The site itself is impressive, high above the left bank of the river. Küchel designed the Gnadenaltar, dedicated to the fourteen *Nothelfer* and enlisted artists of the calibre of the Feuchtmayr brothers to help him decorate it. The brilliant J. I. Appiani frescoed the ceiling.

But the overall genius was Balthasar Neumann. It is said that he initially planned to place the Gnadenaltar in one of the customary spots for such an altar, namely the crossing; but without his knowledge a supervisor of works made this impossible. At any rate, Neumann changed his mind and in a revolutionary stroke situated the altar in the nave. He embraced it in an oval. The notion inspired him to abut on to this oval two more longitudinal ovals, which he then had the audacity to match with a couple of more lateral ones.

These engineering details scarcely matter, as your sensibilities reel before the aesthetics of Vierzehnheiligen. Imaginative, creative engineering has become supreme artistry, at the service of Bavarian rococo.

A trip to Berchtesgaden

Especially where it passes by Lake Chiemsee, the Munich–Salzburg motorway is a scenic drive. Wisely, alongside the lake the Bavarians have laid out an extensive lay-by, for otherwise most of us, distracted from driving by the alluring sight of yachts and wooded islands, would surely smash into the car in front. If you are in a hurry to reach Berchtesgaden you can drive there from Munich along this motorway, turning south just before the Austrian border and taking the road through Bad Reichenhall.

An infinitely more entrancing route is to leave the motorway halfway between Munich and Berchtesgaden at Bernau, and drive south-east along Bundestraße 305 to join the spectacular German Alpine road at Grassau. In this pretty holiday town a fountain and a bust of King Ludwig II of Bavaria front the late-Gothic parish church of Maria Himmelfahrt. Though the south aisle of 1491 and an earlier Romanesque tower have survived virtually unchanged, the rest of the church was greatly extended in 1696 and the first half of the eighteenth century. In 1737 the tower was capped by its gracious onion dome. Inside you can trace the remains of a cycle of wall-paintings completed in the early fifteenth century. A glimpse of Bavaria's old-world piety is offered by the wall-painting in the porch, which dates from around 1700 and depicts a procession on the feast of Corpus Chrisi.

Drive on for three kilometres to splendidly situated Marquartstein, which straddles a river and lies at the foot of a 1,743-metre-high peak. The eleventh-century Burg Marquartstein here remains in private hands, but music-lovers should drive a little way up Bursagstraße to find the house known as 'die Ahna', where a plaque tells you that Richard Strauss lived here between 1894 and 1907. He was married in this town and lived happily here. At 'die Ahna' he composed songs, his symphonic poems and two operas, *Salome* and *Feuersnot*. He took the idea for *Feuersnot* ('Lack of fire') from a Flemish legend, *The Quenched Fires of Oudenarde*, but he twisted the theme to his own ironic purposes. The people of Munich, Strauss decided, had failed to respond properly to his own innovative music. In revenge he conceived his *Feuersnot* as an attack on the city for not having sufficient fire in its belly. Not surprisingly, in 1901 the first performance of the opera took place not in Bavaria but in Dresden.

Marquartstein possesses a parish church built in the 1930s, embellished with some of the weediest wall-paintings I have ever seen. Friends of 1930s' art and architecture will be better pleased with the nine muscular figures on the reredos. Others might like to walk in the fairy-tale and nature park (which you see signposted near the church along Loitshauserstraße).

The seventeen-kilometre route from Marquartstein as far as the Alpine resort of Reit im Winkl runs due south through the village of Unterwössen and an exhilarating narrow gorge. Its houses are decorated, its chairlifts innumerable, and the views from the Grünbühel (which virtually anyone can climb) magnificent. From Reit im Winkl continue along the B305, this time driving north-east through lake-cooled countryside until, after twenty-four kilometres, you reach bustling Ruhpolding, a baroque and rococo town of some 7,000 Bavarians. Here walk up Kirchberggasse to the parish church of St Georg. On the way you pass the presbytery, whose little fountain in the courtyard depicts St Francis and the birds. The steep walk is well worth the trouble and especially rewarding for its fine panorama of the valley below.

The simple stone tower of the parish church supports a double onion dome. Although the west end also remains Romanesque, the glamour of the building derives from the inspiration of Johann Gunetzrhainer, who redesigned the interior between 1738 and 1757. The eighteenth-century pulpit matches the rest in splendour, but nothing in the church surpasses a work of art from a much earlier age, the Romanesque Ruhpolding Madonna, carved in wood around 1230, which you find on the altar to the right of the entrance of the apse. Over the high altar of the church hangs a modern, jewelled cross designed by Professor Karl B. Berthold.

Climb up further to the cemetery, whose seventeenth-century chapel bears tomb-slabs on its walls, both inside and out. You perspire going up and amble gently down, after which pause to sample the cakes and the *Gut bürgerliche Küche* advertised in the shop windows. Ruhpolding's extremely colourful town hall was built only in 1923, but perfectly preserves the charm of a Rathaus built centuries earlier. This centre for winter sports also boasts a museum of local history in the former hunting Schloß. The Schloß itself was built in 1587.

In spite of the whispy clouds floating around their peaks, the mountains of this part of the winding German Alpine route are never menacing. Thirteen kilometres east from Ruhpolding you reach Inzell, a village which somehow conceals a vast number of summer visitors. The Chiemgauer Hof Hotel alone offers 500 beds and a Kindergarten, as well as 140 apartments whose renters cook for themselves, endure body-building torments, have their nails manicured, and swim, without any of the hotel buildings remotely impinging on the skyline. The local inns offer the hungry an *Inzeller Suppentopf* – a liver, meat and vegetable soup – followed by what they call a *Pfandl*, which I conjecture is three different fillets, served with a ragout of mushrooms, plus fresh vegetables and home-made noodles or *Spätzle*. Another local delicacy is braised veal topped with cream (*Kalbsrahmbraten*), usually served with a salad and buttered *Spätzle*. Amazed at the capacity of the visitors' stomachs, I have watched them guzzle all this and finish their meal with *Apfelknödel* and marinated plums.

Small wonder that Inzell also sets out to be a place where the holiday-making sick can recover from the excesses of their workaday lives, or simply from eating too much. Its town hall curiously houses a table-tennis room, a reading room and a salon showing video films. Opposite rises the church of St Michael, founded by Archbishop Albrecht II of Salzburg in 1190. This Romanesque building was burnt down in 1724, and all that remains today of the original is the tower, massively strengthened to sustain the typical baroque onion dome of this region. The new nave, begun in 1727 and finished after two years, was several times restored in the nineteenth century and also in the mid-1930s. Since its redecoration in 1985 it gleams with pride. The organ loft is rapturously beautiful, built in tiers like a sliced wedding cake.

Every window in Inzell, with its winding streets and merry Gasthof Zur Post, looks out on the far from unfriendly hills and crags, though a hint of snow suggests the more dangerous mountains ahead. If you wish to practise hill-walking here, buy from the local tourist office one of the superbly detailed maps called a *Wanderkarte*. The Bavarians have gone to enormous trouble to number and signpost the walks in their sometimes gentle, sometimes taxing hills. Make sure you spot which ones are easy and which are reserved for skilled fell-walkers (*nur für geübte Bergsteiger*). For the most part your leg muscles need to be equal to the demands of walking in the English Lake District, but you can rest in little mountain huts. Each route suggests how long it should take (one way, not there and back), though I have never managed to match these times. From Inzell you walk through beech woods, which thin out as you climb, mingling now with fir trees and then Alpine pasture, with cows staring at you and shaking the bells around their necks. Deer appear too, scrutinizing this intruder before bounding away. Walking through these trees in summer is pleasant simply because they offer such shade. Then comes scrubland. To look down upon tiny houses, towers, valleys and countryside, or else over to the Alps, makes you think you have entered a totally different world.

Drive south-east from Inzell looking for the sign that directs you north-east to Bad Reichenhall. *Hall* is the Celtic word for salt, and Bad Reichenhall has prospered on the salt trade since Celtic times. Salt was never mined here, but simply poured out from wells. Pipelines – which were cheaper than horses-drawn drays – still pump salt to this spot from Berchtesgaden. The salt water has long enabled Bad Reichenhall to set itself up as a thermal spa. But to visit the underground springs and pump rooms of the former Alte Saline or salt works (open most days in summer from 10.00 to 11.30 and from 14.00 to 16.00) is to invite a history lesson in this tremendously profitable spice. The works were built in the first decade of the sixteenth century, though in 1834 Ludwig I had his architects massively transform much of the buildings. Moritz von Schwind also frescoed the chapel of the salt works. You find the Alte Saline by walking from Rathausplatz along

Salinenstraße. The stones of Schloß Gruttenstein, which rises nearby, date from the thirteenth to the seventeenth centuries.

By walking south past the salt works towards the Altstadt and turning right along Kirchgaße, you come to the Romanesque basilica of St Nikolaus. Its modern shell houses a surprisingly ancient interior, cool, narrow, unspoilt – and unexpected, because the church of 1181 was widened in 1860, when the tower was added, so that the exterior in no way announces the glorious interior. Its frescos too are by Moritz von Schwind. Early medieval town walls stretch fitfully from this church, as well as the remains of the Tyroler gate.

Bad Reichenhall is a sizeable town, its centre and environs housing altogether nearly 20,000 inhabitants. Its prosperity today derives as much from its status as a spa and a winter sports centre as from the tourist attractions of its ancient buildings. As I do not ski, or suffer from rheumatism, nor am I much drawn to the roulette and baccarat tables of Bad Reichenhall's Spielbank, I prefer the ancient buildings.

Oddly enough, some of the most attractive turn out to be not so ancient. Rathausplatz centres on a pretty fountain, with lions prowling around its column, which you are surprised to discover was erected only in 1905. The old town hall was burnt down in a terrible fire which raged throughout the night of 8–9 November 1834, so the present Altes Rathaus dates from 1849. The town hall square none the less exudes an attractively old-fashioned air. On its north-west corner stands the Altes Brodhaus with a fine oriel window on its corner, again rebuilt after the fire but modelled on the fourteenth-century building that burned down.

If you follow Poststraße past the Altes Brodhaus you reach the Carmelite church of St Ägidien, built in 1159 in the Romanesque style and partly Gothicized in the fifteenth century. Its tower fell down in 1978, but the speedy Bavarian architects have rebuilt it. St Ägidien has two paintings which, to me, are particularly moving. One (on the wall to the right as you go inside) depicts its parish priest, an opponent of the Nazis who died in Dachau concentration camp in 1942. The other, outside on the apse wall, shows the four horsemen of the Apocalypse riding above the town when it was once more the victim of a fire, this time after an Allied air attack on 25 April 1945, which left 224 of its citizens dead. A legend begs the protection of the Mother of God.

Should you now feel the need for a glass of Bavarian beer, walk around the apse and through an arch on the south side, where you will find that part of the former convent has been turned into the St Ägidi-Keller. The other side of the road is blessed with another pretty fifteenth-century building, the former offices of the salt works. Getreidegasse leads left by this Salzmaierampt to the long, low fourteenth-century granary, the Städtischer Getreidesaal, which has become the local history museum of Bad Reichenhall.

Bad Reichenhall offers a curiously welcome change from most other towns and villages in this region by having remained remarkably Romanesque in its ecclesiastical architecture. At the end of Poststraße rises the Romanesque church of St Johannes. But the finest in the town is undoubtedly the monastic church of St Zeno, rising on the north-east edge of the town. This is the largest Romanesque basilica in Upper Bavaria. Archbishop Konrad I of Salzburg founded it for Augustinian canons in 1208. The propensity of churches for burning down in this region means that part was rebuilt in the late-Gothic style after a fire of 1512. None the less the cloisters and a superb Romanesque doorway survived the conflagration and the rebuilding. Red and grey marble aparts to the doorway a gentleness which entirely suits the carvings of the Madonna and child, worshipped by Saints Zeno and Rupertus. Because one of the monastery's patrons was Frederick Barbarossa, the chapel in the east wing of the cloister carries an inscription, FRIDERI-CUS IMP, acknowledging the imperial generosity.

Berchtesgaden is only eighteen kilometres away, but *en route* you pass through the health resort of Bischofswiesen, one of the five towns that make up the Berchtesgadener Land. The other four are Markt Schellenberg, Ramsau, Schönau am Königsee and Berchtesgaden itself. At Bischofswiesen a sign points you to the left for a five-kilometre-drive to a pilgrimage church you should on no account fail to see, Maria Gern.

Lying just outside Bischofswiesen, the situation of Maria Gern itself is devastatingly charming. Bischofswiesen means 'bishops' fields', deriving its name from land owned by the Bishops of Salzburg when they ruled the Berchtesgadener Land. These green, hilly fields, stretching away to the often snow-clad mountains, surround the exquisite little pink and white church. In spite of its beauty, the artists and architects who created it are scarcely known, save to experts. Two master builders from the Berchtesgaden court, Gabriel Wenig and Jacob Hilliprant, designed the building in the first decade of the eighteenth century. The swirling stucco-work inside is the work of

Joseph Schmidt of Salzburg. In 1710 a devout lay-brother and artist named Christoph Lehrl added the cycle of paintings on the ceiling depicting episodes in the life of the Virgin Mary. He also frescoed the side altars and the organ gallery. I relish the rococo ironwork underneath this gallery. Even the name MARIA sinuously twists above it in the rococo style.

The master who created the high altar was Caspar Schneider, though the magnificent fallen Lucifer and the yet more glorious St Michael, who is about to slay him, are by a sculptor named Andrä Stangaster. The man and woman on either side of the twisting, glittering columns of the altar are Saints Anna and Joachim, the parents of the Blessed Virgin. Two other altars, the altar of the Holy Cross to the left, which dates from 1737, and the Josephsaltar on the right, built a year or two later, are each flanked by pretty young angel-herms carrying elaborate medallions. The artist was proud enough to sign and date the altar painting of the Josephsaltar: *Jo: Zwick inv. e pin: Monachi 1740*. He was Johannes Zwick, court painter at Munich. All this is so glorious that you might almost forget the reason why it is here. Maria Gern was built as a pilgrimage church to house the older miracle-working statue of the Virgin herself, carved in 1666. She is at the centre of the high altar, borne on the clouds of heaven and carrying her infant son. Both are crowned, protectors of humanity, as the ex-votos on the walls of the church proclaim. Often this statue of the Madonna and child is swathed in richly embroidered robes, but I prefer it when you are allowed to see the entire statue. Then you see that Mary stamps on the moon with her foot, and that her divine son is marching like a clockwork soldier.

For refreshment, nearby is the Gastätte Maria Gern, as well as a village of fewer than 500 inhabitants. Return to the town of Bischofsheim, with its clinics, heated swimming pools, its tennis courts, winter sports and a network of paths and walks covering altogether ninety kilometres. Then drive on to Berchtesgaden. The transformation in atmosphere appears to me remarkable, for the spa town of Bad Reichenhall always seems to be filled with greyish persons of my own age, whereas Berchtesgaden bounds with adolescent life. But perhaps this is an illusion.

What is indisputable is the superb site of this altogether charming spot. In the whole of Germany only the Zugspitze rises higher than the 2,713-metre-high middle peak of the Watzmann. Seen from Berchtesgaden itself, the summit to the right of this Alpine peak is the 2,651-metre Hocheck. Across the valley rise eight other peaks, including the so-called 'little Watzmann', which points for 2,307 metres into the skies. Legend has it that the Watzmann represents a ferocious King Watzmann who lived long ago, and that the little Watzmann represents his wife. The seven other peaks are their children. In those far-off days, the tale continues, the whole family dominated the Berchtesgadener Land, viciously putting down anyone who tried to stand up to them. As a result God decided to punish them. One day every member of the bloodthirsty family was hunting in the mountains. A huge storm rocked the mountains, which fell on and buried these evil ones. Two basins filled with their blood – the origin of the lovely lakes now known as the Obersee and the Königsee.

Celtic tribes had been mining salt in this region five centuries before the Christian era. (Their graves have been excavated and sometimes found to contain jewellery and objects that the archaeologists conclude came from as far away as Greece, Egypt and Scotland). As the climate over 200 years or so had become moister and moister, the old ways of keeping food throughout the winter no longer worked. Once it was discovered that salt prevented meat, pork and poultry from rotting, these white crystals became of enormous importance.

Next, around the year 1000, a man named Perther built himself a hunting lodge (or *Gaden*, as Middle High German has it, hence Berchtesgaden) amid these spectacular surroundings. Others joined him, including Augustinian monks, and when the Augustinians of Berchtesgaden took to mining salt, the white crystals also brought them wealth. In the second half of the twelfth century they persuaded the Holy Roman Emperor Frederick Barbarossa to confirm their exclusive rights to excavate it here. Salt is still being mined at Berchtesgaden. Although the Augustinian monks are gone, the Berchtesgaden clergy still bless the mines on the feast of the Epiphany, and the salt miners still proudly parade the streets on Whit Monday.

No visitor to Berchtesgaden should pass up the opportunity of visiting the present-day salt mines, which were opened in 1517. They are still working, still pumping salt to Bad Reichenhall. It is best to make your visit when the sun is shining, so as to remain cool while everyone else is sweltering. When it rains, especially in summer, the queues grow longer, for an annual half-million tourists visit these mines. Even if you have to queue, the visit is well worth the wait.

Before the one-and-a-half-hour trip down the mine begins, everyone dresses in the quaint costumes of salt miners of yesteryear, taking especial care to put on a wide leather belt to protect one's kidneys from the cold below. Then, squatting across a narrow miners' railway train, you travel in the dark through a 600-metre-long tunnel to a huge underground cave, now called Kaiser Franz pit. At this point the value of the miners' costumes becomes apparent, for the way down the next 110 metres or so is by means of a chute, a sort of helter-skelter on which everyone sits with his or her legs stuck out in front of them. The guide warns you not to try to slow yourself down with your feet or your hands, and whoosh! – you reach the bottom, your own rear end slightly warmer. Those who do not feel equal to the chute must laboriously descend a wooden staircase, to join the rest and admire the multi-coloured rocks which contain the salt.

There are two such fearful chutes, the second of which speeds you down to an eerie underground, artificial salt lake. To dig such a lake takes a full year, and before work starts the miners drill to make sure that the rocks contain at least 35 per cent salt. Finally, water is pumped in to dissolve the salt. A boat takes you bizarrely and silently across this lake.

The whole trip is excellently done. At one point underground you enter a little cinema, and a film-show depicts the whole history of the mine, beginning some 60 million years ago when the salt water evaporated and the deposits were formed before the Alps folded over and trapped them underground. For English- and French-speakers, who find German difficult, telephones provide simultaneous translations of the film's commentary. At other points in the visit loudspeakers set in the walls once again enable foreigners to understand in their own language what the guide is saying in German. Miners' equipment, old and new, is on display, as well as fossils, which have been preserved in the mine from prehistoric times.

Finally everyone squeezes into a miners' cage, which lifts them back to the long, narrow train for a pell-mell burst of speed through another long tunnel back to the surface, to the changing-rooms and the mine's restaurant.

Since the Augustinians have led us to the Berchtesgaden salt mines, let us begin a tour of Berchtesgaden itself at their former church, the Stiftskirche of St Peter and St John the Baptist. It stands in the Schloßplatz, which is homely and triangular and cooled by a fountain, with a couple of archways at two of the corners letting you in and out. Its longest side is closed by the former grain and teller's house, founded in 1458 and arcaded a hundred years later. In 1929 an artist named J. Hengge painted its outer wall with a grim war memorial. In the centre is the crucified Jesus. To his right an old man tries to stop his son from going to war. In the next scene the old man and his wife mourn their son's corpse. The face of the dead soldier, his eyes closed now, still wearing his useless tin helmet, is infinitely sad. The memorial was initially devoted to Bavarian victims of World War I, but it has been adapted to include those who died in World War II. The scene depicting the second of these wars is yet more harrowing than the one I have described. 'They gave their lives, their sacrifice is our exortation' runs the accompanying legend (*Sie gaben ihr Leben, ihr Opfer ist uns Mahnung*).

The monastic church of Saints Peter and John the Baptist and the former convent form the other two sides of the triangle. The church sports a couple of symmetrical ancient towers, built in the thirteenth century of reddish-grey stones, with mid-nineteenth-century spires. The Romanesque main doorway, which dates from the second half of the twelfth century, was also partly rebuilt in the nineteenth century. Most of this western façade is in fact entirely nineteenth-century Romanesque, including the two statues of the patrons of the church.

The interior is a graceful delight, the Romanesque nave dating from 1200 or so, the choir from a hundred years later. The splendidly off-centre Gothic net-vaulting of 1515 is entirely at home in this Romanesque masterpiece. Among the treasures of the church are a sculpted Romanesque bucket designed for carrying holy water, and in the entrance to the church a late–Gothic crucifixion, carved in the early sixteenth century. Whereas the Madonna of Maria Gern stamps on the moon with her left foot, the early baroque Madonna in this Stifstkirche is doing the same with her right one. Here too are rich red marble tombs of the Provosts (or *Propsts*) who ruled not just the monastery but also Berchtesgaden. Mitred, vested, carrying crosiers, they include – to the left of the main entrance as you come in – Fürstpropst Gregor Rainer, who started the salt mine we have just visited. The sumptuous choir stalls were carved out of oak in the middle of the fourteenth century.

By now, however, one becomes obsessed by the remarkable number of little galleries in this church, seeming opera-boxes, from which the nobility managed to attend divine worship without mingling with the lower orders. Most of them are on the southern side, on to which abuts the convent and cloisters that first housed the monks, then became the seat of the prince-abbot and finally were transformed into the residence of the Wittelsbachs.

The high altar reminds us how close we are to Salzburg, a mere twenty minutes' drive away, for in the 1660s Bartholomäus von Opstall modelled it on that in Salzburg cathedral. The tabernacle is a lovely work, silver and designed by Franz Thaddäus Lang in 1735. Leave the church by the north side, through its early Gothic atrium, whose tympanum is decorated with a curious picture of God the Father leaning from heaven to raise Jesus from the tomb. Jesus is flanked by his mother and St John, beside whom are the patrons of this church, St Peter and John the Baptist. There is one intruder, the little abbot kneeling on the left who commissioned the painting. On the right his coat of arms identifies him as Propst Erasmus Pretschlaiper. Above his mitre we would be able to read the date of the painting as 1474, but for the antique way in which the artist (Rueland Fruehauf the Elder) wrote the figure 4.

From the north-west corner of the Stiftskirche, if you have a taste for another, quite different church, you can walk the few paces needed to reach a second major house of God in Berchtesgaden, this time baroque in style and built between 1698 and 1700 (though the bottom storey of the tower is late-Gothic). The south wall has it opera box, for notables.

I like all the statues in this church, especially St Roch near the doorway, who is, as usual, showing his wounded leg and accompanied by a dog with a bun in its mouth. The topmost scene of the reredos of the high altar depicts a most elegant St George controlling his prancing charger as he slays the dragon, matched above him by St Michael killing Lucifer. Jesus is portrayed crowned with thorns to the left. An odd error is that his feet are already pierced, though he has not yet been crucified. On the right a sword pierces his sorrowing mother's heart.

The town hall of Berchtesgaden stands opposite the west door of this church, in a street leading back to the centre of the town. Overhanging one of its shops is an exotically ornate wrought-iron sign, depicting a pretzel and a couple of running bakers, laden with cookies. It proclaims that the shop is the Martin Kruis Hofbäckerei. A coffee pot enclosed within the sign tells you that this is a café as well as a baker's. The window below does not belie the sign, with its white and black bread, a sunflower of little loaves baked together, and then innumerable varieties of loaves – *Vollkornbrot, Sonnen-kornbrot, Beystagersemmel, Vitalbrot, Vielkornbrot, Dinkelbrot, Müslisemmel* . . .

Leave until later exploration of the Schloß itself, now a museum, and, through the south-west archway of the Schloßplatz, make your way to the Renaissance and baroque Marktplatz of Berchtesgaden. The inscription on the pretty fountain tells you that it was set up in 1860 'under the glorious reign of King Max II to mark the fiftieth anniversary of the union of Berchtesgaden and Bavaria' (until 1810 Berchtesgaden was part of the Holy Roman Empire). The present fountain rises on the site of one erected here by Churfürst Maximilian Heinrich in 1677, and if you look up at the colourful Hirchenhaus next to it he can be seen painted on the façade, along with his fountain. The other portrait on the façade is of Georg Inbermann, who built the Hirchenhaus in 1594 (save for its tower, which was added at the end of the nineteenth century).

Marktplatz, surrounded by superb burgers' houses, is, like Schloß-platz, basically a triangle. Having once foolishly left my Bavarian hat on an aeroplane, I bought a couple more from one of the nearby shops before walking on into Ludwig-Ganghofer-Straße, named after that merry Bavarian novelist whose most celebrated remark about the Berchtesgadener Land was 'Lord, let the one you love fall into this country.' Turn left out of Ludwig-Ganghofer-Straße into Dr-Imhof-Straße, which leads into Am Anger. At the end of it stands the Franciscan church of St Maria-am-Anger, which P. Kitzinger built between 1488 and 1519 (the tower was added in 1682).

This is a very strange church indeed, bisected by five simple round pillars, from which spring directly the arches of two aisles. There is no centre isle. At the east end the two side aisles meet at the Marienkapelle, built in 1688, a chapel quite different in style from the rest of the church. Adding to the mysterious delights of St Maria-am-Anger is the statue of the Virgin Mary over the altar of this chapel. 'Unsere Liebe Frau am Anger' was copied in Italy around 1500 from the statue of the Madonna in Milan cathedral.

Two other powerful, yet savage carvings adorn this church: a statue of the captive Christ with a sad bowed head, carved in 1689; and, against the third pillar from the west end, the grisly skull-bedecked tomb of Maria Honorata who died in 1713, leaving behind the widowed Landdirektor of Bavaria. Close by St Maria-am-Anger is a tombstone yet dearer to the people of Berchtesgaden. If you leave the church and turn into the cemetery, the first tomb on the right through the gate is that of Anton Adner, who lived between 1705 and 1822, for a staggering 117 years. In Adner's declining years the King of Bavaria paid a family to look after the old man, and in Berchtesgaden you can still drink in the Adnerstübl where they lived.

The National Park House is also next door to this church. An excellent exhibition inside, open daily from 09.30 to 17.30 (except from November to mid-December), outlines the history and aims of the Berchtesgaden National Park. Covering some 21,000 hectares, the park was founded in 1978 to protect not just plants (as had the former Botanical Protection Area) or even plants and animals (as had the Königsee Nature Reserve, founded in 1921) but the whole environment. In consequence the Alpine park authorities have, for example, restored in the park those strange huts whose roofs are held down with stones and whose antiquity is indicated by the name *Kaser*, which derives from the Latin for house (*casa*). Ibex, ptarmigan, black grouse, the snow hare, the snow mouse and alpine chough are preciously guarded, and the deforestation of past years is slowly being remedied.

The National Park House exhibition outlines also the natural history of the Berchtesgaden Alps, as well as the formation of its various rock strata. Finally, a short video show whets your appetite for the best of all the services of Berchtesgaden's National Park House, its guided tours. An annual printed programme allows you to decide whether you wish to spend all day under the expert guidance of a trained leader, or simply spend an afternoon in this astonishingly rich Alpine park. You may choose an exceedingly· stiff climb up the Watzmann, which was conquered only in 1881 and has since claimed eighty-five victims, or take the cable car to the 1800-metre-high Jenner peak and follow a marked climbing path from there.

The Jenner is famed for its stupendous views and for its skiing, as well as for a toboggan run. Less able skiers take the Hirscheck chairlift to the Hochschwarzeck, at the foot of a mountain alarmingly dubbed 'the dead man' (*Toter Mann*). Altogether the region boasts four skiing areas, catering for the experienced, for families and for beginners. No one in Berchtesgaden claims that this region matches any of the huge Austrian ski resorts – if you wish to ski from morning till evening on a new slope every day, this is not your centre; but it is the right place for downhill skiing, for cross-country walks and for nature lovers.

If you prefer wandering alone rather than in a party with a guide, the National Park House can provide you with detailed plans of suggested tours (or *Wandervorschläge*). Some, of course, are restricted only to the experienced hill-walker, and a few German phrases are worth committing to memory, namely, 'closed roads' (*gesperrte Straße*), 'danger of precipices' (*Absturgefahr*) and 'only for experts' (*nur für Geübte*). After that, wandering in the National Park is safe and immensely rewarding.

A walk in the Klausbach valley, for instance, allows you to watch gentle red deer feeding at Hintersee. By feeding these lovely beasts the National Park authorities hope to stop them nibbling at the bark of young trees and killing them. A more exhausting tour takes one up the Mülsturzhorn and the mountain plateau of the Reiteralm, where arolla pine trees have reached 500 years of age, where the adders are as shy as the spring crocuses, where the Alpine roses are as profuse as the salamanders, except that the former come out by day and the latter only by night. To wander on the magic mountain here is to encounter huge fallen rocks, split bizarrely, to climb over the roots of trees growing across paths, and occasionally to be sprayed with water from the rushing torrent. This stream, sometimes developing into a whirlpool, descends from Hintersee. The water is sometimes a muddy brown after rainfall, blue in summer, ice-grey in winter and always ice-cold. Steps lead you mysteriously under rocks. A half-hour walk, say to Hintersee for a cup of coffee, followed by half-an-hour's walk back is romantic and, happily, scarcely rigorous, especially as benches dot the path from time to time.

This Zauberwald lies between the Hintersee and the health and winter sports resort of Ramsau. As you approach Ramsau from Berchtesgaden you pass through a tunnel, which in winter is hung with a mass of icicles. Lying on the stream known as the Ramsauer Ache (which flows into the Königsee Ache at Berchtesgaden), Ramsau itself, though vigorously devoted to offering its guests hiking, skiing, climbing, swimming, fishing and boating holidays, remains peaceful, because the Alpenstraße bypasses it.

Smack in the centre of the town rises its parish church, founded in the early sixteenth century, though its bulbous dome dates from the eighteenth. Inside the church you can see the old family names let into their personal pews, as well as Gothic statues of Jesus and the twelve apostles, sculpted in the first half of the fifteenth century and set on the organ loft. The high altar dates from 1680 and the rococo side altar from 1745.

Ramsau also boasts a pilgrimage church, Maria Kunterweg, on the slope of a nearby hill. On its ceiling is a fresco of the Blessed Virgin Mary triumphing over heresy. The miraculous picture of the Virgin which lies at the centre of the pilgrimage church was painted in 1690 and is enshrined in a high altar carved in 1750.

To reach the magic mountain from Ramsau takes but a short walk, past the Berghotel Gasthof Datzmann, following the path that starts across the road just beyond it. (I used the Zauberwald-Hintersee map from the National Park House and the Berchtesgaden tourist board.) As for the lake itself, sometimes in winter it freezes hard enough for skating, curling and sleigh-rides drawn by little ponies.

Yet more remarkable is the Wimbach valley, consisting of stones and pebbles which are constantly on the move, impelled by the waters flowing under the surface. Erosion over the centuries has sculpted many of the dolomite rocks into bizarre formations. When the water finally emerges, it tumbles headlong through the narrow Wimbach gorge. Incredibly enough, exquisite tiny flowers, such as the dwarf Alpine rose and coltsfoot, manage to find a toe-hold among these shifting stones. Dead Alpine pines mingle with their hardier brethren, which have succeeded in clinging on to life.

The least strenuous mountain walks I discovered in the National Park of the Berchtesgadener Land are reached by taking the Obersalzberg lift near the main railway station up for around 1,000 metres. Even less strenuous, but magnificent, is the drive around the Roßfeld Höhenringstraße – especially if, as I was, you are accompanied by Frau Sabine Kruis of the Berchtesgaden tourist office. This privilege, incidentally, is not something usually put on for visitors, but the tourist office (Königseestraße 2, Berchtesgaden) will give you ample information about this tour – as about all the rest. Look for the signs for Roßfeld and Roßfeldstraße to discover an extremely impressive piece of 1930s' engineering, a circular toll road which winds around the mountainsides for sixteen and a half kilometres from Berchtesgaden and back. Crags and snow rise ahead of you, with deep ravines and distant hills appearing as you climb.

Roßfeld is an area much frequented not only by skiers but also by sunbathers, who lie on hotel terraces, order coffee and develop a fine tan. Eventually Bavaria lies on one side and Austria on the other. As we drove, a hang-glider in his sack floated over Austria at eye-level. We reached the village of Oberau, which resembles an enormous ski school. Since this whole region is a climatic and health resort, even as you drive you feel yourself getting physically better and better. Over the centuries the Bavarians have endowed several of these mountains with human characteristics, and in truth the one known as the sleeping witch is exceedingly realistic, her profile displaying a long hooked nose, a curved chin, a young pointed breast and a witch's scrawny body.

The mountain inns here (all of which close around nine o'clock in the evening) vie with each other in their specialities. Frau Kruis took me to the Graflhöhe. Part of the restaurant is a traditionally built Bavarian farmhouse, with stones holding down its roof. And the cream-puffs of the Graflhöhe have earned its owner – as his father before him – the honorary title of cream-puff baron (*Windbeutelbaron*). Looking out from his terrace over the village of Schönau and, to the far left, at the bobsleigh run, I ate a colossal mixture of cream and ice-cream. (Of the six varieties on offer I had baulked at the one *gefüllt mit Sauerkirchen* and chosen one with *Sahne und Vanilleeis*.) Frau Kruis alleged that the portions were huge because people managed to walk off the excess after their snack. And a twenty-minute stroll further down the mountainside, she told me, leads you to an inn specializing in huge *Schnitzeln*. 'Eat one, walk up to the inn of the *Windbeutelbaron*, buy a cream-puff and then fast for three days,' she said. The very thought made me thirsty, so I asked for a glass of wine. 'The only real Bavarian wine is beer,' the *Windbeutelbaron* insisted, and he brought me a huge stein.

All of which has taken us a long way from the National Park House and St-Maria-am-Anger. Berchtesgaden itself is moderately hilly and, when staying at the splendid Hotel Geiger, which stands uphill back from the road from St-Maria, I was pleased to discover that a bus stops at the church and runs directly to the hotel entrance. The hotel itself is like everyone's dream chalet and has been in the hands of the Geiger family since 1863.

To learn from Herr Geiger some of its history is also to realize how much has changed in this corner of Bavaria over the last century. In this predominantly Catholic land I wondered why Herr Geiger himself is a Protestant, until he told me that his family came from East Prussia. On retiring here, his grandfather bought a farmhouse and his wife, fearing that it would be too lonesome living in Berchtesgaden, decided to enlarge the place and turn it into apartments in which people could gather to play bridge. Eventually the apartments were attracting people from St Petersburg, Scotland, Naples, Philadelphia ... Frau Geiger kept a diary, which still exists, listing their peculiar characteristics. And she found herself having to train waitresses and servants in the most elementary skills. As she wrote to a friend in Lithuania, 'You cannot believe how dumb the girls are here. They have seen only a spoon.'

In today's prosperous Bavaria it is instructive to learn of the poverty of the comparatively recent past. Herr Geiger's father took over the hotel in 1929, on the eve of the Depression. He added proper heating to the hotel, running water and bathrooms – 'at least a few,' smiled his son. During the Depression, the family indulged in a serious discussion over food, which ended when his father decreed that each member could have either butter or jam on bread, but not both.

I spoke of the gargantuan meals offered in most Bavarian restaurants, which evoked Herr Geiger's comment, 'Think how many poor farm people have in past days sat in this very room, eating badly: meat once every two weeks at the most.' The prince-bishops, he told me, gave everyone just enough land to feed the family and not a hectare more. The people still had to pay tithes to the Church, and if they wanted more income they were obliged to work either in the salt-mines or in the forests. Herr Geiger himself likes to run his hotel with a hint of French cooking, so that the food is light enough to fill those who are sitting in cars all day and substantial enough for those who want to climb in the national park.

Then we talked of politics. 'One of the problems with Berchtesgaden,' Herr Geiger remarked, 'is that people say, "Berchtesgaden: that's all Nazis."' From my own observation two facts are certainly true about Hitler and Berchtesgaden. First, a good number of souvenir shops do a brisk trade selling illustrated booklets depicting Hitler and his Nazi friends lording it over Obersalzberg. Second, the Nazis' visual impact on the town and region remains today almost nil. The future dictator undoubtedly liked the region. Hitler began renting a chalet from Frau Kommerzialrat Winter in 1925 and bought it from her four

years later. For his fiftieth birthday the people of the town created for
the Führer a stunningly sited Teehaus often referred to as the Eagle's
Nest. Despite the extraordinary feat of engineering necessary to give
access to this spot, which is 1,834 metres high on a spur of the Höher
Goll, the ungrateful Führer did not like it and went there no more than
five or six times.

He did, however, continue to relish his lovely chalet. Soon he was
joined here by Hermann Goering and Martin Bormann, who also
found themselves houses and built lavishly. This was where Hitler
received those celebrated – some would say notorious – diplomats,
Prime Ministers and royals. But the sole memorial that remains to the
whole Nazi regime is the monumental railway station built by Albert
Speer in 1937 to receive these dignitaries. For the rest, in 1952 the US
forces had the houses of Hitler, Goering and Bormann destroyed.
They thought twice about demolishing his guesthouse, the Platterhof,
and in the end took it over as a rest-home for American servicemen and
renamed it the General Walker Hotel.

The first distinguished foreign visitor to be welcomed by Hitler at
Berchtesgaden was Lloyd George, Britain's former Prime Minister,
who came in 1936. Next arrived the Aga Khan, followed on 22
October 1937 by the Duke and Duchess of Windsor, exiled from
Great Britain after his abdication. Herr Geiger's father filmed their
arrival, and the film remains in his son's keeping. Two days later,
Mussolini's son-in-law Count Ciano, Italian Foreign Minister, was on
his way. His train, Herr Geiger told me, was twenty minutes late, and
the guard of honour broke ranks to allow through a farmer with his
oxen. At that precise moment of chaos, with some crying to the farmer
'forward' and others 'go back', the train whistled into the station.

So they all came, a long list of exalted personages desperate to do
some deal with Hitler: the British Foreign Minister Lord Halifax, the
Austrian Chancellor Kurt von Schuschnigg, British Prime Minister
Neville Chamberlain, the Japanese Ambassador, Crown Prince
Umberto of Italy, King Carol of Rumania and the Foreign Minister of
Poland. Finally, in the month before World War II was declared, the
British Ambassador Nevile Henderson arrived on his impossible
mission to preserve peace in Europe. Thus, and because many such
continued to arrive as the Führer's guests throughout the war (includ-
ing in 1943 the French statesman and collaborator Pierre Laval),
Berchtesgaden and Hitler seem indelibly and unfortunately linked.

Personally I am glad that Albert Speer's railway station remains, for it is a fine piece of 1930s' architecture. Yet I hope these few paragraphs of mine do not contribute to the myth that so unfairly links the Nazi dictator with this town. 'From the business point of view,' said Herr Geiger, 'Hitler brought people here.' He added that in 1942 his uncle was sentenced to death for observing that he did not see many tangible results of the Hitler regime (his sentence was commuted to life-imprisonment). Herr Geiger himself saw Hitler about a hundred times, and had this to say about him: 'He was impressive to hear and see, but you felt that what he had to say came more from his feelings than his brains!'

It seemed much more pleasant to remember more gracious visitors. Indeed, one of my host's earliest memories was of handing flowers as a boy to the old Queen Mother of the Netherlands, who arrived at his father's hotel in her carriage, with other carriages bearing her baggage. I looked up the date and found that she came in September 1929. The SPD leader Willi Brandt also stayed here. Herr Geiger is a leading member of the CSU party in Berchtesgadener Land, but one of Berchtesgaden's SPD politicians told Brandt, 'He's a convinced CSU man, but he's also a good hotel keeper, so we'll let you stay here.'

For a further, and this time visual, history lesson you should join one of the guided tours around the Schoß at Berchtesgaden. This former monastery, seat of the provosts when Berchtesgaden was Germany's smallest province, was taken over by the Wittelsbachs when the town became Bavarian in 1810. The tour begins in the cloister, whose capitals are decorated with cute Romanesque faces. There are (to my mind) too many rooms filled with ancient weaponry, hunting rifles, muskets and guns. But the first room, a graceful Gothic dormitory, houses four carved masterpieces: St George and the dragon, carved around 1480 by Erasmus Grasser, the saint's foot resting nonchalantly on the beast's mouth; an 'Annunciation' of 1520, carved by Veit Stoss; and two wings of an altar carved by Tilman Riemenschneider. One depicts the resurrection of Jesus, the other the scene on the Mount of Olives when Jesus prayed and his three closest disciples slept. Sleeping St John has been given sweet, curly red hair.

In the centre of the next room but one stands a curiosity, a table intricately carved in 1519 out of Kehlheim stone. Among its incised devices is a six-part Palestrina motet. In this room do not miss a fine picture of Venus and Cupid by Lukas Cranach the Elder. The

Wittelsbach portraits in the next room, though no great masterpieces, are hung in a fascinating fashion. On one wall hang the Bavarian branch of the family, which stayed Catholic. On the other are the Palatinate branch, which converted to Protestantism.

The great dining room of the Schloß is a bizarre affair, for its table is laid out like a formal garden (supposedly the one at Schloß Nymphenburg), with 1755 Meissen pottery representing parterres, statues and cypresses. As the tour progresses through elegant rooms with royal portraits, do not miss the single earring which King Max I Joseph sports. There are portraits of King Ludwig I, but alas I saw none of the fiery temptress Lola Montez, who so infatuated the king that his cabinet was mocked as the 'Lolaministerium'. In the end Ludwig's inability to leave Lola forced him to abdicate. The last room of the whole tour is devoted to Prince-Regent Luitpold, who became regent in 1886 because both Ludwig II and his brother Otto I had been declared insane. His long reign lasted until his death in December 1912 in his ninety-first year. Two contrasting paintings in this room have been well hung, close to one another. One shows Luitpold ready to set off hunting in his ninetieth year. The second shows him in 1825, aged four, dressed as a little curly-haired girl.

The tour ends here, just as the long Bavarian dynasty was itself about to end. In November 1913 Luitpold's son was declared Ludwig III, nine months before Germany entered World War I. In 1918 a Berlin pacifist and an independent socialist named Kurt Eisner proclaimed a republic. The deposed Ludwig III fled. Although, as the republic spread throughout Germany, Eisner vigorously defended the rights of Bavaria, he himself had only a few months to live. In February 1919 he was assassinated by a Bavarian nobleman.

Today's Bavarians remain content to be republicans living in a free State. A friend of Bavarian tourism, dressed in his national costume of short breeches and long stockings (quaintly, since we met in a London hotel), once told me he was sorry he had taken off his hat, for, he averred, one should do that only in church, as a sign of subservience to no one but God alone. Yet at the same time these republican Bavarians remain proud of their history, as the State coat of arms indicates. Its central shield of white and blue diamonds derives from the heraldic symbol of the Counts of Bogen, a symbol inherited by the Wittelsbachs. Its four quarters represent the Upper Palatinate (a golden lion against a golden background), which now represents

Schwabia, and a silver rake on a red background, representing Franconia.

A more intimate view of Berchtesgaden's local history is provided by the Heimatmuseum. Its home is the unpretentious pink-and-white Schloß Adelsheim, which was built in 1614 at the end of Schrof-fenbergallee (just off Salzburger Straße). On display are some of the works of Berchtesgaden's celebrated woodcarvers, whose twentieth-century descendants will sell you children's toys and Christmas decorations in the town's shops. With few exceptions, I prefer to drink in the atmosphere of a place in its ancient streets rather than in its local history museums. Nonntal is just such a street, the oldest in the town, with little doorways (people were smaller in the past than they are now) peeping out from delicate façades.

At Berchtesgaden the historical legacy includes a royal villa, built in the mid-nineteenth century for King Max II and his wife Marie to the designs of Friedrich von Gärtner. Their royal portraits adorn its façade. Other historical legacies incorporate some rare bibulous treats. The Augustinian provosts, for instance, patronized local brewers. Prince-bishop Ferdinand II is especially venerated for order-ing the foundation of a monastic brewery in the early seventeenth century. You can visit Berchtesgaden's brewery (the Hofbräuhaus) on weekdays between 08.00 and 19.00, on Saturdays between 08.00 and 12.00 and between 16.00 and 19.00, and on Sundays between 10.00 and 12.00 and between 16.00 and 19.00. Since the brewery also has a Bräustübl, built in 1910, where you can quaff its products, here is a suitable moment to mention the three main types of Bavarian beer: *Hell*, the normal light ale, *Weiß*, made with much more yeast; and the dark malt *Dunkel*. In Berchtesgadener Land alone there are some twenty breweries, many of them private, their beers sold within four or five weeks of brewing and therefore always fresh.

One evening Frau Kruis telephoned to say that she would drive me to one of Bavaria's private breweries, the only one in the neighbour-hood of Berchtesgaden. We took Route 20 from the town, driving towards Bad Reichenhall. Ahead, the profile of the sleeping witch was clearly visible. On the right at Bischopfswiesen we reached the Brenner-Bräu with its restaurant, developed out of a three-and-a-half-centuries old guesthouse and post-house. Its owner, Herr Hermann Neudecker, proudly took me round the vats, which produce a monthly total of some 900 litres of *helles*, unfiltered beer.

You can see these vats through windows giving on to his restaurant. That evening, however, we ate in the open air under the chestnuts (for a true Bavarian beer garden can be shaded only by chestnuts). Our most intriguing dish was called, in the Bavarian dialect, *Obatze*: a soft cheese that had been shredded and mixed with butter, lighter cheese, salt, pepper, paprika, onions and parsley. Shovelling *Obatze* on to black bread, having a beer, eating, talking, and downing another beer was a most inviting experience. As we ate, the sun sank behind the Kehlstein, and its golden light winked through the windows of the Eagle's Nest.

The same prince-bishop who founded the brewery at Berchtesgaden also granted to a family named Grassl, who lived at Unterstein, the right and duty to keep the Alpine meadows in order and to dig up the roots of gentian plants in order to distil from these an amazingly powerful Schnapps. The Grassl family still brews this Schnapps in Berchtesgaden. Initially they built huts high on the mountain slopes, nearby which the genetian (or *Enzian*) roots were dug up, distilled and then laboriously brought down into the town, to delight the monks, their visitors and everyone else.

For a guided tour of the modern Grassl distillery, drive along Bergwerkstraße across the bridge on the right, just past the Hofbräuhaus. Turn left where you see the sign for Gewerbegebiet Gartenau. I was shown round this distillery, which employs some hundred workers, by one of the three directors, Herr Beierl. He told me first of all that you do not sink an *Enzian* fast, like a normal Schnapps, but slowly. You drink it, he continued, at any time of the day. ('It helps you to get up in the morning.') He added, 'For us it is a medicine.' You drink it, too, in an ice-cold glass, but no colder than five degrees, for any colder and *Enzian* would taste worse. '*Zum wohl*,' he said, and I downed my glass and immediately felt better.

In the distillery you need not drink, but simply smell, for the aromatic Schnapps to warm your heart. Modern copper and ceramic stills have replaced their older prototypes of wood, but these are still on show. As well as a guided tour, a film depicts the techniques of producing *Enzian* over the centuries. The Schnapps, I learned, is allowed to mature in ashwood vats stored in cool cellars. Four types of gentian roots are used – yellow, spotted, red and the Hungarian variety – producing two different sorts of *Enzian*. The Grassl family has even endowed a research chair at Munich university to further the cultivation of these most valuable plants.

At the end of your visit you can buy the Schnapps in its pleasingly ancient brown bottles. Before I could put my hand into my purse, Herr Beierl kindly gave me a couple. Returning to my hotel, I sampled only one glass, for on that same day the Hotel Geiger was hosting a Bavarian evening to greet midsummer's day, the feast of St John (*Johannistag*). A traditional Bavarian five-piece band – zither, guitar, trombone, double-bass and accordion – regaled us. White and blue Bavarian bunting decorated the tables, as well as the chandeliers (which happen to be in the shape of wooden wheels). The special menu for the evening included boiled beef (*Tafelspitz*), which I gobbled down, while quaffing beer. The waitresses were in excellent fettle. When I apologized to one for disturbing her by asking for a toothpick, she gave me five and said in English, 'I have lots of time with the toothpick. When you want more, I'm here again.'

At ten o'clock that evening a bonfire was lit on the side of the hill. My memory fades a little, but I still have a vision of Herr Geiger in his Bavarian national costume feeding the fire with a pitchfork, of the cow-bells hanging in the main room, of the gleaming turquoise ceramic stove (the *Kachelofen*), of everyone returning from the bonfire to listen to the band singing, and of one of my happiest evenings for ages.

Such a happening takes place in the restaurants of many Bavarian towns and villages on the feast of St John, often with clog-dancing and yodelling as well as music. The word they use for it is a *Gaudi*, the Latin for pleasure. Traditional customs are powerfully alive here. On the evening of 5–6 December, for instance, Santa Claus (that is, St Nicholas) fights against twelve evil spirits known as *Butt'nmandln*. Men dress up as these spirits, with cow-bells around their waists, visiting homes, and children peep out and pretend to be frightened. Santa Claus comes along too, checking whether the children's names are in his gold or his black book. Named in the gold book, they are given nuts, chocolates and oranges. Named in the black book, they are pushed into the snow.

On the four Thursdays before Christmas children dress as shepherds, wander around singing, and are given presents. The Schloßplatz at Berchtesgaden also houses a Christkindlmarkt, with small wooden huts selling presents and, of course, *Enzian*. Many of these festivals are accompanied by the shooting of fake bullets from handguns, the noise echoing in the mountains. Is it a privilege or not for a bride to be awakened at four o'clock on the morning of her wedding day with such merry huntsmen shooting away?

Recovering, the following morning, in Herr Geiger's swimming pool, I gazed up at the mountains surrounding Berchtesgaden and decided I ought to mount to the Eagle's Nest. The easiest way is to drive for five kilometres from Berchtesgaden railway station, following the signs for Obersalzberg-Kehlstein and parking when you reach Hintereck. Buses then take you along a twistingly spectacular private road, through five tunnels and then directly up the north face of the mountain. Impassible in winter, this six-and-a-half-kilometre long road is open only from mid-May to mid-October. The final tunnel takes you as far as a lift which, in less then two minutes, transports everyone to the Kehlsteinhaus itself. Hintereck is 750 metres above sea level. The Kehlsteinhaus is 1,087 metres higher. Altogether the journey takes about an hour.

The Eagle's Nest is now a decent restaurant and coffee-house. Even here you are not at the summit, and to follow the pathway up to it could take another couple of hours. In good weather the views – not simply of the surronding mountains but also into Austria as far as Salzburg and down to the Königsee – are astounding.

A trip along the Königsee is our final venture into Berchtesgaden's National Park. Again you reach it from the town's main railway station. Regular buses run from here to park at the village of Königsee which, I have to admit, is touristy, with shops selling the usual useless trinkets. But nothing can spoil the atmosphere created 300 metres further on by the blend of green lake and, on three sides, pine-clad cliffs and peaks. A boat trip to and from Schönau am Königsee takes an hour and a quarter. You glide along slowly, driven by electricity so as not to pollute the National Park with oil-based fuel. Quaint, weather-boarded boathouses give way to the quiet lake. Its depth, gouged out long ago by a glacier, reaches 220 metres, and its walls (as underwater films have revealed) fall sheer to the bottom. On your left the Röthbach waterfall rushes headlong down for 400 metres, disappears underground and re-emerges into the nearby Obersee. Halfway across the lake, the ship stops, windows are opened, and one of the crew blows a fanfare on the trumpet, the notes uncannily thrown back by the echo from the cliffside. Then the trumpeter comes round for a tip. According to local legend two emperors, Charlemagne and

Barbarossa, lie under the surrounding mountains.

As you approach Schönau am Königsee you notice the curiosities of its pilgrimage church, St Bartholomä. Its little red domes swell out from the roof like half-inflated balloons. One tower is capped by an onion dome; the other has a rounded cap. But compared with what we have already seen in Bavaria, baroque St Bartholomä is not great shakes architecturally, once you get inside. Annually on 24 August a pilgrimage here still takes place. Daily visitors taste the *Schwarzreiterl* a fish delicacy from the lake itself, in the nearby restaurant.

This is where the composer Max Reger found peace and where Sigmund Freud spent summer holidays. The romantic artist Caspar David Friedrich was also inspired here. If you continue to the end of the lake, you can walk on to Obersee. Mountain walks here take from three to three-and-a-half hours. Otherwise, have a drink or meal at the Gasthaus and then take the ship back on its silent journey.

1   *Angels and cherubs unfold a swirling canopy over the altar of Balthasar Neumann's baroque church in the Residenz at Würzburg to reveal the Holy Trinity and an ecstatic Virgin Mary.*

2 (Above) *Bamberg's former town hall, half-Gothic, half-rococo, seems to float in the middle of the River Regnitz.*

3 (Opposite) *St George despatches the dragon on top of the column of the Renaissance fountain in the market place of Rothenburg ob der Tauber.*

4 (Above) *The River Inn washes the unspoilt town of Wasserburg.*

5 (Opposite) *A defensive Schloß transformed into Renaissance elegance: Burg Traunitz at Landshut.*

6 (Below) *The pilgrimage church of Maria Gern near Bischofswiesen stands in green pastures, while beyond rises the Watzmann.*

7 (Above) *The twin Gothic spires of Regensburg cathedral beckon the visitor across the early twelfth-century stone bridge, Germany's oldest.*

8 (Opposite) *Schloß Neuschwanstein, set on its wooded peak, looks across the lake and, to the right, at Schloß Hohenschwangau.*

9 (Below) *The lavishness that bankrupted King Ludwig II of Bavaria: the main staircase at Herrenchiemsee.*

10   *Ettal monastery, whose domed rococo church derives its Italian aspect
from the architect, Enrico Zucalli, who rebuilt it in the late eighteenth century
after fire destroyed the ancient buildings.*

Altötting and the heart of Bavaria

For a town of scarcely more than 12,000 inhabitants, Altötting at first sight seems to have an unusually large (and elegant) central square and an inordinate number of churches. No fewer than three churches grace this square, the Kapellplatz. In it stands a baroque fountain topped by the Madonna and her child, placed here in 1637, the gift of the Archbishop of Salzburg. The Madonna also appears painted on countless walls in the town; and dealers in holy goods, the twentieth-century equivalent of the money-changers of the Jerusalem Temple, sandwich their shops between cafés and churches and sell statues, candles and other such religious bric-à-brac. These mementoes include Pope John Paul II pocket watches, which I swear I saw on sale at the Gasthof Scharnagle, opposite the Hotel Zur Post.

The reason for all this trade can be found in the tiny chapel in the middle of the square, for it enshrines the Black Madonna of Altötting, a miracle-working statue which has made this town the greatest pilgrimage centre in all Bavaria. No more than twenty-six metres long and fifteen metres wide, this Heiligkapelle is one of Germany's oldest churches. It embodies an octagon, which was possibly the baptistry of the palace of the eighth-century rulers of Bavaria. Today this octagon is known as the chapel of grace. Since the fourteenth century it has housed an image of the Virgin Mary and the infant Jesus, carved in limewood in Lorraine around 1300.

Over the centuries smoke from innumerable candles has blackened the Virgin Mary's features. Why has no one restored the statue to its original colour? The answer lies in the Christian habit of assuming that the Jewish Scriptures, which Christians designated as the Old Testament, can be interpreted as referring to their own faith. In the book known as the Song of Songs a woman reciting a love poem proclaims, 'I am black, but comely.' For centuries Christians have applied this Jewish text to the mother of Jesus, and in consequence any carving of the Madonna which turned black with age or smoke was perceived to have become over the centuries an increasingly accurate reproduction of Mary. Such a Black Madonna is the carving of the Virgin Mary at Altötting.

She also works miracles. In 1489 a three-year-old Altötting child fell into the River Inn and drowned. The distraught mother and her companions rushed into the chapel of grace, laid the dead child on the altar, and before the image of Mary and Jesus begged for the restoration of the infant. Their prayers were heard. The three-year-old apparently awoke from death. As news of the miracle spread, more and more pilgrims came to Altötting to venerate the black statue. Miracles multiplied. In 1520 a local artist decided to depict over fifty of them on small Gothic tablets. These still hang in the ambulatory of the chapel of grace, a covered walkway stretching around three sides of the church and added in 1494. Some 2,000 other ex-votos have joined them, cramming every conceivable space of this ambulatory, including the roof, depicting blessings and miracles that have flown from pious devotion to the Black Madonna.

Looking for twentieth-century ex-votos on the south side of the ambulatory, I spotted that the Black Madonna of Altötting must have accompanied the sons of Altötting to the battlefields of World War II. An ex-voto of 1970 depicts an injured athlete, revived and after four months declaring, 'Through the intercession of the Mother of God of Altötting I am once again recovered – thank you a thousandfold.' Another of 1975 shows a farmer rescued from the horns of an irate bull. It seems to me that the Madonna could have been spared some miracles if only a tractor-driving school had been set up in the town. This part of the building is full of accidents on farms. Tractors continually back over little children. As late as 1983 another tractor, its load and driver dangerously topple over. The Black Madonna saves them all.

Many of these votive paintings, thanking the Black Madonna for her mercies, remain wonderfully rustic, though the young man and woman engaged in restoring them seemed to me, as I chatted with them, sophisticated artists. I asked the bearded man whether his was a dying trade. 'No,' he replied, 'several of us do this throughout the whole of Bavaria.'

Devotion to the Madonna who inspired these paintings remains intense, and today Altötting is annually visited by half a million pilgrims. In the early years of this century so many were arriving here that no church in Altötting was big enough to accommodate them. In 1910 the Munich architect, Johann Schott, was commissioned to design a neo-baroque church large enough to house 6,000 worshippers at once. It stands just outside Altötting's Kapellplatz, to the north-west.

Each Sunday evening in summer, and of course on the eve of and on the feast of the Assumption (15 August), pilgrims still gather as evening draws on in this huge papal basilica, dedicated to St Anne, the mother of the Virgin Mary. Then, carrying lighted candles and singing hymns in honour of the Blessed Virgin, they process to the Kapellplatz, circling the chapel of grace and finally receiving the blessing of the Black Madonna. Yet more remarkable is the fact that many of these pilgrims arrive here not on the special trains laid on by the German state railway but on foot. When I was there on the five hundredth anniversary of the first miracle, some 300 had arrived from Freiburg alone, and although it was not Sunday, as I ate my evening meal between quarter past eight and nine at the Hotel Zur Post they processed with their candles around the square.

It is rarely easy for a tourist to see much of the Black Madonna at Altötting, for priests lead virtually continuous worship by the altar of grace, as crowds flock inside. The faithful repeat the Hail Mary, sing *Kyrie eleison* and then burst into the verses of 'Praise to the Lord, the Almighty, the king of creation'. I peered beyond them at the late seventeenth-century altar of grace, which almost dwarfs the Black Virgin and her child. It is a home far more lavish than the humble one in which the mother of Jesus must actually have lived at Nazareth. In chased silver to the sides of the niche you can see the family tree of

Jesus. On the right is a statue of a young Prince Maximilian Josef of Bavaria, worshipping the Madonna, whose intercessions had cured him of an almost fatal illness in 1737. The ten-year-old boy has prettily curled hair, and although he has reverently placed his helmet on the ground, his sword is still sheathed and swings against his knee. The statue to the left, created by Georg Busch in 1931, reveals that the aura of sanctity has not yet deserted Altötting. It represents St Konrad of Parzham, a Capuchin monk beatified in 1934 by Pope Pius XI. He had spent forty-one years of his life at Altötting, distributing food to the poor, caring for children and preaching the gospel.

Nowadays the Capuchin monks take most of the responsibility for the pilgrimages to Altötting. The mortal remains of St Konrad lie on display in a glass shrine in the Capuchins' monastic church, Bruder-Konrad-Kirche, which was built in the 1650s and widened in 1754. Originally dedicated to St Anne, it was re-dedicated to Konrad after his beatification. Its interior has, alas, been modernized. Children who say a prayer beside the statue of the Blessed Virgin near the door of this church (once the home of the Altötting Franciscans) still receive a morsel of bread as a present. A further treat is to take a drink of water from Brother Konrad's fountain nearby, by the entrance to the present Capuchin monastery. After you have sipped, take spiritual comfort from the fact that the water runs over another bit of the dead saint's mortal remains. You sample a drink of dusty relics.

After sampling this particular holy water, I felt it was perhaps time to eat and wash away the saintly dust with a glass of beer. Here Bavarian food is at its most succulent. Once I saw on the menu of an Altötting restaurant the word *Lingerl* and asked the waitress what it meant. She replied, 'You need to be a Bavarian for me to explain.' Then I walked back to Kapellplatz. Such is the religious impact of Altötting that the first time around you do not realize how fine are the secular buildings in this square. The Rathaus sports a double onion dome and tower. The dormer windows of its roof peep out like eyebrows. The whole dates only from 1908. Next to it stands the Hotel Zur Post, which dates back far longer, to the time when it belonged to the court in the Middle Ages and afterwards became a guesthouse of the monastery at the other side of the square. The beautiful classical monastic buildings were designed by the Italian architect Zucalli and built in the late 1670s. Part of them serves these days as a school of music, and from the open windows sacred song permeates the square for most of the day. Next to it lies the town's cemetery, with a twentieth-century way of the cross in red marble, undramatic but pleasing, and a little gurgling fountain.

Altötting boasts a secular history longer than its dominant religious one. In the mid-eighth century the dukes of Bavaria made the town the seat of their official residence. The Frankish King Karlmann chose to be buried here. (His corpse, laid in the Stiftskirche or collegiate church, which rises next to the Heiligkapelle, was lost, discovered during the restoration of 1965 and put to rest again under the high altar.) Emperor Otto the Great declared Altötting an imperial possession. Yet only in 1845 did the spot gain the right to hold markets, and only in 1898 was it designated a town.

Religious and secular history always intertwine in Bavaria. The Wittelsbachs, rulers of Bavaria from 1180 to 1918, grew more and more attached to the Black Madonna. Some of them entrusted their most precious parts – their hearts – to her care. The more humble hearts are buried under the floor of the chapel of grace. The more arrogant ones are preserved in elaborate urns opposite the altar. The hearts of Kaiser Albrecht VII and his Kaiserin Maria Amalie are enclosed in the most splendid urn, sculpted in 1745 by the rococo master Johann Baptist Straub. Here too, in 1886, in a heart-shaped urn was placed the heart of poor mad king Ludwig II.

Rising beyond the chapel of grace at Altötting is the double-steepled collegiate church (or Stiftskirche), founded by the Wittelsbachs in 1499 and dedicated to Saints Philip and James. Its cloister dates from the second half of the fifteenth century. The architect Jörg Perger designed the rest, and the church was finished in 1511. Once again the immense thrust of pilgrims was responsible for a new building, for this Stiftskirche replaced a Romanesque building that could no longer accommodate everyone coming to Altötting to venerate the Black Madonna. In consequence this early sixteenth-century church houses fine earlier works of religious art, in particular the leafy twelfth-century font under the choir gallery and a Romanesque doorway of 1254. The late-Gothic font in use today, however, dates from 1501 and is chiselled not with leaves, but with the baptism of Jesus himself. Another magnificently carved doorway dates from 1511.

The vaults of the Stiftskirche of Altötting are simple and, because of that, beautiful. If you look back towards the organ case and the balustrade of the choir, both dating from 1724, you spot a grisly device. On top of the clock to your right a skeleton, representing death, swings his scythe once a second. In truth, as the handy guide to the town tells you, these days four of us die every second; but this skeleton almost certainly dates from the plague of 1634, when the grim reaper took a hold on Bavaria and probably took only one a second.

Often tourists neglect to visit church treasuries, but that of the Stiftskirche at Altötting is a must, if only to admire the little golden horse (*das goldene Rössl*). Created in Paris in 1392, a statue of the Blessed Virgin and her child sits in a bower, guarded by angels. King Charles VI of France and his marshal worship on either side of the bower. Walk down the steps which lead down underneath the bower to find the king's page, keeping under control his spirited white horse. The page wears one red boot and one white. Then find your way to the cloister of the parish church, for a staircase leads from here down to the chapel of St Peter. Here reside the bones of the superb Field Marshal Johann Tserclaes Tilly, who commanded the army of the Bavarian elector during the Thirty Years' War. Out of devotion to the Black Madonna, Tilly himself decreed that here should be his last resting place. Those with a taste for the macabre can peer at his skeleton through a glass window let into his coffin.

A helicopter bearing Pope John Paul II, whose veneration of the Blessed Virgin Mary is legendary, landed here on 18 November 1980. I realized the importance of the huge square when my hostess, Frau Gabriele Tandler of the Hotel Zur Post, Altötting, told me that 80,000 persons gathered here to welcome him. His sculpted self blesses the square from a wall, next to which rises the early eighteenth-century church of St Maria Magdalena. Once the home of the Jesuits, it is the last of Altötting's churches that I urge you to look inside. Its high altar by Josef Doppler of Salzburg dates from the very end of the eighteenth century, and above it is displayed the Maltese cross. The latter is a relic of the time when the Jesuits were dissolved and the church was taken over by the Maltese order. All the furnishings of St Maria Magdalena are of a very high order, and the pulpit of 1697 is particularly magnificent.

How can the tourist see anything going on in Altötting when the Kapellplatz of Altötting is packed with pilgrims? The answer, I suggest, is to book the two rooms of the Hotel Zur Post (which has stood here since the 1280s) overlooking the square. From these

windows of an evening the softly lit spires and buildings are enchanting. How can the tourist escape all-pervading religiosity, even if, like
me, he or she sympathizes with the religious spirit of this pilgrimage
town? The answer again is in this same hotel, whose solarium and
swimming pool are modelled on some pagan Roman original. A
couple of Roman lions spouted water on me as I swam. As I bubbled
away in the Wellenbad, boisterously happy Bavarians hooted and
jumped into the heated whirlpool half an inch from me.

Then I realized it was a Friday and grew Christian again. In the hotel
restaurant I chose a fish dish, following the ancient rule of the Church
that one should – to some extent – fast on a Friday. This was not much
of a fast, since that evening I ate a turbot served in a dill sauce with
mushrooms, accompanied by a large mixed salad. Then followed
strawberries and loads of cream. As usual throughout the night every
bell in every belfry of the churches of Altötting chimed the hour and
reminded me of the perils of gluttony.

Religion has its charms, some of them slightly embarrassing as well.
Close by Krezentienheim Straße is a remarkably naïve stone panorama
of the way of the cross and the crucifixion. More acceptable to me is
the diorama which depicts the whole history of the pilgrimage, from
1489 to the twentieth century, beginning with the distraught parents
of the dead child, continuing through the building of the Stiftskirche,
re-creating the lowest point of the veneration of the Virgin when
Protestants infested (so to speak) this part of Germany. Tilly and
Kurfürst Maximilian I are blessed by the Black Madonna. The image
flees to Salzburg to escape Protestant wrath. It returns to ensure that
the Bavarians survive the assaults of the French and the Swedes in
1648. In 1681 it blesses the holy alliance against the Turks. It succours
Altötting during several devastating fires. And so the holy tale goes on,
until the diorama depicts pilgrims of our own day winding their way
into the centre of the town.

Altötting profits from its beautiful situation, the surrounding
countryside blessed with lakes, woodlands and hills. The Alps here are
giving way to the older, gentler hills. From the Verkehrsampt (in the
Rathaus, open from Monday to Saturday between 08.00 and 12.00
and between 14.00 and 17.00) I obtained one of those useful
Wanderkarten and, following its instructions, found myself walking
the most gentle ups-and-downs, rather as if I were in the English
Cotswolds. The *Wanderkarte* proved extremely practical once away

from the main roads, taking me by stretches of fields, meadowlands and farmlands, and alongside prosperous-looking farmhouses with red-tiled roofs and colourfully stacked window boxes. Some of the roads are clearly ancient, especially those running below the level of the fir trees and beech woods. Unlike the routes around Inzell, these are not numbered, but they are well-signposted.

Only three kilometres north-east of Altötting, Neuötting am Inn entrancingly beckons you into its walls from its cliff above the Inn valley. To call this market town new (*Neu*) makes sense only in relation to old (*Alt*) ötting, for we first hear of Neuötting under the name *forum novum Odingen* in the year 1231. The contrast between the two towns could not be greater. Neuötting is a classic medieval market town, consisting of a long, long, wide Marktplatz closed in at either end by a gateway. The southern gateway bears a most impressive coat of arms, dated 1792, although the gateway itself had of course been guarding the town for the previous 500 years. Neuötting also boasts a Pfennigturm, a tower which from 1240 until 1486 housed the town mint.

Arcades, some of them pointed, some of them round and shallow, add to the charm of the houses flanking the square, as do the intricate wrought-iron signs which overhang them, a bull's head in the centre of one of the most ornate telling you that this is a butcher's shop. One is surprised to see painted over a butcher's in Neuötting a picture of the Lamb of God, dated 1797. Next to the shop is a narrow alleyway whose ancient walls are kept apart by buttresses. The archway leading into the alley is decorated with a painting of St Nicholas, patron saint of pawnbrokers and furnished here with his three golden balls.

For centuries the arcades fronting the shops of Neuötting have sheltered farmers and their wives, selling flowers, vegetables and fruit, and so they do today. Those houses that have lost their arcades compensate by their classical decoration: swags, naked little putti, and ancient heads set between the second- and third-storey windows. The blue-painted Gasthof Krone is a notable example of the latter, its doorway wide and welcoming and big enough to let through a coach and horses, its beer cool. The upper storeys of the house opposite are equally elegant, and the town hall has a particularly fine façade. It also once served as the granary of Neuötting, and you can see in the middle of its battlemented roof an opening from which (I guess) once poked a crane to drag up the sacks. You can also make your way into the double-arcaded courtyard of the former toll-house, which now has a happier function as the venue for summer concerts. Some of the houses are dated, but I think these dates refer not to the original building but to the year when coats of arms were painted on their façades.

The men and women of Neuötting love dressing up in traditional Bavarian costume and parading to the music of brass bands. At Fasching the men also sport a curious version of Mexican costume. As for the Neuötting male-voice choir with its zither accompaniment, it must be seen as well as heard to be believed.

St Nikolaus is the patron of the marvellous brick parish church of Neuötting, whose crocketed stone spire rises for seventy-eight metres at the north end of the Marktplatz. The architect of this church was Hans Stethaimer, who was born in Burghausen in 1360 and died at Landshut in 1432. Building began in 1410 and was not finished until long after his death, although he did see the completion of the spire in 1429. The delicate ogival vaulting inside the church was completed only in the 1620s. A clock at the end of the north aisle is dated 1588. During the Renaissance and the baroque eras, St Nikolaus, Neuötting, was continually altered, but in the late nineteenth century a parish priest named Heinrich Dachs decided that the whole building should be re-Gothicized. From his time dates the high altar, carved in 1896. The altar in the chapel of St Sebastian, installed in 1776, is the only major eighteenth-century work of art to have escaped this restoration.

Such details matter little beside Stethaimer's overall conception of a huge hall church, its lines rendered even more slender by the optical illusion of having the upper-storey windows taller than the lower ones. The vaulting of the chancel is particularly pretty. Only after enjoying the whole ensemble should one start exploring the details: the chapel of the Holy Cross (the easternmost of the north side), created in 1440; next to it the chapel of the twelve Apostles, created six years later and frescoed in 1596; the lovely organ case of 1642; and the rococo statue of Bishop Nicholas, again carrying three golden balls as well as waving a giant crosier.

If you drive north-west along the B299 from Neuötting in the direction of Landshut, after twenty-two kilometres of flat and then rolling country you reach the pretty town of Neumarkt-Sankt Veit. Its plan is that of Neuötting, a long Stadtplatz guarded at each end by a medieval tower and gateway (the lower one, or Unteres Tor, dated 1542), though none of the houses have arcades. Halfway up the

Stadtplatz is the extremely well-restored late-Gothic church of St Johann. It was built around 1450 and boasts a neat Gothic spire. Ogival entrances prepare you for the ogival arches inside, whose bosses depict God the Father, God the Son and God the Holy Spirit, as well as the Blessed Virgin Mary. Mary also figures startlingly on the reredos of the altar nearest the nave on the south side, where a sword literally pierces her heart as she grieves over the sufferings of her son.

On either side of the altar an artist in 1578 added two excellent wall-paintings, the one on the left depicting an equally dangerous sword. The Jewish patriarch Abraham is about to slay his son Isaac with it. An angel boldly stops him by grabbing hold of the point of the sword, thereby risking cutting the angelic hand to ribbons. On the other side the corresponding wall-painting depicts Mary Magdalene meeting the resurrected Jesus and supposing him to be a gardener. Underneath both paintings are earlier treasures: on the left a 'Deposition' dated 1505, on the right a carving of the scene when three of the disciples of Jesus slept while he prayed to be spared from death. Since this scene has been crammed into a tiny space, one of them has to sleep sitting up.

The faded chancel wall-paintings, done in 1450, portray the visit of the Magi to Mary and her child. As I was making out the scene, a woman came into the church and greeted me. In response I observed that there were some beautifully restored works of art here. 'Anything can be made beautiful by spending money,' she sourly replied.

Sitting in the square and sipping a beer I reflected on human sourness. In this exquisite spot it was hard to believe that on 24 April 1809, during the Napoleonic wars, a battle should have taken place at Neumarkt-Sankt Veit, but this is clearly stated on the modern fountain opposite the Gasthof zum Post, on which stands a little bear, part of the town's coat of arms.

Walk out of the town by the Unteres Tor to find, after a gentle five minutes' climb, the largest Gothic church in these parts, the onion-domed St Veit (Johann Michael Fischer added the dome in 1765). All that one can visit, of the monastery which once stood here, are the exquisitely clean public conveniences next to the monastic brewery (the Kloster Bräuerei AG St Veit). Great iron doors lead into the church, where you discover an ogival organ loft with a classical organ case and a clock. Mighty funeral slabs have been set into the walls, including two powerful images of dead abbots underneath the organ loft. At the end of the eighteenth century the architect Johann

Nepomuk della Croce created for this church a sumptuous high altar. The golden, espiscopally-clad figures flanking it represent St Rupert and St Vitus. In the picture in the middle of this altar St Vitus is being martyred and is also receiving his reward in heaven.

On our way to Landshut, a mere thirty-eight kilometres further north-west, we should certainly allow ourselves to be detained by another charming village with an extremely fine church. The B299 crosses the River Vil into Vilsbiburg, its noble gateway and tower all that remain of the fifteenth-century walls and fortifications. Little windows allow light into the Torturm today, and its octagonal top hosts a useful clock. Park and find to the left of the tower the former Heilig-Geist-Spital, a hospice founded in 1476 and finished in the first half of the sixteenth century. Its present-day function is to house the local history museum of Vilsbiburg, which sounds boring enough until you learn that it also incorporates the basically fifteenth-century hospice church (with a delicate Gothic gallery at its west end).

This, however, is not the church that should detain us. High above the town to the right rises the early fifteenth-century church of Maria Himmelfahrt. Built out of pale brick, its impressive octagonal belfry is topped with an onion dome added at the end of the seventeenth century. Red marble tomb slabs line the porch, with a knight and his family kneeling before the risen Lord on the left. On the right a chubby Mary, carved in 1514, sorrows over her dead son. The carvings on the church door outline the fall and redemption of mankind, with Adam and Eve's expulsion from the Garden of Eden overlooked by the Madonna in glory surveying the scene from heaven. Other panels show Jesus crucified and an angel catching his shed blood in a chalice, while Mary and St John flank the cross, and the scene when St Thomas doubts that he really has met his risen Lord.

The ogival vaults and the bosses of the church are excellent. A late Gothic carving of the Madonna and child hangs on the north wall, her son as merrily comical as any baby of his age. Here is a fresco of the martyrdom of St Sebastian, painted in 1546. But our main reason for coming to this church is the stunning reredos of the high altar. Carved in the late-Gothic era, it depicts not only the Blessed Virgin but also those fourteen saintly helpers of mankind, whom we have already come across in the church of Vierzehnheiligen. Each is identified by an emblem, St Erasmus, for example, by his spindle, St Catherine of Alexandria by the wheel on which she was broken. This is the moment to name them all. Along with Erasmus and Catherine here are Saints George, Blasius, Barbara, Dionysius, Christopher, Pantaleon, Vitus, Cyriacus, Eustachius, Achatius, Margaret and Aegidius.

The rest of Vilsbiburg is by no means without interest. In 1979 the citizens erected a fountain topped by St Dionysius (who holds his own severed head, as he does on the reredos of the church), to commemorate the five hundredth anniversary of the granting of a market to the town. The pink building nearby, the former Rathaus, was rebuilt in 1652 after a fire destroyed the old one, and then enriched in 1727. Next to it stood the old brewery, but in 1897 the citizens of Vilsbiburg decided to replace it with the present, entertainingly neo-baroque building.

Drive through the town gate, this time turning not right towards the church but left towards Landshut. The capital of Lower Bavaria, Landshut is superbly sited between wooded hills and the River Isar. Park your car and walk to Altstadt, to enjoy an Erdinger beer while sitting and admiring this long street, which is blessed with a church at each end. The centre of Landshut (the environs being a modern city) is a perfectly preserved medieval and Renaissance gem, picturesquely basing itself on two wide and long parallel thoroughfares, Altstadt and Neustadt, which are linked by narrow little streets called Gassen. The beauty of the one we are sitting in, Altstadt, derives in part simply because the green, pink, white and yellow gables of its Gothic houses, its shops and their awnings are set on a gentle curve. On the west side covered passages, as well as narrow cobbled streets, lead through the houses. Altstadt stretches towards the medieval church of St Martin, whose brick spire rises to a height of 133 metres. From the ridge of the hill beyond the church, Burg Traunitz dominates the city.

The second Wittelsbach Duke of Bavaria, Ludwig the Kelheimer, built Burg Traunitz in 1204. Half a century later, in 1255, Upper and Lower Bavaria were divided for the first time, and Heinrich XIII, who became Duke of Lower Bavaria, made Landshut his capital. Lower Bavaria prospered far more than Upper Bavaria, so that by the mid-fifteenth century the Dukes of Bavaria-Landshut were all dubbing themselves 'the Rich'. After the death of Duke Georg the Rich in 1503, the covetous Upper Bavarian Wittelsbachs disputed the succession. The result of a savage little war was that Duke Albrecht IV, who had ruled Upper Bavaria since 1467, became head of a united duchy. He made Landshut his second capital.

Albrecht IV died in 1508 and his sons Ludwig X and Wilhelm IV agreed to rule the duchy together. Their decision was decisive in transforming Burg Traunitz into one of the most entrancing castles in Bavaria, for Ludwig X and his exceedingly artistic successors moved their court there. Even on a hot summer's day, a visit to Burg Traunitz is well worth the climb from the end of Altstadt or Neustadt. It opens (except on Mondays) between April and September from 09.00 till 12.00 and from 13.00 till 17.00, closing one hour earlier during the rest of the year.

On the way up to the castle you pass a statue of Duke Ludwig the Rich, who ruled Bavaria-Landshut from 1450 to 1479. It seems curious to me that he is dressed so martially, since his chief gift to Bavaria was that of culture. In 1472, for instance, Ludwig the Rich founded Bavaria's first university. Three years later, amid pageantry of unbelievable splendour, the eighteen-year-old Hedwig, daughter of the King of Poland, came to Landshut to marry Ludwig's son, the future Duke Georg the Rich. For seven days the tradesmen and guesthouses of Landshut served every citizen, high and low-born, at the duke's expense. Since 1903 the people of Landshut have re-enacted this celebrated *Landshuter Hochzeit* every three years. When I was there in 1989 benches along the whole length of the Altstadt provided seats for the spectators. Alas, the tradesmen and guesthouses were not serving meats and ale free.

The rest of the pageant seems remarkably authentic, simply because the heart of Landshut remains authentic. Two thousand costumed players throng the streets, which are hung with bunting. In the town hall the nobles dance. A hundred young women form part of the bride's retinue. Flags wave, drums beat and flutes whistle, while jesters and morris-dancers make merry in the streets. Medieval music once again plays in Burg Traunitz and in the Residenz, while below the Burg jousts and tournaments are once again fought.

Whether you visit Landshut during the festival or not, the houses of the old city breathe this history. The Papperbergerhaus, No. 81 Altstadt, built around 1400 and arcaded in 1681, is where the Emperor Friedrich III stayed for the wedding. No. 299, a late-Gothic house with a nineteenth-century façade, is where the wedding feast took place. Its arcades of 1453 had just been built. The fabulous, triple-gabled town hall (No. 315 Altstadt) is in fact an assemblage of three fourteenth- and fifteenth-century houses. The delightful oriel window on one corner was added in 1570. Its Gothic façade dates from 1860. The whole turreted ensemble offers everything you expect from a German Gothic town hall, including a balcony for public announcements and the ceremonial appearance of important personages.

Around 1880, commissioned by King Ludwig II of Bavaria, the Munich artists Rudolf Seitz, August Spieß, Ludwig Löfftz and Konrad Weigand decorated the Prunksaal, or State Room, of the town hall with scenes from the famous wedding, thus incidentally inspiring the citizens of Landshut to start re-enacting it. In these charming scenes burghers and knights, equestrian trumpeters and drummers, bishops, archbishops and ladies all honour the princess, who rides demurely in her coach. The men handling the magnificently plumed white horses are dressed in Polish costumes. Guests are shown arriving from Saxony, a massive dappled grey carrying both a burgher and his lady who rides side-saddle behind him. And the great ones also arrive, Margrave Albrecht Achilles, Kurfürst of Brandenburg, and his wife Anna of Saxony walking on foot ahead of the richly robed Emperor on his black charger, accompanied by his son Maximilian.

This room with its massive green-tiled fireplaces, its mighty chandeliers and mightier wooden beams is, of course, much older than these paintings. It derives from a patrician house built after a fire had ravaged the city in 1342 and acquired by the city in 1386. We know that it was widened in 1475 for the marriage celebrations. But its present Gothic style owes much to the work of the architect Georg Hauberisser in 1880.

Opposite the town hall Duke Ludwig X built his Stadtresidenz between 1536 and 1543. Ludwig embraced the new learning. His court even embraced for a time the teachings of Martin Luther, and Ludwig also became enamoured of northern Italian architecture. After a visit to Mantua he commissioned in the Stadtresidenz of Landshut the first Italian Renaissance building on German soil. The main inner courtyard speaks more of Michelangelo than of Germany, its arches rising from round pink columns and decorated by alfresco murals. Thomas Hering chiselled limestone medallions depicting the labours of Hercules for the Italian room, whose arched ceiling was painted by Ludwig Raufinger with scenes from both Holy Scripture and Greek mythology – the second themes a sure sign that the Renaissance had reached Germany. Today the forty rooms of this beautiful palace form the city and regional museum, housing exhibits dating from the early Stone Age through baroque sculpture to the homely lives of nineteenth-century burghers. The Prunksaal is an eighteenth-century confection of stucco, and the eighteenth-century living rooms house the Landshut picture gallery. It hangs a fair sprinkling of European baroque masters, as well as work by local artists dating back to the sixteenth century.

The Archbishop of Salzburg conducted the celebrated wedding in St Martin's church, which was built between 1389 and 1500. Its style, once one has admired the parish church of Neuötting, is instantly identifiable as that of Hans Stethaimer, and its spire, the tallest brick-built spire in the world, is dubbed the Stethaimer after its creator. A couple of unsuitably playful crowns of thorns circle the topmost storey.

The first impression, as you enter the church, is one of extreme height and gracefulness. I do not pretend to know how this brilliant architect achieved this stunning effect, but here are three clues. The ribs of the vaults spring directly from two rows of slender stone columns, each reaching twenty-two metres high. The aisles add to the airiness by being as long as the nave. And the long, narrow windows have next to no tracery to interrupt their upward thrust.

The furnishing is sparse, so as not to interrupt the flow of the church, but virtually everything in St Martin, Landshut, is marvellous. Stethaimer's altar, carved in freestone in 1424 and given a baroque upper half in 1664, depicts rows of saints, beginning with a carving of the patron. The Gothic pulpit dates from 1422; the sculptures of the chancel from 1450. Gothic canopies in the aisles shelter painted terracotta figures created between 1460 and 1480. (I greatly like John the Baptist, preaching from a Bible, his bare legs ready to step at a moment's notice into the River Jordan.) Michael Erhart carved a great crucifix in 1495 to hang at the entrance to the chancel. The choir stalls, carved around 1500, are filled with intriguing scenes. (Samson rides on the back of a doomed lion at the end of the stalls on the left. The canopies are peopled with bizarre animals, gesticulating choirmasters, saints, apostles, fools and devout ladies. Once again St Martin slices his cloak in two and gives half to a beggar.) The organ screen dates from 1620.

All the tombstones are worth exploring, especially that of Dr Martin Vair, co-founder of the university of Ingolstadt, Landshut and

Munich, who died in 1481. Only the stained glass of 1945 by Franz Högner is mocked by the surviving medieval glass. By general acclaim, the finest monument of all in the church is Hans Leinberger's Madonna, carved in the second decade of the sixteenth century and gracing the right aisle. Mary's face meditates on the future of her child, while the infant himself seems about to set off on a hundred-metre sprint.

In 1980, when the foundations of this church were being strengthened, part of the earlier thirteenth-century Romanesque church was discovered, and a circular staircase leads down to its remains. A previous restoration of 1950–1 uncovered the remnants of fifteenth-century and baroque frescos on the walls and pillars.

The outside of the church is as fascinating as the interior. Five flamboyant Gothic doorways shelter earlier Gothic porches. Their stone gently contrasts with the red brick of the church. Once they were black, but restoration is bringing back their true tones. The outside walls bear tombstones and epitaphs of long-dead worthies. One of these memorials is both moving and of supreme importance. An alleyway leads round the south side of the church of St Martin to St Martinsfriedhof. On the south side of the church, in between two of the superb porches, is a bust of an old man, Hans von Burghausem himself, architect of this church. This is the oldest self-portrait bust in German art (unless, as some assert, it was carved by the architect's son).

The lined face of Stethaimer, who died in 1631, broods quietly, and he has humbly portrayed himself as a corbel, holding up a carving of the suffering Jesus. Underneath the bust of Stethaimer is his coat of arms – fittingly, a couple of set-squares. On the left is the coat of arms of his first wife, on the right that of his second. The inscription lists his masterpieces: St Martin and the Heiliggeistkirche in Landshut; the choir of the Franciscan church in Salzburg; the parish churches of Neuötting and Wasserburg; and the Carmelite church at Straubing.

A little way further on stands the Frauenkapelle, a fifteenth-century chapel whose interior the city architect Wolfgang Eheham transformed in the early eighteenth century into a little rococo treasure. F. J. Lederer painted the newly stuccoed interior with scenes depicting the miseries of the War of the Spanish Succession and the motherly care shown by the Blessed Virgin Mary to Bavaria. But the main reason for making sure you go inside this church is the carving of the Gothic statue which adorns the rococo altar, a calm Madonna and child which was being peacefully carved while the rest of Landshut was consumed with excitement over its royal wedding. Just beyond this church you find the house where Stethaimer himself lived from 1408 to 1415.

Take Theatinerstraße, just south of the church of St Martin, to admire the fifteenth-century gate, the Landtor, part of the city's medieval fortifications and defended by a couple of square battlemented towers. Then walk back along the curving Altstadt to reach Stethaimer's other masterly church in Landshut, Heiliggeistkirche. This time one of his tricks for giving an illusion of remarkable height has been to set the mighty brick tower to the side of the main church, unlike his design at St Martin, which places it squarely above the west end. He began building the Heiliggeistkirche in 1407, and after his death his son took over as architect, dying himself in 1461, one year before the building was finished. Across the road is the Heilig-Geist-Spital, a hospice founded by the citizens of Landshut in the thirteenth century. The present early eighteenth-century building was designed by Johann G. G. Hirschstetten and the same Martin Eheham who transformed the Frauenkapelle from Gothic to rococo. On its façade of 1728 someone painted the Holy Trinity, who now ride in heaven above a clock.

Zweibrückenstraße leads from here across the river – two bridges being necessary because the waters divide at Landshut into the Grosse Isar and the Kleine Isar. Inevitably one of the little streets leading off from here is called Fischergasse. In between the two streams stands the church of St Sebastian, built in the late fifteenth century and transformed into a baroque church in the early 1660s. Passing the war memorial to the fallen of the 1870–1 war, the route takes us as far as the Seligenthal monastery, which Ludwig the Kelheimer and his wife Ludmilla von Bogen founded in the thirteenth century. Both lie here, their carved wooden figures standing stiffly on their tomb in the Afra chapel of the monastery church.

Such was the transformation wrought in the eighteenth century by the architect Johann Baptist Gunetzrhainer, the artistry of Johann Baptist Zimmermann and the Munich stucco genius Egid Quirin Asam that you would scarcely guess that this church was once Romanesque. Zimmermann's painting of the coronation of the Virgin decorates the dome, her divine son and God the Father sharing the honour of placing the crown on her head, while a dove representing the Holy Spirit hovers above. All the altars are giddy rococo creations, the side ones – dedicated to St Anne and the Madonna – especially so. To find a couple of lovely earlier works, namely a 'Deposition' and a 'Last Supper', both carved at the beginning of the fifteenth century, look in the chapel of St Agatha beneath the nuns' choir at the west end of the nave. This Nonnenchor also houses a mid-thirteenth-century crucifix, one of those in which Jesus is depicted hanging from a real tree.

The church contains another splendid tomb, that of Duke Ludwig X, who died in 1545, his robes thick and powerful, his long whiskers equally impressive. You can see another relic of a previous era in the former refectory: a very early thirteenth-century fresco of the coronation of the Blessed Virgin Mary, far more restrained than J. B. Zimmermann's fresco on the dome of the monastery church.

The whole monastic complex dates from the same era as the transformed church, enclosing a quiet courtyard with a formal box garden and a fountain. On the outside wall of the church Our Lady, painted on clouds, unusually acts as a sundial.

Return past Heiliggeistkirche and take Herrngasse left to find yourself in Neustadt, the second lovely wide street of Landshut, laid out in 1338 to match Altstadt. The church of the Ursalines is immediately beside you. Several of the gabled Gothic houses in Neustadt were given an elegant rococo aspect in the eighteenth century. In the seventeenth century the Jesuits built at the far end a fine classical church. Once again you see Burg Traunitz towering above the city. Halfway along Neustadt, close by the 1914–18 war memorial, turn left down Regierungstraße. Ahead, beyond the houses, rises the brick tower of the church of St Jodok which, it is said, was a practice effort by Hans Stethaimer before he designed those of St Martin and the Heiliggeistkirche.

Before we reach it, however, our route takes us to the former monastic church and monastery of the Dominicans. Most of its shell dates from the thirteenth and fourteenth centuries, but its façade is strictly classical, added at the end of the nineteenth century. Inside, Johann Baptist Zimmermann once more applied his touch, transforming the church in 1749 into another pile of rococo exuberance. This monastery was founded in 1271. The monks had the ironic misfortune to rebuild their monastery in 1802, a year before the secularization of

Bavaria which forcibly dissolved them. Today the convent houses the State administration.

Finally, from the side of the monastery church, gaze in wonder at the huge, brick hall-church of St Jodok. Nearby I decided to eat an amazingly inexpensive and satisfying meal in a working-men's bar. On the wall hung the following inscription:

> *Betrifft: Kredit!*
> *Ich Dir nix Pumpen,*
>   *Du böse!*
> *Ich Dir Pumpen,*
> *Du nix wiederkommen.*
>   *Ich böse.*
> *Besser Du böse!*

which is, I suppose, a Bavarian dialect version of the English 'Please don't ask for credit, since a refusal often offends.'

If you follow the B11 south-west from Landshut towards Munich you pass through Kronwinkl. Its Schloß, first built in the eleventh century and repeatedly rebuilt until the seventeenth, was once the family seat of Bavaria's oldest noble house, the counts of Preysing. From here it is worth taking a lingering look back at Landshut, with the spire of St Martin and Burg Traunitz both clearly visible. Then drive on to Moosburg an der Isar, with its picturesque old houses, a sixteenth-century Schloß and no fewer than three medieval churches. If you have time, do please go inside the Romanesque Benedictine monastery church, which from the twelfth to the fifteenth centuries was transformed into a superb minster. Between 1511 and 1514 Hans Leinberger worked here creating an incredibly rich high altar, which stretches up almost to the ceiling. The medieval sarcophagus of St Kastulus is also worth seeking out. Kastulus was a Roman martyr whose bones the Benedictines somehow got hold of and brought here some fifty years after the foundation of the monastery in 750.

Continue south-west and you reach Freising, just over thirty-five kilometres from Landshut. For centuries Freising and not Munich was the seat of the Bishops of Bavaria. In consequence it boasts an outstanding cathedral, rising on the Domberg and dedicated to the Virgin Mary and St Corbinian. Building began around 1150. As you go inside, look in the doorway for the little statues of the Emperor Friedrich Barbarossa and (peeping over his shoulder) his wife Beatrix.

Corbinian was an eighth-century missionary, whose bones now lie in the perfectly preserved Romanesque crypt. The cathedral boasts a curious 'beasts' pillar' on which carved dragons wrestle with human beings. The brothers Asam in the early eighteenth century gave the interior of this church a stuccoed beauty which, because of its comparatively restrained style, seems to me quite perfect. Hidden behind it is the so-called former Dom, a late-Gothic church of 1346 dedicated to St Benedict. West of the cathedral is another fine church, St Johannes, built between 1319 and 1321. The prince-bishops' Residenz stands on the west side of the Domberg, built over three centuries, beginning in the fourteenth.

If I were to choose for a visit one other church out of several fine ones in Freising it would undoubtedly be the monastery church Neustift, which the Italian Giovanni Antonio Viscardi designed in 1705 and which both Johann Baptist Zimmermann and Franz Xaver Feuchtmayr decorated. To add to its glamour, in 1765 Ignaz Günther built for this church a lavish high altar.

Over the centuries Freising has built up a remarkable collection of religious art, now on display in the diocesan museum. The Benedictines brought another useful gift to Freising: that of brewing beer. Founded in the mid-twelfth century, their Weihenstephan brewery is the world's oldest. Now owned by the State, it houses an institute of brewing run by Munich university, and is well worth a visit, if only for its excellent beer garden. A litre or so of Weihenstein beer happily washes down a dish of Freising's wild mushrooms and dumplings (*Pfefferlinge mit Semmelknödel*).

Seventeen kilometres south-east of Freising lies a completely different little town, Erding. Its great brick parish church of St Johannes der Täufer, a late-Gothic three-aisled basilica, boasts a high altar with a terrific nineteenth-century reredos and a crucifix of 1525 by Hans Leinberger. The Saviour's side has been viciously gashed, and his mouth hangs open in agony. I puzzled over an intricate late-Gothic altar-relief in this church, depicting the Last Supper. Why is everyone taking this sacred meal standing up? Wondering why the mighty stone belfry stands so far from the church, I discovered that it was once quite separate and served as the town watch tower.

From the corner of Kirchgasse you enter Lange Zeile, where, emerging from Mass one Sunday, I had the good fortune to discover the start of a clothes market, which arrives at Erding only five or six times a year. Straight ahead from the west end of the church is Landshuterstraße, leading into Schrannenplatz, at the far end of which rises Erding's sole surviving medieval gate. The Schöner Tor was built around 1500 and the bulbous dome added in the early 1660s. Today the bulky white gateway and tower are picturesquely sandwiched between a couple of yellow-painted houses with red-tiled roofs.

Because of a disastrous fire in 1648, many of the houses in this sweet town date from the following centuries, especially the eighteenth. A few older ones survive. Erding's small town hall, for instance, built in 1648, is No. 1 Landshuterstraße. Once it was the home of the Counts of Preysing. Schrannenplatz houses the fourteenth-century church of Our Lady, which was restored in 1665, secularized in 1803 and is now a little art gallery. Directly opposite is a pretty sixteenth-century house. And to the south side of the Schöner Tor stands the hospice of the Holy Ghost, built here in 1444. A little archway leads between this Heiliggeistspital and the contemporary Heliggeistkirche (whose high altar was made in 1793) to the fourteenth-century brick defences of Erding, near which I discovered the welcome bar known as the Heiliggeisthof.

Just outside the town is a pilgrimage church, Maria Verkündigung, built in the 1670s in the baroque style. Now drive due east to join the B15, which the Germans – with their canny eye for tourism – have decided is part of the Ferienstraße, or holiday road, from the Baltic to the Alps. This road runs south through Dorfen, which nestles by the River Isen. Dorfen's pilgrimage church of Maria-Dorfen is an oddity. Though built in 1782, it is one of the earliest classical buildings in Bavaria, instead of following the usual rococo style of such churches. Inside is the fifteenth-century picture of the Virgin Mary which draws the pilgrims. One of the ubiquitous maypoles of Bavaria rises near the church in Dorfen's wide market square. Drive on by way of Haag, whose massive medieval watchtower looms over you, and where you can pause to visit a garden of rock formations created by an Ice Age glacier.

Further south along the B15 the route reaches Wasserburg am Inn, a walled town beautifully situated on the River Inn. The peninsula on which it rises juts out into the river opposite a romantic-looking Schloß built by the dukes of Bavaria in the fifteenth and sixteenth centuries. This splendid site is matched by every inch of the rest of Wasserburg. A bridge over the river leads directly to the wide and handsome, battlemented Brucktor, a town gate built in 1374 and renewed in 1470. A couple of bearded and moustachioed knights were painted on the outer wall of the gate in 1568 for further protection. You pass through the gate to turn directly right and park in the Marienplatz. Then walk back to the gate, for inside it is, on the one side, a woodcarver's shop and, on the other, an art gallery specializing in works dating from the twelfth to the twentieth century. This was once part of Wasserburg's Heiliggeist-Spital, founded in 1341 and in part built in 1380. The collection on display belonged to a connoisseur named Günter Dietz. It includes Romanesque frescos, Renaissance prints, baroque masterworks and French Impressionist paintings, and does not stop until it reaches Pablo Picasso. You can visit the museum from May to September (except on Mondays) between 11.00 and 17.00 and at other times of the year between 13.00 and 17.00.

Marienplatz is filled with good things. The former tollhouse (Altes Mauthaus) was once the home of the dukes. Built in 1497, it received its present satisfying Renaissance façade (which includes three unassuming oriel windows) in 1530. A plaque on No. 23 declares that the religious poet Johann Kaspar Aiblinger was born there in 1779. On the other side of the square the sixty-five-metre-high medieval watchtower now serves as the church belfry and has been given a little spire. Wasserburg suffered a great conflagration on 1 May 1874, but a legend on the church door tells you that this building was saved from destruction by the intervention of the Blessed Virgin Mary. Thank heavens, for the tiny interior of this fourteenth-century church is beautiful, with the same Madonna holding her baby son on the high altar.

Beyond the church is the stern town hall, built by Jörg Tünzl in the late 1450s and seemingly in two powerful parts. Coats of arms fill its blank windows, and you can follow a guided tour of the interior on the hour. A playful contrast is provided across the square by the rococo façade which J. B. Zimmermann gave to the Kernhaus in 1738.

Walk round Alte Schranne into a second, equally delightful arcaded square which calls itself Herrngasse. As you walk you notice that No. 4 Salzenderzeile must once have been a warehouse, for a decrepit crane still pokes out of its top storey. The late-Gothic Herrenhaus, built for a rich abbot, is now Wasserburg's local history museum. In spite of some notable pieces, this is one of those collections I prefer to miss, save for the chance of exploring the building that houses it. For my liking, you see too many leather harnesses of yesteryear.

At the far end of Herrengasse turn right into Kirchplatz to come upon a rarity. The apse of the church of St Jakob is painted with a medieval tree of life depicting Adam's sin and our salvation. In an ungentlemanly fashion the artist has actually left Adam out of the picture, portraying only the naked Eve with an apple in one hand and a skull in the other. He has compounded his prejudice against women by giving the serpent that tempts her the head and breasts of a woman.

The church has a proud, square tower with Gothic ornaments. Hans Stethaimer began building it in 1410, followed by Stefan Krumenauer in 1445 and Wolfgang Wieser in 1461. The nave of the church is brick, the tower and apse stone. Statues of St Peter (who seems to have lost one of the keys to heaven) and St Paul guard the entrance. The interior is virtually as the architects left it, apart from a richly carved Renaissance pulpit, on top of which stands St James, dressed in his pilgrim's hat and carrying his pilgrim's staff. The brothers Martin and Michael Zürn designed this pulpit in 1639. St James also perches, similarly equipped, on a fountain set up in 1988 outside the church presbytery (which was built in 1496). What I do not understand is why his toes are peeping from underneath his robe. Since he has so far to walk, the pilgrim apostle is traditionally the sole one of the twelve who wears boots.

Our last drive before returning to Altötting is to wind along the lovely Inn valley north-east as far as Mühldorf. Just outside Wasserburg am Inn on the Mühldorf road is the church of St Achatz (look out for Achatzstraße on the left). Wolfgang Wieser rebuilt this church in the 1480s. The reason it lies outside the town is that St Achatz served the spiritual needs of the local leper colony.

Lying but fifteen kilometres from Altötting, Mühldorf am Inn could not be more different in character. As its name indicates, it prospered as a mill town. Also a walled town, it boasts a long, wide Stadtplatz, busy and partly arcaded, with a fountain of 1692. In 1906 J. Widmann painted one of its gateways with the scene of a medieval battle. Even so, these once fearsome defences have been adapted for peaceable pursuits. A twentieth-century family has made its home in part of the tower. The three-storeyed arch above the gate has become the Hotel-Restaurant Altöttinger-Tor. Beyond it meanders the wide River Inn.

The other gateway and tower of Mühldorf, known as the Nagelschmied-Tor, rises for thirty-five metres. You can still see the slits that once guided its portcullis. Built and rebuilt between the thirteenth and the fifteenth centuries, this gateway-tower is now the home of Mühldorf's local history museum, reached by rickety wooden steps covered with slippery pigeon-droppings. Outside stands a mild-looking halberdier, carved in stone. Apparently when the bridge over the River Inn was blown up towards the end of World War II, the force of the charges flung this poor halberdier into the river.

The Frauenkirche at Mühldorf began as a Capuchin monastery in 1643, and a metal monk still acts as its weather-vane. The thirty-five-metre-high tower dates from 1856. The stern doors, the heavy arcades of the town hall and its battlemented gateway are lightened by its Renaissance features. The whole Stadtplatz is unspoilt, rendered all the more charming by the variety of its decorated houses, some of which sport pretty oriel windows. It boasts no fewer than three more baroque fountains, beside the one we have already seen.

Kirchgasse leads from the Stadtplatz up to the church of St Nikolaus. Its powerful stone tower is Romanesque; signs of the zodiac decorate the medieval entrance, as do gargoyles and faded frescos. The rest is light, rococo, exquisite – redesigned and built by Alois Mair between 1769 and 1775. One of the paintings on the dome (all of which are by Martin Heigl) depicts the Council of Nicea, when St Nikolaus lost his temper and threw a right hook at a heretic. On the left in a glass case is displayed an extremely grisly skeleton, which turns out to be St Deodoratus. A little chapel here displays a bizarre tufa grotto. To step from the nave of the church into the tower, with its Gothic arches and a gravestone depicting the Last Judgment (with people busily clambering out of their tombs) is to take a remarkable mental and artistic leap from the eighteenth century back into the Middle Ages.

Nearby is a detached, eight-sided war memorial chapel. On closer inspection it reveals itself as medieval, dedicated to St Johannes and built around 1350. Brick pillars hold up its graceful arches. A hundred years later another chapel was added at the east end of this rotunda. The fresco of St Johannes dates from the fifteenth century. Another fresco depicts St George killing the dragon, complete with a crowned maiden. The treasures of this hidden gem include a stunning Gothic winged altarpiece and a touching *pietà*.

In Kirchplatz beyond the chapel of St Johannes stand a war memorial museum and a Weinstube. I chose the Weinstube. Then I drove back to the Hotel Zur Post in Altötting. After such a long, though scarcely gruelling tour, I thought it right to feast on *Kalbsrahmbraaten mit Butterspätzle* (roast veal and noodles), served with a salad, followed by *Gebackene Apfelknödel mit marinierte Pflaumen* (baked apple dumplings and marinated plums).

Oberammergau

Everyone has heard of the Oberammergau passion play. And it stirs mixed emotions in many breasts.

Like the pilgrimages to Altötting, the origin of the Oberammergau passion play lies in a miracle. This occurred during the Thirty Years War, which began in Prague in 1618. Bohemian Protestants in that year had been enraged at being denied the right of assembly. They flung out of a fortress window two emissaries of the Catholic emperor, as well as a private secretary. (Fortunately, the three victims fell into a dung-heap outside the castle wall and thus landed softly, escaping unhurt.)

Inevitably when war started, the Catholic rulers of Bavaria supported the emperor. Initially their general, the redoubtable Tilly, routed the Protestant forces, but even he was no match for the army commanded by the Swedish King Gustavus Adolphus. In September 1631 Gustavus Adolphus's Protestant troops crushed Tilly's army at the Battle of Breitenfeld. Soon they had taken Würzburg, and the following May, having decisively defeated Tilly in a conflict by the River Lech, they invested and took Munich.

'You would not recognize our poor Bavaria,' lamented the Emperor Maximilian. 'Villages and convents have gone up in flames. Priests, monks and citizens have been tortured and killed at Fürstenfeld, at

Dießen, at Benediktbeueren and in the Ettal.' As the soldiers marauded and the people starved, the plague added to the toll of the dead. It was no new scourge in Bavaria. During the first half of the sixteenth century 38,500 people had died of the plague in Augsburg alone. Keeping a deadly note of its ravages, the imperial city lost another 20,500 in the second half of the same century, and another 34,000 in the first fifty years of the next.

Starving people offered little resistance to this Black Death. Because the land was not rich enough to support the great influx of troops, harvests were destroyed by the soldiers and granaries robbed. One of Wallenstein's armies lived for a whole week on fruit alone, with the consequence that every soldier suffered grotesquely from dysentery. The plague became an epidemic.

Throughout this time the village of Oberammergau escaped unscathed. Its council decreed that no one from outside Oberammergau should be allowed in, and armed guards protected the charmed spot. Yet the plague was not far away. Close by, in Kohlgrub, you can still see a plaque on the church wall recording that of the whole population only two couples remained healthy, all the rest having been struck down. These two had made a vow that they and their descendants would keep the church in perfect repair, should they manage to survive.

Even closer to Oberammergau lies the village of Eschenlohe. Today a bright, clean Bavarian town, overlooked by the chapel of the ruined Burg, it boasts a parish church, St Clement, designed by Johann Michael Fischer in 1773 and enhanced with a rococo tabernacle by Johann Baptist Straub. In midsummer 1632 Eschenlohe was a village of desperate citizens, wondering who would next catch the plague from his neighbour. Their former church boasted a painting of St Sebastian, which is still in the present building. Sebastian was reputed to be a powerful defender of the faithful against the plague, but in 1632 he failed the citizens of Eschenlohe.

Unfortunately for Oberammergau, one of its citizens worked in Eschenlohe as a farmhand. Kaspar Schisler seemed unaffected by the plague, and when he learned that his native village had decided to go ahead with the annual celebration of its patron saint, he decided to return home. Easily evading the guards, he brought with him the plague. According to a later Oberammergau chronicle, dated 1733, he returned to Eschenlohe to die. His infected wife and children followed him to the grave, and other villagers now fell sick and died. Oberammergau's parish register in the early seventeenth century did not record the deaths of children, but it does record the inevitable news that the parish priest, Primus Christeiner fell sick and died, followed by his successor, Marcellus Fatiga, and their unfortunate verger and grave-digger, Hans Stückl. On the feast day of Saints Simon and Jude, 28 October 1632, eighty-four adults were recorded as dead of the plague in Oberammergau.

The promise made by the two surviving couples in Kohlgrub reveals the sole method of defence available to those who were faced with some deadly peril. The village council of Oberammergau decided on a similar promise, if God should lift the plague from their people. In July 1633 all those who could still walk processed to the parish church. There they vowed that, should the plague be lifted from them, for ever they and their children would re-enact the passion and resurrection of Jesus. Some of them, declares the chronicle of the village, already had the marks of the disease on their faces and bodies, but from that moment no single person died of the plague in Oberammergau.

Passion plays were not unusual in this part of Bavaria. Indeed, as late as the mid-nineteenth century the Bavarian villages of Brixlegg, Kohlgrub and Mittelwald were still performing them. The villagers of Oberammergau had performed such plays in the past, and in 1633 they had a play ready to perform. In the fifteenth century the monks of Saints Ulrich and Afra had written their own passion play, and a mastersinger named Sebastian Wild had got hold of and rewritten it. It must have been a merry spectacle. The plot, which still survives, includes numerous devils as well as Lucifer himself. Sebastian Wild's prologue begins with a speech asking the spectators to receive the play with deep reverence. A devil immediately appears and reads a letter from Lucifer advising them to treat it with contempt.

In fulfilment of their vow in 1634 the villagers of Oberammergau borrowed this play. Ten years later they performed it again. Unlike the passion plays of Brixlegg, Kohlgrub and Mittelwald, that of Oberammergau has been faithfully performed virtually every decade since that time. When I visited Oberammergau in 1984, the year of a special three hundred and fiftieth anniversay performance of the play, the players were no longer using the Augsburg text. The people had tired of it after only two performances. The original text is now covered with strips of paper obliterating passages they disliked and suggesting new sections of more acceptable dialogue.

Fortunately, the devils did not disappear, although a merrily vulgar scene which they enacted for some time has, alas, disappeared from the twentieth-century text. When Judas, the betrayer of Jesus, hanged himself, we learn from the Bible that his entrails fell out. For several performances the local butcher would create these entrails out of bread and sausage-meat. As they fell out, a horde of devils would rush on to the stage and gobble them up.

This knockabout drama was soon changed. Monks from the nearby monastery at Ettal were enlisted to soften its features. More devils were added, but these exhibited improvingly spiritual sins, such as envy and covetousness, rather than the fleshed-out wickedness of the earlier demons. By stressing the danger of eternal damnation, a further air of gloom was added to the passion play. Few liked the result. In 1750 Father Ferdinand Rosner, parish priest of Oberammergau, wrote a completely new version, in the style of an Italian opera and consisting of long, rhyming couplets set to music. No one liked this either, although it was performed again in 1760. Slowly the version was modified. Under threat from the secularizing tendencies of late eighteenth- and early nineteenth-century Bavarian princes it somehow survived, until in 1803 the monastery of Ettal was suppressed.

One monk carried on living there. Othmar Weiß also became parish priest of Eschenlohe. A doctor of the university of Ingolstadt, he now decided to run the local brewery as well as serving as a parish priest. He completely rewrote the Oberammergau passion play, basing it entirely on the Bible, save for the scene where St Veronica offers her scarf to wipe the sweat from Jesus' face as he carries his cross to Calvary. Weiß also kept one of the innovations of Ferdinand Rosner, the 'living tableaux'. These consisted of eighteen scenes from Jewish history as recorded in the Bible. Crowded with actors, the scenes are entirely motionless, frozen spectacles.

This is basically the play you see today, although as we shall see, further modifications have been forced on the Oberammergauers. Othmar Weiß was fortunate that a composer named Rochus Dedler had become schoolmaster and organist at Oberammergau. Deeply influenced by Mozart and by baroque eighteenth-century music, Dedler orchestrated Weiß's new text, interpreting the action with sacred songs. Weiß was also lucky that Alois Daisenberger, who became parish priest of Oberammergau in 1845, when asked to revise his text remained extremely faithful to Weiß's version, simply shortening scenes, cutting down tediously long speeches and omitting passages that slowed down the action. Daisenberger had the good sense to leave Rochus Dedler's music entirely intact.

The passion play at Oberammergau is thus no medieval survival but a performance and text that have been repeatedly modified over the centuries. What has survived all these changes is the tenderly human treatment of the biblical characters who throng the stage. Mary still desperately laments over her dead son, as she did long ago. 'My dearly beloved child, must I now live without you? Dead as you are, I still love you. Every woman in the world, join in suffering with me! Help me to mourn my son.'

The international renown of the Oberammergau passion play was given an immense boost in 1871 when the English travel firm, Thomas Cook, began bringing tourists to see it. (The year was 1871 because the 1870 performances had been delayed for twelve months owing to the Franco-Prussian War.) In the same year the Prince of Wales (the future Edward VII) took his bride there, travelling supposedly incognito but staying in the home of the man playing Jesus. Nine years later Thomas Cook had its own agent permanently in the village during the season to look after British guests. By 1890 a railway track from Munich had reached nearby Garmisch-Partenkirchen.

In that year the satirist Jerome K. Jerome went to see the play and published an account of his experiences in his *Diary of a Pilgrimage*. His story, in my view, comes as a necessary antidote to some of the over-pious gush that has been written about the play. First he complained that the performances went on too long. They still do. Next he noted an occasional lack of conviction in the acting. Jerome K. Jerome was convinced that he could have taught the traitor Judas Iscariot far more about evil than he had ever learned in Oberammergau. 'This actor was evidently not acquainted with even the rudiments of knavery,' he wrote. 'I wanted to get up and instruct him in them. I felt there were little subtleties of rascaldom, little touches of criminality, that I could have put the man up to, which would have transformed his Judas from woodenness into breathing life.'

Yet the satirist left the theatre deeply impressed. 'The crowded audience that sat beside us in the theatre yesterday saw Christ of Nazareth nearer than any book, however inspired, could bring him to them; clearer than any words, however eloquent, could show him.

They saw the sorrow of his patient face. They heard his deep tones calling them.' These words remind me of a comment by Hans Christian Andersen who, as a Danish Protestant, had come with reservations to see the Oberammergau passion play. As he confessed afterwards, 'Never shall I forget the passion play at Oberammergau, so completely did it surpass all my expectation. I could not think of it beforehand without being scandalized at the idea of seeing Jesus acted on the stage; but as it took place here, in religious faith, full of fervour, all offence was taken away.' Hans Christian Andersen added, 'The whole religious play has a majesty, a simplicity, something so strangely absorbing that even the most irreligious must needs be dumb.'

These apparently innate skills possessed by the people of this little Bavarian village obviously derive from the long tradition of the whole affair. Actors and directors of the passion play build on, and also rely on, the interpretations and achievements of their predecessors. It is fascinating to trace a villager's participation in the play over the years. Anton Preisinger, for instance, took the role of Jesus both in 1950 and in 1960. He had played an angel in 1922 at the age of ten, and twelve years later he portrayed Lazarus, whom Jesus raised from the dead. His was a noted family of Oberammergau actors, for in the production of 1930 Mary Magdalene was played by Anton Preisinger's sister, Hansi.

The passion play has made Oberammergau into Bavaria's richest village. So many visitors press to see it – more than a million spectators came in 1984 – that the villagers now elect two persons to play the principal roles on successive evenings, a wise precaution in case one should fall ill and the production be cancelled. Max Jablonka (who runs a shop selling, among other goods, artificial Christmas trees) and Rudolf Zwink (a dentistry student at Munich university) both took the part of Jesus in 1984. Two quite different girls, one chubby and black-haired, the other slender and blonde, played the Virgin Mary. As I talked to them, to some of their parents, and to other members of the cast, it became clear to me that these village actors and actresses were passionately committed to the Christian faith and, in spite of the immense profits made by the Oberammergau passion play, to the integrity of the demanding enterprise in which they were engaged. As Hansi Preisinger once observed, 'The Oberammergauer does not feel as if he were acting in a theatre. To us the play means keeping faith with the sacred vow of our forefathers.'

In truth their play has rarely been performed without controversy. At the time of the Enlightenment the Prince-Elector of Bavaria, Maximilan Joseph, along with the Archbishop of Salzburg, decided that the 'ludicrous and disagreeable effect of bad acting, plus the intentional buffooneries' at Oberammergau brought scandal on the Church and religion. They determined to ban the passion play. The Oberammergauers boldly ignored the ban. In 1810 another elector threatened to fine the villagers thirty *Reichstaler* if the play went ahead. A deputation of Oberammergauers persuaded the Munich court that all they were presenting was a harmless country festival.

More recent controversy has been provoked by the role of women in the play. Christian Stückl, elected director of the 1990 performances, decided to abolish the age-long and absurd notion that although married men could play Jesus and his apostles, no married woman, or indeed any woman aged over thirty-five, could take any of the leading roles in the play. As Christian Stückl put it, 'It is quite a problem when Jesus dies at thirty-three and Mary, his mother, looks a mere twenty-one.' His decision created uproar among the Oberammergau traditionalists. Historical research supported the new producer, for the rule barring married or middle-aged women had been introduced a mere 120 years earlier. Yet passions rose. Said one traditionalist, 'We don't wish to see ugly old women on the stage.' Retorted a woman ally of Christian Stückl, 'For too long we have seen ugly old men on the stage.'

Such outbursts usually disappear when the performances begin. Even so, a powerful objection to the traditonal interpretation of the Christian story has been mounted in recent years by both sensitive Christians and devout Jews. Even as early as 1860 an English Christian, Dean Stanley of St Paul's Cathedral, perceived that parts of the passion play were traducing the Jews. The text of the Oberammergau passion play, he observed, had transformed the ancient Jerusalem council, or Sanhedrin, 'unintentionally it may be, but, if so, the more impressively' into 'the appearance of a hideous caricature of a great ecclesiastical assembly'.

These anti-Semitic nuances took on a far more sinister aspect with the coming to power in Germany of Adolf Hitler. The people of Oberammergau, like many others, welcomed the new Führer. At the three hundredth anniversary performance in 1934 spectators read in the preface to the text a tribute to the new spirit that Hitler had brought to his adopted country. 'Instead of imminent ruin, we experienced the fortune of a new life which unites us all in our race,' it ran. 'Is there any other time more favourable in these days of the suppression of the anti-Christian powers in our fatherland to remember the price the Son of God himself paid for his people, the people who adhere to him and to his banner?'

Hitler himself came to see the passion play in 1934, and (although in private an unbeliever) declared himself pleased. His table-talk, in July 1942 when the Holocaust was about to emerge in all its terror, stated that the play 'convincingly portrayed the menace of Judaism'. Pontius Pilate, the Roman governor who had weakly acquiesced in the execution of Jesus, seemed to Hitler to embody 'a Roman so racially and intellectually superior that he stands out like a firm clean rock'.

After the defeat of the Hitler regime no one could afford to be insensitive to accusations of anti-Semitism. The villagers decided to commission Father Stephan Schaller, of the nearby monastery of Ettal, to write a new version of their passion play. Controversy still raged, especially when the Oberammergauers rejected the priest's new text. Schaller himself was incensed. 'The Oberammergauers do not wish to be anti-Semitic,' he declared, 'but history has passed them by.' He went further in adding, 'The locals believe they have one irrefutable argument to prove themselves right: an enormous financial profit at the end of the season, making them the richest village in Bavaria.'

Such commercial instincts proved decisive in finally excising anti-Semitic elements from the Oberammergau passion play, for in 1970 the American Jewish Congress urged every citizen of the United States to boycott the production. Distinguished Americans, such as Lionel Trilling, Leonard Bernstein and Arthur Miller, concurred in the boycott, as did the celebrated German authors Günther Grass and Heinrich Böll. In 1978 Hans Mayr, elected producer of the 1980 performances, chaired a committee to amend the text. The Committee cut out a totally unhistorical section depicting the Jerusalem Jews, who changed money in the temple precincts, as stirring up hatred against Jesus. For the first time Jesus' own nationality emerged in the passion play. Jewish visitors to Oberammergau were welcomed as 'brothers and sisters from which our Saviour came'. And the discourteous references to the Pharisees were finally excluded from the play.

At last the play involved a judgment on all men and women, not just on those who put Jesus to death. The words of the crusading Victorian journalist W. T. Stead, who came to Oberammergau in 1890, finally coincided with what was actually represented on the stage of the passion play theatre. 'The Passion Play has at least done this – it sets us discussing the conduct of Caiaphas, Pilate and Judas as if they were our contemporaries, as if they were statesmen at Westminster, judges at the Old Bailey, or administrators in India,' he wrote. For W. T. Stead the High Priest Caiaphas, who helped to condemn Jesus to death, was not some alien being, but 'the great prototype of the domineering and intolerant ecclesiastic the world over'. He went further in asserting that 'there is a latent Caiaphas in every heart'.

This, I believe, is the most valuable function of the Oberammergau passion play. Many people, however, will visit this enchanting corner of Bavaria in those years when no play is being performed. They will not be disappointed in simply exploring the village of Oberammergau itself. The sole ugly building is the passion play theatre itself. Advertising the Jubilee Performances of 1934, Thomas Cook's brochure rightly observed, 'The theatre itself is roughly like an airport shed.' Even so, it has its virtues, for every spectator can see the action perfectly (which cannot be said of most London theatres), and by some accoustical miracle every single word spoken on the stage can be heard without amplification. Out of season you can go behind scenes to admire the hundred-year-old costumes, the armour and the spears which serve as props for the passion play. In a quest for total realism the crown of thorns worn by the actors playing Jesus is woven from thorn brought here from the Holy Land.

This airport shed is fronted by a modest, effective statue of Jesus, riding on an ass into Jerusalem, and is surrounded by a beautiful Bavarian village in a magnificent setting. Oberammergau, lying some 916 metres above sea level, is set in the valley of the River Ammer at the foot of the Bavarian Alps. To the south Mount Kofel, surmounted by a huge cross, rises to a height of 1,343 metres. The Sonnenberg to the west is topped by its uppermost peak, the 1,565-metre-high Pürschling. To the east the Laber rises even higher, and when the air is clear you can see as far as the highest peak in Germany, the superb 2,966-metre-high Zugspitze.

The Kofel is the mountain best loved by the villagers. Early in the morning every 24 August the young men of Oberammergau climb the slopes adjoining the Kofel, bearing kindling and logs. They arrange them in the shape of a crown, a cross and the symbols 'LII'. The symbols refer to mad King Ludwig II of Bavaria, whose birthday occurred the following day. As night falls the kindling sets the logs ablaze, and torch-carrying citizens process behind brass bands to the centre of Oberammergau, where they let off rockets and fireworks.

One morning I lay in bed in Oberammergau forgetting that it was the feast of Corpus Christi. Suddenly the bells of the parish church began to ring out. After half an hour of these bells I felt constrained to get up – fortunately in time to see a procession which included the parish priest holding a sacred Host under a canopy. Led by the local musicians, he wended his way to celebrate Mass at an open-air altar erected outside the passion play theatre. Most of the women in the procession were dressed in traditional full blue skirts, with white blouses, lace-edged petticoats, white hand-knitted stockings and black silver-buckled shoes. The men wore grey jackets, white shirts overclad with embroidered braces, coloured silk neckerchiefs and leather knee breaches. This, I learned, was the livery of the Bishop of Freising, in whose territory Oberammergau lay until 1803. This Eucharist was accompanied by a splendid choir.

My informant told me of one ceremony that I have yet to see at Oberammergau (I gather that it also occurs throughout the whole of this region of Bavaria.) The Thursday before the second Sunday before Christmas is called *Klopfersnacht*, which means the night for knocking on people's doors. In the evening the children parade the streets singing songs about Mary and Joseph, who found no resting place, save a stable, when she was carrying Jesus. Like Mary and Joseph, they knock on every door they come to. Unlike Mary and Joseph, the children are rewarded. As soon as a door is opened, they cry in Bavarian dialect '*I bitt Enk um an Oklopfat*', which means 'give me a tip'. The same profitable rigmarole occurs again on New Year's Eve.

In the village the outside walls of several of the houses on whose doors these children knock are exquisitely painted. The technique used in decorating them is known as 'air painting' (or *Lüftlmalerei*). The greatest *Lüftlmaler* of Bavaria, Franz Zwinck, was born in 1748 and made his home in Oberammergau. Adapting the skills of Italian church decorators, he applied his own art to the humble homes of the villagers. He painted the so-called Pilate's House at Oberammergau in

1769 – the spiral staircase leading to the house is a fine example of Franz Zwinck's ability to create perspective; a second is the Gerold-haus. He decorated houses with hunting scenes. Once he laid a bet with a milkmaid, promising to paint on her house a portrait of the Virgin Mary before she managed to churn a pail of butter. Zwinck won the bet.

When it comes to religious services, my own preference is for Mass in Oberammergau's parish church rather than outside its brutal theatre. By the seventeenth century, before Oberammergau grew rich on the profits of the passion play, its church was so decrepit that the villagers decided to pull it down and rebuild. In 1736 they chose as architect Franz Schmuzer. He created a minor rococo masterpiece, whose lines and convolutions continually trick the eye. He brought in Matthäus Gunther to depict on the dome the martyrdom of Saints Peter and Paul, joint patron saints of Oberammergau parish church. He himself decorated the choir with a painting of the Virgin Mary. And Franz Zwinck, the *Lüftlmaler*, was available to create frescoes of *trompe-l'oeil* balustrades. Schmuzer crowned his work by bringing in the sculptor Franz Xaver Schmädl to fashion a magnificent high altar and scarcely less lavish side altars. Cherubs, twenty-five of them, slide up and down the sculpted curtains of the high altar. Saints Peter and Paul, and Saints Joseph and Joachim, flank this altar, sculpted in white and crowned with golden haloes.

Yet this remains a humble village church. Underneath the choir loft is a simple memorial to the nine sons of Oberammergau who, in the early nineteenth century, went to war in Russia and never returned. Beside the gleeful skeleton it depicts a weeping mother. And on the north side of the church is a chapel dedicated to the Holy Trinity, which includes a statue of St Gregory Thaumaturgos. He is there because at this time the River Ammer frequently overflowed its banks, and one of the reputed skills of Gregory Thaumaturgos was to prevent flooding. Opposite stands an altar dedicated to St Anthony, patron saint of pigs.

Alois Daisenberger, who in the nineteenth century re-drafted the text of the passion play into what is basically its present form, was buried in the graveyard of this church in 1883. The bust on his tomb was sculpted by Otto Lang of Munich. One side bears the inscription 'His works survive him' (*Seine Werke folgen ihm nach*); the other side the inscription 'Let us keep his ideal holy' (*Sein Vorbild sei uns heilig*).

Do not forget to pause also beside the tomb of Rochus Dedler, on the north side of the parish church. The inscription on this monument to the creator of the music of the Oberammergau passion play announces that it was 'erected by friends and pupils in memory of our unforgettable teacher'.

Oberammergau is a winter sports centre, with a ski-lift taking athletes up the mountainside. After visiting the shops and the local history museum, both of which display the celebrated woodcarvings of Oberammergau craftsmen, it is time to leave the village and tour its environs. The B23 leads north-west to its sister village, Unterammergau. I used to swim in the Adriatic with the village schoolmaster of Unterammergau, who would frequently tell me that the place where he lived was quite as attractive as the far more famous Oberammergau. He was right. Excellent hostelries and guesthouses here surround another lovely church. St Nikolaus, Unterammergau, fell into ruins during the Thirty Years War. When the war was over the parishioners decided to rebuild it. They managed to finish the tower by the end of the century, and in 1709 they began building the present baroque church.

Far less ornate than the church of Saints Peter and Paul in Oberammergau, the church of St Nikolaus is none the less beguiling, with delicate frescoes and a high altar created by Franz Xaver Schmädl. On the south side of the nave an altar carries a picture of the martyrdom of St Veit. The naked saint is surrounded by faggots; soldiers set light to them; and in heaven a cherub proffers Veit his martyr's crown. The baroque organ dates from 1777. The chapel of the Holy Blood, which was stuccoed and painted by Schmuzer in the mid-eighteenth century, contains a phial said to hold a drop of the blood of Jesus himself. This holy blood was brought to Unterammergau from Italy in 1734. How it reached Italy from Jerusalem remains unexplained.

Continuing north-west from Unterammergau the B23 reaches Rottenbuch. And three kilometres south of Rottenbuch you reach a piece of technological history: the Echelsbacher bridge was Germany's first reinforced concrete span, thrown across the River Ammer in 1929 and arching eighty-nine metres above the deep cleft of the waters. I prefer Rottenbuch, with its superb monastery, once belonging to the Augustinians and later taken over by the Benedictines. The square tower of the monastery church carries several clocks and, in case they all fail, a sundial as well. With the help of Franz Xaver Schmädl,

Josef Schmuzer of Wessobrunn transformed its interior into a rococo riot. Schmädl created the feverish high altar, dedicated to the birth of the Blessed Virgin. The pulpit, canopied and golden, supports a cherub whose horn blasts a silent fanfare for the angel bearing the tablets of the Ten Commandments above. Behind the preachers glitters the sacred heart of Jesus. Apparently flying beside the pulpit are two evangelists, St John, identified by his eagle, and St Matthew, identified by the head of a bull.

Balthasar Freiwiß built the organ in 1747. Its three parts are delicately set together, a pink marble arch supporting the choir organ. Franz Xaver Schmädl's extreme playfulness expresses itself in the cherubs he set along the long, canopied apse, playing fiddle, flugelhorn and kettle-drums, while one sings from a golden sheet of music. Since this was once an Augustinian convent church, Matthäus Günther in 1741 was commissioned to decorate the ceiling with a painting of the death of St Augustine. Few seem to mourn his passing in this picture, while the pagans assail the Christian world.

Rottenbuch monastery was founded by Duke Welf I, and Schmädl sculpted a ridiculously pompous, even fey statue of him on the left choir stalls, a little dog peeping up at its master. Schmädl, I think, was more successful in portraying an ill-tempered St Paul, to the right of the high altar. In all this richness it comes as a surprise to discover the late-Gothic Madonna and child, dating from 1483 and possibly by Erasmus Grasser. Mary is giving her obviously overfed infant a golden apple.

Peiting, our next stop along this route, is a winter sports centre which also boasts a couple of fine churches. The pilgrimage church of Maria unter dem Egg was built in the mid-seventeenth century. The church of St Michael has a rococo pulpit and a high altar created by Schmädl in 1758, but it has managed to retain its gothic chancel and its Romanesque tower and crypt. If you walk up the hill set with stations of the cross, the Kalvarienberg offers a superlative view of the surrounding mountains, and a *Wanderkarte* directs walkers along the luscious, so-called König-Ludwig-Wanderweg between here and Rottenbuch.

Just beyond Peiting rises a town whose walls have survived virtually intact from the fifteenth and seventeenth centuries. Washed by the waters of the Lech, Schongau is a health resort offering ski schools and sailing on the nearby Schongauer See. This part of Bavaria is known as the Pfaffenwinkel or clergymen's corner. Ancient moors, meadows and forests, Bavarian farmhouses, gently rolling countryside, lakes and mountain streams have combined to create a blissfully beautiful land. The König-Ludwig-Wanderweg is matched in beauty and quietness by the Lech mountain trail (the Lech-Hohenweg). It is possible to glimpse virtually the whole of the Pfaffenwinkel, its eleven lakes sheltered by the mountains, from the top of the 988-metre-high Hohen Peißenberg, where the monks of Rottenbuch set up a meteorological observatory as early as 1781. The main tourist and information office for the Pfaffenwinkel is here in Schongau, at No. 1 Schloßplatz. The town also boasts a baroque church, Maria Himmelfahrt, built by Domenikus Zimmermann, enriched by Franz Xaver Schmuzer and frescoed in 1748 by Matthäus Günther. The Spitalkirche is dedicated to the Holy Spirit and was built in the sixteenth and seventeenth centuries, as was Schongau's cemetery chapel. This Helig-Kreuz-Kapelle dates from 1689.

Alt-Schongau also boasts a Romanesque basilica, dedicated to St Michael and built around 1220. Spot the saint slaying a dragon on the west entrance. Inside is a Romanesque font and on the high altar a large wooden crucifix, carved in the early thirteenth century. As for Schongau's secular buildings, the Schloß is a kindly-looking late-Gothic building and the Steingadener Richterhaus dates from 1493. Although the Ballenhaus of 1515 was altered in the nineteenth century to make it more suitable as a town hall, this former warehouse remains stern enough, its narrow windows peering out across the calm Marien-platz towards the statue and fountain of Our Lady.

Drive west now for twenty-six kilometres along the B472 to another beautifully sited little town, to which the Bishops of Augsburg would repair in order to hunt. Their hunting lodge, designed by a native of the town, Johann Georg Fischer, adorns the central square of Markt-oberdorf. In 1732 Fischer also re-designed the parish church which stands next to it. Clearly a man who considerably respected the architecture of previous years, this architect blended his own rococo fantasies with the older Gothic structure, adding an onion dome to the tower which had guarded the church since 1680. Abraham Bader, a masterly stucco artist from nearby Mindelheim, and the court painter Franz Georg Hermann of Kempten, came to Marktoberdorf to enhance Fischer's work with their own splendid decoration.

Kaufbeuren lies thirteen kilometres north along the B16. The praise heaped on Berchtesgaden by the novelist Ludwig Ganghofer becomes still more persuasive when you remember that he was actually born in this spot in 1855 – long before it had expanded to its present size. His birthplace still stands in Kirchplatz and is marked by a plaque. Mementoes of Ganghofer, including portraits of the author and his friends, as well as manuscripts of his work, make a visit to the local history museum (Heimatmuseum, Nos 12–14 Kaisergäßchen) unusually rewarding. It opens every weekday except Mondays from 09.00 to 11.00 and from 13.00 to 16.00, and on Sundays between 09.00 and 12.00. The west end of Kaisergäßchen ends in a T-junction, where you turn right along Am Breiten Bach to reach the Franciscan nunnery of Kaufbeuren. This was the home of another celebrated citizen of the town. Founded in 1261, it achieved fame from 1682 to 1744 through the holy mystic Crescentia Höß. Her mortal remains still lie in the convent in a glass coffin.

This town is the perfect setting for Bavaria's oldest children's festival, the *Tänzelfest*. On the third Sunday in July over 1,500 children dress in medieval costume to depict Kaufbeuren's history throughout the centuries. Its *pièce de résistance* is the ceremonial welcome given by the town to the Emperor Maximilian I, who is said to have instituted the whole festival in 1497. A free imperial city from 1286 to 1802, old Kaufbeuren has preserved impressive medieval walls and sturdy towers. The most imposing is the fifteenth-century Fünfknopfturm. From this tower you can walk along the battlements to reach Kaufbeuren's finest monument, the chapel of St Blasius, which rises quaintly by the town walls. Begun in the early fourteenth century and finished in the next, this chapel houses a late-Gothic masterpiece, a high altar which Jörg Lederer carved in 1518. Beautifully sculpted saints – Stephen, Christopher, Blasius, Erasmus and Ulrich – as well as the Madonna enrich this winged high altar. The paintings on the altar are by the local artist Jörg Mack.

Before leaving Kaufbeuren spare time to see another fine late-Gothic church, St Martin, which stands in the very centre of the town, its mighty tower shading the Hafenmarkt. Of its Romanesque origins all you can see today are the chiselled font and the entrance pierced in the south wall. If, as I do, you relish nineteenth-century Gothic town halls, walk from this south porch and turn left along Kaiser-Max-Straße to be as surprised as I was to discover that in 1881 the omni-competent architect Georg von Hauberisser built for Kaubeuren not a Gothic but a Renaissance one. He brought along Director Lindenschmidt of the Munich Academy to paint the frescos in its assembly room. Then drive twenty-seven kilometres north-west to Mindelheim.

On the way you will see signs directing you right to one of Bavaria's most celebrated spas. Bad Wörishofen was Germany's first *Kneipport*. The name *Kneipport* derives from that of its remarkable priest, Sebastian Kneipp, who lived from 1821 to 1897. In 1849 he originated the cure known as Kneippism, whereby various forms of hydrotherapy, massage and other such tortures assisted men, women and children with wasted limbs back to health. He himself, it seems, was inspired to invent the cure when his chronic consumption was apparently cured after he plunged recklessly into a freezing pool. The techniques he developed from this experience made Kneipp famous. In 1886 his book was even translated into English, as *My Water Cure*, though his cure never really caught on among the cautious British. Bad Wörishofen did, however, succeed in enticing to Bavaria American President Theodore Roosevelt. The Dominican monastery where Sebastian Kneipp served the people of Bad Wörishofen is a fine building, with late-Gothic elements blending into Franz Beer's rebuilding of around 1720 and decoration by such geniuses as Domenikus Zimmermann. I also suggest that you visit the parish church of St Justina, which boasts a saddle-tower of 1520. For information about the spa in general and its cure in particular, apply to the Kurverwaltung, No. 1 Zweigstraße.

As you drive from Bad Wörishofen to Mindelheim, Schloß Mindelburg rises on the hill which it has dominated since 1370. Mindelheim itself is still surrounded by parts of its medieval town walls and defended by three of its old towers. St Stephen is an early eighteenth-century parish church which is becoming a cornucopia of baroque treats, as the ecclesiastical authorities bring here for safekeeping religious treasures from other churches in the region. Its tower dates in part from the fifteenth century. Again, breaking my habitual caution about local history museums, I do recommend visiting the Heimat und Turmuhrenmuseum in the monastic buildings at No. 2 Hauberstraße. The armoured knight whose statue defends the town hall square is Georg von Frundsberg. He flourished in Mindelheim in the early sixteenth century. As for the church of Our Lady in Memmingerstraße, it houses a moving carving of the Holy Family, dating from around 1515, and is fronted by a cool fountain created in 1662 and dedicated to the five wounds of Jesus.

Magical Memmingen lies twenty-seven kilometres south-west along the B18. Five gates and five towers surmount its medieval walls. Each of the town gates has a pleasing individuality, the Wesertor octagonal and topped by a curving roof, the Kempter Tor square yet elegant, its windows oddly offset. The Ulmer Tor, a delightful creation of 1445, is entirely windowless. Its clock is flanked by painted saints and above its shallow archway is painted the double-headed imperial eagle. The defensive open spaces by these walls have been transformed into sweet parkland. As for the Lindauer Tor, it gained its present form in 1648.

This was an Alemmanic hamlet which the Franks made into a royal residence. By 1288 Memmingen had become an imperial city. It was a stronghold of the peasants during their revolt of 1525, and in the Weinmarkt they formulated their twelve revolutionary principles, which ultimately led the nobility and Martin Luther to turn against them. By 1530 the citizens of Memmingen had adhered to the principles of the Reformation. As a result, at the beginning of the Thirty Years War, the Protestant champion King Gustavus Adolphus of Sweden made the town his headquarters. The towers of its churches match in variety the towers above the town gates. The bells of St Martin, the greatest church in this city, are supported by a massive tower from which protrude quaint gargoyles. The tower of the Kreuzherrnkirche becomes more and more playful as it reaches into the skies. At the end of the seventeenth century its interior was rendered equally playful by Wessobrunn artists. The Frauenkirche is decorated with delicate frescos that were rediscovered only in the late nineteenth century. The vault of its choir is equally delicious. To say more about St Martin, the unpretentious arches inside the church are entrancing. In both St Martin and the Frauenkirche are carvings and mid-fifteenth-century frescos by Memmingen's most famous artist sons, the Strigel family.

Every aspect of the old town pales before the picturesque effect of the waters which mirror its ancient houses. These too are resplendent. Especially notable are the Parishaus, an elegant four-storeyed classical building of 1736, the Renaissance town hall of 1589 (its façade dates from 1765), the half-timbered house of the weavers' guild (the Weberzunfthaus), the Fuggerbau of 1599, the patrician Hermannsbau of 1765 and the altogether delightful seven-roofed Siebendächerhaus, built by the tanners of Memmingen in 1601. Its overhanging roofs sheltered their hides as they dried. Each July the stream which runs through the town has to be dredged with special hoop-nets (or *Bären*). The catches are weighed in the Marktplatz. A new fisher-king is elected and the old one routed. Then the night-watchman walks his ceremonial round, and Memmingen continues to carouse until the small hours of the morning.

To see the dramatic effect of church towers mirrored in water, drive south-east from Memmingen to Ottobeuren, which is not only another Kneipp health resort but also the gorgeous spot where the Benedictines founded an abbey in 764. The present monastic buildings, including the two masterly eighty-five-metre-high church towers, are mostly by Johann Michael Fischer. The interior of this church is ravishing, as one might expect from the work of J. B. Zimmermann and J. M. Feuchtmayr, not to speak of Carl Riepp's baroque organ.

From here return south-west to the A7 motorway and drive on to Kempten, not only the capital of Bavarian Allgäu but also its cheese centre. Walled Kempten is ancient, but although some Roman stones are said to support its walls, the best place to examine the Roman (as well as the Celtic and Alemannic) remains of this town is in the local history museum at No. 1 Großer Kornhausplatz. Otherwise make your way to Residenzplatz and the former residence of the prince-abbot, a 140-metre-long palace built by Michael Beer in the late seventeenth century. During the reign of Abbot Anselm von Reichlin-Meldegg its state rooms were greatly enriched between 1730 and 1742. The rococo architect responsible was Johann Georg Übelhör. In front of this palace stands St Lorenz, the first major baroque church to be built in Bavaria after the Peace of Westphalia was agreed in 1648. Michael Beer and Johann Zerro were its architects, and the masons began building in 1652. Beer and Zerro chose to design a church not after the Bavarian or Austrian fashion but in the Italian style.

Walk south-east from here towards the River Iller to find first Kempten's Rathaus and then the church of St Mang, the apostle of the Allgäu. Mang was a missionary from St Gall. The British dub him St Magnus. Kempten town hall is a gem, an onion dome crowning the gable end with its graceful double flight of steps. All this glamour is based on a building that dates principally from 1474. In front of the town hall spurts a Renaissance fountain set up by Hans Krumppe in 1601. And in the surrounding streets rise houses with mid-eighteenth-century rococo façades. As for St Mang, this unpretentious three-aisled basilica dates from 1427 and boasts a couple of sixty-six-metre-high towers.

Drive forty kilometres south-west to reach Füssen and you find yourself joining the spectacular German Alpine road which we last encountered on our way to Berchtesgaden. This curving route takes us through the mountain *Kneipport* of Mittelberg, through Nesselwang, another health resort whose parish church has a neo-baroque decoration of 1906 which I do not much admire, and increasingly into a region of ski-lifts, superb panoramas and winter-sports centres.

The narrow streets of Füssen exude Bavarian charm. A monastery dedicated to St Magnus was founded here in the late eighth century on the site of his tomb. Today its eighteenth-century successor exudes Venetian charm, rising white and cool on the same spot. On one side of the cloister you suddenly spot that the balcony and pillars you are looking at are a *trompe-l'oeil* trick. The monastery church, originally a Romanesque basilica, was transformed by the baroque architect Johann Jakob Herkomer in the second decade of the eighteenth century. He had studied architecture in Venice, hence its Venetian aspect. The pews are perfect miniature examples of early rococo, the organ and organ-loft fantastically carved. Not long afterwards Herkomer's great-nephew, Franz Karl Fischer, designed the quaint and atttractive Spitalkirche which stands outside the monastery. Its west end resembles the gable of a patrician home, painted by one of those homely *Lüftlmalerei* who so much enhanced this part of Bavaria. Homely is the best adjective for Füssen. Even its Schloß, once the home of the prince-bishops, is a mild-mannered gentleman's home. What makes the place utterly delightful are its six lakes. The prettiest is the Alpsee, the largest the Forggensee, an artificial lake created by a dam across the River Lech. Alas, the village of Forggen, from which the lake takes its name, now lies submerged. Steamers ply above the drowned village.

At Füssen signposts direct you to the *Königschlößer*, the fantastic castles built nearby by mad King Ludwig II and his father. They form in part the subject of the next chapter of my book. At this moment our plan is to arrive at the splendid winter-sports resort of Garmisch-Partenkirchen. To reach this spot you can travel by way of the delicate countryside of Reutte in Austria. The twin towns of Garmisch and

Partenkirchen were united only by the Olympic Games of 1936. They have enormously profited since then from the two stadiums built for those games, one devoted to skiing (with four leaps and room for no fewer than 80,000 spectators), the other to ice-skating (and welcoming 12,000 spectators). A rack railway takes sixty-five minutes to pull you partway up Germany's highest peak, the 2,966-metre-high Zugspitze. At the Schneefernerhaus, 2,650 metres above sea level, you must change to a cable car, which whisks you up the rest of your journey in four minutes. The 1,780-metre-high Wank, which juts up to heaven to the north-east of Garmisch-Partenkirchen, offers equally outstanding panoramas. The other noted peak overlooking this town is the Alpspitze, reaching an altitude of 2,628 metres. No fewer than fifty-three cable cars carry visitors to the peaks of the Wetterstein range, and 290 kilometres of footpaths have been marked out for hill-walkers. (The local information office offers no fewer than 111 suggested routes, ranging from gentle strolls to gruelling hikes.) The municipal park of Garmisch-Partenkirchen was laid out in 1928 and today is filled with music and dancing. Eternally beats out the traditional song, which runs, in Bavarian dialect, *'s gibt nur oa Loisachtal aloa, a Zugspitz und an Waxistoa* ('There is but one Loisach valley, one Zugspitze and one Waxenstein').

If you wish to explore the architectural delights of the town itself, do not miss J. M. Schmuzer's elliptical pilgrimage church of St Anton, nor his Neue Pfarrkirche, dedicated to St Martin and enriched by the brilliance of Wessonbrun artists. Matthäus Günther painted the frescos on its ceiling. Old St Martin sports on its walls some beautiful late-Gothic frescos depicting Jesus's Passion, as well as a massive portrait of St Christopher dating from the thirteenth century. If you wish to improve your health, swelter in the saunas, or bask in the winter sun, the hot-water pool and the open-air gymnastic tortures of this Kneipp resort.

The congress hall in Dr-Richard-Strauss-Platz reminds one that the composer Richard Strauss lived here, dying at the age of eighty-five in the Richard-Strauss-Villa (in Richard Strauss-Straße) on 8 September 1949. As I write, his eighty-six-year-old daughter-in-law Alice still lives here in Strauss's former home. The Nazis made him their court musician. He did not understand them. They dismissed him, because he insisted on performing works by the Jewish composer Mahler and using the Jewish librettist Stefan Zweig for his comic opera *Die schweigsame Frau*, which was based on Ben Jonson's *Epicene, or the Silent Woman*. Together with his wife, the shrewish soprano Pauline de Ahna, he survived ostracism by the Nazi regime. After the Third Reich collapsed in ruins he wrote of his relief that 'the most terrible period in human history, the twelve-year reign of bestiality, ignorance and anti-culture' was over. As he lay dying, he exclaimed that the experience exactly matched his own tone-poem 'Death and Transfiguration'.

Drive north from here for nine scenic kilometres to Kloster Ettal, which lies a mere four kilometres from Oberammergau. Although the Benedictine monks who inhabited this monastery were driven away in 1803, members of the same order returned in 1900. Today it is a working (that is, praying) monastery. The name of the valley in which it stands derives from a Guelph named Ethiko, who ruled this region in the tenth century. Eventually the Wittelsbachs became supreme here. In 1327 after a pilgrimage to Rome, one of them, Ludwig the Bavarian, brought back a miracle-working statue of the Blessed Virgin Mary. Suddenly, the local tale runs, his horse genuflected. This was a sufficient sign for Ludwig to found a monastery in Ethiko's valley.

After a fire burned down most of the old abbey in 1744, the precious statue remained intact. The monks commissioned the Italian Enrico Zucalli to rebuild their church. Keeping to the original twelve-sided plan, Zucalli created a superb rococo church (indeed, in my view, one of the finest in Bavaria), topped by a magnificent cupola which was itself surmounted by a lantern more than fifteen metres high. In the mid-eighteenth century an artist named J. J. Zeiller painted the interior of this cupola with more than 400 figures, depicting the glories of the Benedictine order. A master stone-mason named Josef Lindner came from Salzburg to create a new high altar fit for Ludwig the Bavarian's miraculous Virgin. As for the delicate pink and white organ and organ loft, it constitutes yet another Bavarian masterpiece by J. B. Zimmermann. Johann Baptist Straub contributed six marvellous side-altars and an even finer pulpit. This beautiful white church is surrounded by green lawns. On the feast of the Blessed Sacrament I have seen monks, priests and layfolk joyfully process to its doors, which they had earlier decorated with fir branches.

For centuries the monks have distilled what they proudly describe as 'the original Ettalklosterliqueur'. Their rebuilt monastery, Jerome K. Jerome judged, rather than acting as a house of prayer, 'now serves the more useful purpose of a brewery'. For once I feel I must disagree with this merry satirist.

A passion for princely castles

The two best-known castles in Germany perch high on peaks near Schwangau. Signposts directing you there from Füssen bear the legend *Königschlösser*. The two castles suddenly appear on the mountainside – to the right, turreted Schloß Hohenschwangau, pale yellow and brick-red, to the left Schloß Neuschwanstein, Disney-land come alive.

Some hundred feet lower than Neuschwanstein, Hohenschwangau, surmounted by a white swan, stands where in the twelfth century the knights of Schwangau built themselves a stronghold. Napoleon Bonaparte razed it. In consequence we see today not a medieval castle but a nineteenth-century dream of the Middle Ages. Between 1832 and 1837 King Maximilian II of Bavaria (at that time still only crown-prince) employed a theatre architect named Dominik Quaglio to build it on this 'swans' rock'. The pine-covered peak, dominating both the Alpsee and the Schwansee lakes, offers a superb view of the Allgäu's greatest reservoir, the Forggensee. The theatre architect produced for the king a splendidly theatrical castle.

This delightful confection is a complete hybrid of styles, basically medieval but with a dozen surprises at every turn. By 1837, when Dominik Quaglio died, the king was already living in part of his unfinished Schloß. He turned to an architect he had already commissioned in 1831 when building an impressively Germanic neo-Gothic church, Mariahilf, for the suburb of Au in Munich. Joseph Daniel Ohlmüller now brought the work at Hohenschwangau to a successful conclusion – except for the court building (the Kavaliersbau), which was added in 1851 by the architect G. F. Ziebland, who had just finished the majestic pile in Munich's Königsplatz that houses the Staatliche Antikensammlungen.

The fourteen rooms which you can visit at Hohenschwangau do include one authentic medieval piece, an altar of 1460 in the chapel. On the way to this chapel there are photographs of Maximilian's two sons, Ludwig and Otto. Their eyes already look wild, and both died mad. Ludwig consoled himself by continually building his own fairy palaces and castles out of some wooden building blocks he had been given on his seventh birthday.

The basic theme of the Schloß is instantly proclaimed at the entrance by statues of two great former Wittelsbach rulers, Emperor Ludwig the Bavarian and the Elector Maximilian I. Hohenschwangau rises as a tribute to the majesty of the Wittelsbachs. Generously, Maximilian II also acknowledged the glories of his dynasty's predecessors, the Guelphs, who ruled from 1070 to 1180 and whose deeds are depicted here in the Welfzimmer.

The swan surmounting the Schloß is matched by innumerable swans inside it. Throughout Hohenschwangau frescos by Moritz von Schwind and Wilhelm Lindenschmidt illustrate the legendary deeds of Germany's medieval chivalry, and above all those of the knights of the swan. (The themes of the twelfth-century Lohengrin saga, painted on the walls of the Schwanenrittersaal by Lorenzo Quaglio and Michael Neher, directly influenced Richard Wagner, who would often stay here with Maximilian's elder son, the future King Ludwig II.) Swans decorate the seats and the centrepiece in this great room, the centrepiece a silver gift sculpted by Andreas Fortner in 1842 and paid for by the citizens of Munich as their wedding present to Maximilian. A massive silver chandelier is also decorated with swans. Entranced by romantic notions of the medieval knights of the swan, Maximilian II often went so far as to dress up in medieval costume before venturing out to feed the real swans, whose descendants still swim on the Alpsee.

The artists who decorated Schloß Hohenschwangau did not forget to include among the heroes of Germany, Martin Luther. And Charles Martel slays an enemy. On the table of the mighty reception room (or hall of heroes) is a huge, gilded bronze depicting the saga of the

Nibelungen. On the walls of the Autharizimmer the Lombard King Authari eternally woos Princess Theodelinde. He is here because she was the daughter of a Bavarian duke. Theodoric, King of the Ostrogoths, makes his due appearance. And in the splendid hall built for Ludwig's mother, Queen Marie Friederike, Maximilian commissioned paintings depicting the lives of women in the Middle Ages. They hunt with falcons; they play the harp; they read to their children – alas, something Marie never did for her own sons. Her husband's study is similarly decorated, though in his case with scenes of the daily life of a medieval knight.

The most bizarre room of all is the queen's bedroom. Crown-prince Maximilian had visited Turkey in 1833 and decreed that this room should be decorated in the oriental style. Sultan Mohammed II gave the settees. Moritz von Schwind painted Maximilian's own bedroom with suitably enticing maidens, their nakedness conveniently excused by the fact that they are the stuff of medieval legend.

Yet this oddly thrilling Schloß was a real home, its rooms warmed by a tiled *Kachelöfen* designed in the Gothic style. In the hall of the Hohenstaufens is the piano on which Richard Wagner would play for Ludwig. A gilt-framed portrait of the future king (dressed as a knight of St George) stands beside a bust of the composer. Ludwig had become passionately devoted to Wagner at the age of thirteen. When he heard his first Wagner opera (*Lohengrin*) in 1861, passion turned to obsession. Wagner was fleeing his creditors when Ludwig became king in 1864, but the monarch sought him out and even paid them off. Small wonder that Wagner once exclaimed, 'The king understands me like my own soul.' As for Ludwig, he promised to banish for ever from the composer 'the pretty cares of everyday life', so that Wagner could spread the mighty wings of his genius. Ludwig set the composer up in a house overlooking the Starnberg Lake. The two met daily at nearby Schloß Berg, and Ludwig summoned the architect Gottfried Semper to design a theatre for his idol.

Over the coming year Ludwig's ministers became increasingly alarmed at the unstable king's besotted relationship with the musician. The relationship led to Wagner being nicknamed 'Lolotte' by his enemies, a reference to the adventuress Lola Montez who, by becoming the mistress of King Ludwig I, had eventually brought about his abdication. The tangle grew even more disturbing for the king's ministers, for just as *Tristan and Isolde* was about to receive its first performance, the police arrived at Wagner's apartment to take his possessions as security for his debts. To save the day the wife of a distinguished music critic, Cosima von Bülow (for whom Wagner had developed a scarcely concealed romantic passion and with whom he was shortly to elope), sped to the king's treasury and returned with 2,400 florins. When Ludwig saw *Tristan and Isolde* he instantly dubbed it his favourite opera. Yet by the end of 1865 even he could not resist the pressure to send Wagner away. His entire Cabinet threatened to resign. The queen-mother joined forces with the Bishop of Munich-Freising in attacking Wagner's profligacy. 'Now they have finally set the dogs on me,' the composer lamented. 'Your Majesty has to choose between the love and respect of your loyal subjects and your friendship with Richard Wagner,' declared the Minister of State Ludwig von der Pfordten. The king's great-uncle brought up the spectre of a revolution against the sovereign, adding that the army would certainly join it. In December the distraught king begged his friend to leave Bavaria, if only for a few months, quoting as they parted some words from Wagner's *Götterdämmerung*: 'Though sundered, who can separate us?'

Ludwig's fevered love for the composer did survive. Three years later he told Wagner of his plans to build a new Schloß, which would rest on a peak even higher than that of Hohenschwangau. His inspiration was the great castle of Wartburg – famous as the refuge of Martin Luther – but he also planned Neuschwanstein as a monument to his idol Richard Wagner. To provide a base for this castle, part of the mountain peak was blasted away. Although only fifteen rooms were completed out of the sixty-five intended by Ludwig, the achievement is remarkable. Again a theatre designer, this time Christian Jank, provided the basic scheme. Shimmering white, Neuschwanstein rises to the east of Schloß Hohenschwangau. The best view is from a vertiginous ironwork bridge, a forty-four-metre span, which in 1855 was thrown across the Pöllat gorge a hundred metres above the gushing waters.

You climb up to the Schloß from the parking lot, taking half an hour on foot or using either the prosaic bus or the romantic horse-drawn carriages. As at Hohenschwangau, guided tours take place (apart from public holidays) in summer between 09.00 and 17.30 and in winter between 10.00 and 16.00. Ludwig's architects who created this fantasy were principally Eduard Riedl, George Dollmann and Julius

Hofmann, assisted by another theatre designer named Christian Jank.

Initially the rooms are Gothic. Apart from the Wartburg in Thüringia and Château Pierrefonds in France (restored by Viollet-le-Duc and seen by Ludwig on his way to the World Exhibition of 1867), Wagner's influence is everywhere. The whole upper courtyard is even based on a set designed in 1867 for the second act of *Lohengrin*, which had been performed in Munich in that year. The entrance hall is decorated with scenes from the Nordic legend of Sigurd, the basis of Wagner's Nibelungen cycle. The dining room is illustrated with scenes from *Tannhäuser*. The murals of the king's study, painted by Joseph Aigner, boringly depict Tannhäuser's song-contest and entrancingly depict him in the Venusberg with the goddess of love, along with other beauties and cherubs. In this mural only Tannhäuser is fully clothed. Ludwig's study, a curious mixture of styles confected by Julius Hofmann, also boasts a chair in which no one could sit comfortably. On his desk is a little statue of Lohengrin.

The furniture of the king's bedroom is magniloquently ornate and took fourteen craftsmen four years to make. Here the decorative Wagnerian theme is *Tristan and Isolde* (as is the theme of his living room). Over Ludwig's bed is a canopy frighteningly matching that of a medieval tomb. For the king's ablutions, running water poured from a swan's beak beside the bed. For his devotions, a prayer stool and devout paintings are situated at the other side of the bed. Next door is a little chapel, whose Gothic triptych was carved by Julius Hofmann of Munich. The stained glass depicts the holy death-bed of Ludwig's patron saint, King Louis the Pious of France. Scenes from the life of the troubadour Walter von der Vogelweide decorate the toilet. Tannhäuser appears again in the main hall of the Schloß.

Then the architectural style quits the Gothic, even though Ludwig had told Wagner that he intended to build 'a true castle of the old German knights'. The style of the throne room is Byzantine, and indeed it resembles rather more a Byzantine church than the spot where Ludwig planned to sit and indulge his megalomaniac dreams – a resemblance enhanced by the fact that since work stopped when the king died, the throne room was never fitted with a throne. Its inlaid marble floor embodies over 2.5 million small pieces. A massive golden chandelier weighing 900 kilogrammes, courtiers' galleries and golden walls (on which are painted saints between palm trees) add to the glitter. The atmosphere of a Byzantine basilica is reinforced by scenes from the life of Jesus, by pictures of the twelve apostles and six royal saints, and by the sight of St George and the Archangel Michael both, as usual, slaying their enemies. But Wagner is never far away, and the minstrel's gallery (inspired by that at the Wartburg) returns to the theme of his last opera, *Parsifal*. Accoustically perfect, this hall was never used in Wagner's or Ludwig's lifetime. Today the Sängersaal regularly houses concerts (about which the Schwangau Kurverwaltung, at No. 2 Münchener Straße, will provide information).

I do not think that Schloß Neuschwanstein is either refined or subtle. It is quite simply audacious. The winding staircases (their columns occasionally fashioned as palm trees), the balconies, the piped water and hot-air vents of the kitchens are all remarkable pieces of engineering. The balconies and the vistas brilliantly exploit the surrounding countryside and the four lakes: the Schwansee, the Hopfensee, the Forggensee and the Bannwaldsee. Schloß Neuschwanstein might have been even greater, had not Ludwig's madness and extravagance finally taxed his ministers to depose him and place him under house arrest in Schloß Berg, where he had so often met his adored Wagner. In that same year, 1886, on Whit Sunday he and his physician, Dr Bernard von Gudden, went for a walk along the lakeside. That evening their bodies were recovered from the water. One of von Gudden's eyes was blackened, as if he had fought with the deposed monarch, perhaps trying to stop him from committing suicide or escaping from his semi-captivity. The autopsy revealed a yet more sinister finding. Ludwig's lungs were clear of water. If the king had not died by drowning, how had he died?

And was he really mad or simply inadequate? The shrewd Otto von Bismarck, Prime Minister of Prussia, may have thought Ludwig inadequate but certainly not insane. Throughout the complex political events surrounding Ludwig's reign, beginning with the Austro-Prussian War, which broke out in 1866 when the young king was scarcely twenty, Bavaria reluctantly supported Austria, the losing side. When the next conflict broke out, the 1870–1 war between France and Prussia, Bismarck sought and gained Bavarian support for Prussia. In return he did his utmost to save the Bavarian king from his worst excesses. He also spotted the alarm caused among the king's enemies in Munich in 1886 when Ludwig began planning to reform his administration. 'The ministers wish to sacrifice the king,' Bismarck correctly observed to the Bavarian envoy to Berlin, 'because otherwise they will not be able to save themselves.'

Bavaria had paid Prussia 30 million gulden in war reparations after the 1866 conflict. After the 1870–1 war she received back nearly 600 million gulden for partly surrendering her sovereignty to Berlin. Bismarck also made sure that Ludwig himself received 2 million gulden. Even this subsidy though, could not stop the enormous rise in Ludwig's personal debts, caused by his mania for building. By 1886 these debts topped 6 million gulden, nearly one-and-a-half times his annual personal income. Yet his schemes grew yet more grandiose. Twenty kilometres west of Neuschwanstein lay another ruined castle, Falkenstein. In 1883 Ludwig decided to re-create it as an enormous Gothic Schloß. When the court architect Georg Dollmann prudently decided to design a much more modest affair, Ludwig contemptuously threw aside Dollman's plans and brought in more pliable architects. By now Ludwig's dreams had shifted from building a Gothic castle towards creating a huge palace in the Byzantine style.

At the same time as this potentially ruinous scheme was being prepared, Ludwig was also directing the building of a hunting lodge, the Hubertuspavillon, which was to rise in the Ammer forest not far from Neuschwanstein. Its name was a strange one, since St Hubertus was noted not for killing stags but for protecting them. The king had no intention of ever using this place as a hunting lodge, and had chosen St Hubertus as the patron to demonstrate his hatred for the sport. Work began on the folly in 1885. By the following May two building companies had applied to the courts for the settlement of unpaid bills to the tune of 100,000 gulden. Ludwig was heartbroken. 'Now that everyone knows the frightful state of my financial circumstances and my beloved building has had to stop,' he wrote, 'the greatest pleasure of my life has been taken away.'

Yet there was still no certainty that he was deranged. One of his physicians emphatically denied it, blaming his building extravagances on 'those venal, egotistical, lying flunkeys, who formed his set and encouraged his fantasies'. By 8 June 1886, however, four other medical men were willing to diagnose paranoia, along with what they dubbed Ludwig's 'original or primary madness'. Ludwig was placed under house arrest, and his uncle Luitpold took over as regent.

Mad or not, the life of Ludwig II was undoubtedly an amalgam of misfortune and eccentricity. In 1871 he sat through a performance of the Oberammergau passion play entirely alone. To each actor he gave a silver spoon, save for a mortified Judas, who received a tin one. Moved by the spectacle of the passion play, Ludwig next commissioned a massive statue of the crucified Jesus, his mother and St John to be set up on the north side of the Kofel. By 1875 the statues were ready to be transported from Munich to Oberammergau. The socket for the cross alone weighed 480 hundredweight, and not surprisingly the steam locomotive pulling it up from Oberau to Oberammergau gave up halfway there. Eighty firemen and relays involving a hundred horses laboriously dragged it to its destination. Ludwig decided that a special carriage was needed to bring from Munich the statue of St John. On the way the carriage overturned, and the statue of the saint toppled over, crushing to death a master stonemason and one of his assistants.

When the whole crucifixion group was finally assembled, Ludwig arranged for it to be consecrated on the birthday of his widowed mother. Each year on the anniversary of the consecration he would arrive at its foot and pray, both for Marie Friederike and for his younger brother Otto. Ironically, he hated both of them. 'I shall never cease to revere her because she has the honour of being the mother of the king,' he ambiguously said of Marie Friederike, adding swiftly, 'At times she overdoes the mother and underplays the queen.' As for poor Otto, Ludwig once tied him up, threatened to decapitate him and would probably have done so, had not a courtier appeared and stopped him. Small wonder that Otto was insane by the age of twenty-nine.

To see both the king's waywardness and his inspiration at their greatest, visit the third of his splendid Schlösser, Linderhof. First, however, make sure to visit the charming village of Schwangau before leaving the region of Hohenschwangau and Neuschwanstein. From this exquisitely sited climatic health resort extends a network of seventy-five kilometres of walking routes (signposted in yellow on brown posts and climbing up to 900 metres), another fifty kilometres of hiking paths (signposted in blue on white and climbing up to 1,000 metres) and yet more mountain hiking routes (signposted in black on white, reaching from 1,100 to 2,000 metres). Yellow gentians, Alpine roses, black salamanders brush against your feet, and an occasional mad hang-glider seems to brush against your arm. The shy chamois dart nimbly away.

As for the Tegel mountain lift, it whisks you from 800 metres to

1,700 in ten minutes. The Tegelberg ski stadium sets out to welcome families and offers runs for novices and experts. And when any one of the four neighbouring lakes freezes over, tourists abandon swimming and fishing and take to curling, skating or riding in sleighs pulled by tough little horses. Dressed in leather shorts, waistcoats and feathered hats, the citizens blow their long Alpine horns, play in the town brass band or bring their cows to drink at the town fountain (which is topped by a bearded statue of Schwangau's patron saint, the Irish pilgrim St Coloman, he and his horse unkindly standing on a bullock). Schwangau's churches include an entrancing one, set by a lakeside and dedicated to the Irish pilgrim, on whose feast day (15 October) the neighbourhood erupts in pagan and religious merriment.

Now make your way to the one palace Ludwig's architects managed to complete. You reach Schloß Linderhof by driving four kilometres south from Füssen through the country dedicated to St Ulrich, where you reach Ulrich's bridge and even an Ulrich's bridge guesthouse. Thirty-six kilometres later, in and out of Austria (so you will need your passports and, by law, a simple first-aid kit in the car), you drive by way of Reutte, and alongside the waters of the Plannsee, to Schloß Linderhof.

Since Ludwig II was rejected by his mother (and in turn rejected her), and his father could barely bring himself to talk to the boy, let alone go walking with him, one is tempted to guess that throughout his life he searched for other people on whose roles he could model his own behaviour. At Schloß Linderhof, the adored hero of the king was not Richard Wagner but the long-dead French 'Sun King', Louis XIV, who had arrogantly declared, '*L'état c'est moi*'. Accordingly, Ludwig made an anagram of the words and called his Schloß, which stands near Kloster Ettal 'Meicost Ettal'. The Sun King's statue stands in the entrance hall of the Schloß. Louis's motto, *Nec pluribus impar*, is embossed on the ceiling. As Ludwig increasingly withdrew from society after 1880, he preferred to dine alone at Linderhof, accompanied only by the busts of Louis XIV and Marie Antoinette. They came, Ludwig observed, only when he asked them. They left when he bade them go.

On his visit to the World Exhibition in Paris, Ludwig had inevitably gone to admire the château of Versailles, and the Petit Trianon at Versailles is the chief inspiration of Schloß Linderhof. Georg Doll-mann designed the palace. Karl Effner laid out its impressive gardens, which include statues of dolphins, Venus and Marie Antoinette, and a fountain that gushes up to thirty metres – another reminder of Versailles. Lifesize statues of Louis XIV and Louis XV of France respectively adorn the western and the eastern parterres.

The genius of Richard Wagner reappears here in an astonishing Venus grotto, with colourfully illuminated, fake stalactites and stalagmites and scenes from the first act of *Tannhäuser*, depicting the interior of the Hörselberg. A shimmering picture of Tannhäuser on the Venusberg was painted inside this cave by August von Heckel. Ludwig would sail through this overwrought grotto in a punt resembling a mussel-shell. This quaint boat is still on show, floating in the technicolour cave. Fortunately, in 1867, ten years before the grotto was completed, Werner von Siemens had invented the dynamo. Siemens was commissioned to instal twenty-four of them, complete with rotating plates of coloured glass in front of twenty-four arc-lights, in order to keep the colours constantly changing in the three grotto caves. Since Ludwig liked to be punted through them at night, warm air heated the caves. And a machine was installed for creating artificial waves when he decided on a sail.

Dollmann's Schloß is petite compared with Effner's garden. Its fountain depicts Flora, the goddess of spring, and was sculpted in pewter by Michael Wagmüller. A Neptune fountain fronts a fabulous cascade at the back of the Schloß. A terraced Italianate park is surrounded by three summer houses. Effner also drew on French baroque gardens, formal and graced with statues. He merged it all into the informal, so-called English garden style, and the whole finally shades into the forest. To all this Ludwig added a quaint touch by buying a Moorish kiosk from a Berlin railway magnate and erecting it here. This pavilion boasts four corner towers shaped half as minarets and half (it seems to me) like pepperpots, as well as an oriental cupola. Inside, Ludwig set up a throne, fashioned as a peacock, which he had brought from Paris in 1877. Among the other accoutrements of the Moorish kiosk are a white marble fountain and a Persian hookah shaped like another peacock.

The kiosk looks genuinely oriental inside, though the purply colours are garish. I wish I had seen the *Hundinghütte*, which Dollmann designed and which stood close by. Built around an ancient ash tree, it matched the setting of the first act of Wagner's *Valkyries*, whose performance Ludwig exulted in at Bayreuth in 1876. At times the king would take it into his head to sleep inside this crude, old Teutonic hut, lying on a bed covered with bearskins and drinking himself to sleep with mead from a horn. Alas, the *Hundinghütte* burned to the ground in 1945.

Other aspects of Ludwig's eccentricities appear inside the Schloß. One is the quantity of vases he assiduously collected, set out in the hall of mirrors. Another is one of his famous devices, a *Tischlein-deck'-dich*. These were tables set over a trap-door. Since Ludwig far preferred to dine alone (except in the company of his knights of St George), without even casting his eyes on the servants, he would sit by the table, pull a bell and wait for his servants to crank the table down through the trap-door. They would furnish it with food and drink, before winding it up again to their solitary master.

Curiously enough the king seemed happier in this relatively modest home than in any other of his palaces. He stayed here longest, and Linderhof is the only one to bear the royal coat of arms, set on the ornate gable above the three balconied entrances and topped by a statue of Atlas. Presumably this strange man who went riding at night in a cloak modelled on that of Louis XIV felt closest at Linderhof to acting out his chosen monarchical role. Three royal coats of arms were embroidered on the blue silk drapes of the king's bedroom, from whose enormous canopied bed Ludwig could see through the window across the Graswang valley to a tumultuous waterfall and the mountains. Since Louis XIV's ceremonial getting up and going to bed were an important part of court ritual, with slavish noblemen fighting for the right to be in attendance, a couple of small pictures on the bedroom walls depict these absurd rituals. As Ludwig hated company, however, at Linderhof he went to bed and rose alone.

Peacock statues abound at Linderhof, in part because Ludwig hated flags, as symbolizing war, and preferred the magnificently plumed bird, in part because their overwrought colours fitted in with the lush décor of nineteenth-century Bavarian rococo. Red, gold, yellow, lilac, white, blue and pink lavishly splash over the walls, carpets, furniture and ceilings. Yet somehow, in spite of every extravagance, Schloß Linderhof remains an intimate home.

Not so Ludwig's fourth great Schloß; yet Herrenchiemsee should on no account be missed by a visitor to Bavaria. It lies on an island a couple of hours' drive away from Linderhof, in the beautiful Chiemsee area. We have already visited Bavaria's largest lake, but only to see the lovely parish church of Maria Himmelfahrt at Prien am Chiemsee, and perhaps also to rise over the superb countryside in one of the hot-air balloons (I forgot to mention), which boost themselves upwards with the intrepid guests of the Yachthotel, Chiemsee. Now is the time to remedy my neglect of the very many other delights of this lakeside resort.

As such it is of course crammed with clinics. Because of its proximity to Italy, the town also boasts Italian as well as Bavarian restaurants although in my visits to Prien I have never eaten in one. If you arrive by train from Munich or Salzburg carrying a picnic, you can eat it in a little park just beyond the local tourist office (the Kur-und-Verkehrs-amt), which happens to be conveniently situated at No. 3 Bahnhofsplatz.

Then walk the few yards to explore first the parish church, followed by its separate, Gothic onion-domed baptistry of St Johannes. Less glamorous than the parish church but equally moving, it is surrounded on three sides by arcades, which shelter mementoes to the dead in successive wars beginning in 1870 (though the arcades were erected as Prien's war memorial only in 1923). Its legend reads, *Ein Volk, das seine Toten nicht ehrt, ist nich wert zu leben* ('A people which does not honour its dead is not worthy to live'). Professor Friedrich Lommel sculpted the statue of St Catherine for the fountain abutting the memorial. One Saturday I glimpsed here hope for the living, as well as these sombre mementoes, when a priest in a golden cope emerged from the parish church, leading a family to baptise their little boy in this sacred building. Only the child himself failed to enjoy the ceremony, refusing to accept the lighted candle proffered him by the priest and bawling throughout the whole holy rite.

Beyond the church, to the left as you approach it from the railway station, narrow arcades lead to the former town hall, which now houses one of the little galleries that offer precisely the right amount of fare for the culture-sated visitor. The Galerie im Alten Rathaus at Prien opens every day except Mondays and Thursdays from 10.00 to 12.00 and from 15.00 to 17.00. Its exhibitions offer an intimate glimpse of local life, sometimes hanging local artists of the past, such as the portraitist, landscape artist and wall-painter Paul Kaloff, who was born in 1877 and died here in 1951. Another artist whose minor, but in no way boring, works I have seen in the Galerie im Alten Rathaus is Princess Clara of Bavaria, the sister of Prince-Regent

Luitpold, who lived from 1874 to 1971. The last time I was there works by an entertaining modern cartoonist were on show. Gerhard Brinkmann (who signs himself G. BRI) produces not only cartoons but also, as I had not known before seeing this exhibition, witty three-dimensional pieces, such as a merry barrel organ worked by a little electric motor. A magician miraculously raised a lady into the air without visible support. A sword-swallower plunged deadly steel into his throat. Together with other visitors I found myself giggling aloud at G. BRI's drawing of bewildered tourists on a visit to Greece who come upon a centaur and cannot decide whether to offer him a cigarette or a lump of sugar.

Prien's local history museum is another such gem. Housed in a very pretty three-storey house with painted walls and little shuttered windows, the date MDCCCXXXVII inscribed over its door, it is situated in the pedestrianized zone north of the parish church at No. 1 Friedhofweg. The organizers of the exhibition have thoughtfully set alongside the lovely local costumes of yesterday black and white photographs of people actually wearing them. I like very much the ladies' hats of old Prien. Another room houses a magnificent wooden loom. The baroque room is quite different, with a delicate faience *Kachelofen* warming portraits of a couple of baroque-looking clerics. One of them, named Augustinus Fuchs, was painted around 1795, his hair cropped and tied in a little bow. He was the last provost of the Augustinian canonry of Herrenchiemsee. When it was dissolved in 1803 he became parish priest of Prien and died in the town in 1825.

Since we are beside a great lake, here are old fishermen's nets and fragile boats. Since this is hunting country, the museum houses targets for shooting matches – but not just boring bullseyes. Instead the round targets, peppered with holes, are painted with houses and rustic scenes. What I wonder, did Jakob Eilenrichter and Elize Etermann think when a target decorated to celebrate their wedding on 11 April 1866 was shot to pieces by their guests?

Musical instruments, kitchens and the over-elaborate (as we would consider it) interior of a nineteenth-century home remind one of the future domestic life together of the happy pair. Since we are in a land of a long Christian tradition, here are also displayed the seventeenth-century iron door of the parish church, rustic holy paintings and a horrific seventeenth-century carving of the scourged Jesus. A mid-seventeenth century carving shows Jesus at home in Nazareth. The biggest rustic carving of the nativity I have ever seen occupies quarter of a room, climbing around the corner. The setting is obviously the Bavarian Alps, with people hunting in the mountains, but everything eventually converging on the infant Jesus.

Bavarians have been kind to me. The Prien local history museum was closed when I first arrived to see it, and its guardian was taking a drink with a friend. The door was happily open, so I knocked. When I explained my purpose, the guardian kindly allowed me to go round the exhibition by myself, provided that I turned out the lights. I cannot ask others to take advantage of his affability, so I record that opening times are from Tuesday to Friday between 10.00 and 12.00 and 15.00 and 17.00, and on Sundays simply between 10.00 and 12.00.

Just beyond the local history museum you can wash the dust of the past out of your throat in a restaurant serving Hacker-Pschorr, a beer that has been brewed in Munich since 1417. Every Monday in the Weißbräustuben of this hostelry takes place one of the *Heurigen* wine-bibbing evenings deriving ultimately from Austria, with homely traditional music, singing, 'atmosphere' as the landlord puts it, humour and, of course, wine and beer. This hotel has also taken up the habit of hosting special food weeks: a noodle week in April, in May an asparagus week, a Hubertusweek in October and in November a Swiss week. As we have learned from King Ludwig II's aborted Hubertuspavillon, the Hubertus week is particularly touching, since the locals arrive to guzzle venison carved from the flanks of the deer that Ludwig so laboured to protect. Small wonder that one of the carvings on the maypole which graces the centre of Prien (as one does many another Bavarian village and town) depicts a pig, its front trotters clasped in prayer, begging for mercy from the bloodthirsty butcher.

You can take an inexpensive taxi ride from the station to reach the harbour of Prien, from which steamers sail to the islands in the lake, on one of which stands Ludwig's Schloß Herrenchiemsee. Far more romantic is to ride to the harbour by the Chiemseebahn. The rolling stock of this railway consists of a couple of late nineteenth-century steam locomotives, in their original green livery. They puff and whistle their way along one-and-a-quarter miles of single-line track, pulling carriages capable of holding 350 persons. This is the oldest steam train in the world still plying its trade.

It stops at the harbour beside the café, *Weinstube* and Hotel

Luitpold am See, a Bavarian family hotel where I have happily lodged in exploring this magical region. I remember returning there late and deciding that I needed at least one *helles Bier* before dropping into bed. Only two old codgers were taking a last drink in the bar, both of them as wrinkled as the portrait of old Prince-Regent Luitpold himself on the dining room wall. One of them yawned and staggered away. The yet more wrinkled one wove his way over to me. 'It's pleasant and peaceful now,' I observed. 'Who wants peace when you can drink another beer and have a laugh?' was his response. He called out, 'Herr Ober', and bought us both (me a complete stranger) another half a litre of foaming *helles*.

So we chattered away. Then I bought him a drink. Then I too wandered fairly steadily to my room and fell asleep, first however listening to the Bavarian national anthem as the television also went to sleep. I sincerely hope that no Bavarian considers me discourteous in saying that whenever today I hear those stirring words:

> *Gott mitt dir, du Land der Bayern,*
> *deutsche Erde, Vaterland!*
> *über deinen weiten Gauen*
> *ruhe seine Segenshand*

I remember with glee first of all that delightful geriatric whose brain was unfuddled, whose generosity made me welcome and whose jokes remain unrepeatable.

From Prien Stock just by the hotel you can make three different trips on the pleasure boats that sail the 82.5 square-kilometre lake. The first, *Zum Königschloss*, merely takes you to the largest island, the Herreninsel on which Ludwig built his Schloß, and then brings you back. The second trip, dubbed the *Kleine Rundfahrt*, takes in the second island, the Fraueninsel, as well. The third *Große Rundfahrt* visits not only these islands but also Gstadt, Chieming – at the eastern end of the lake – and Seebruck, at the northern end. If there is a long queue at the harbour kiosk, remember that you can buy tickets on board the ship.

Tours in English take place from May to September at 10.00 and 14.00. You can, of course, break your journey and rejoin a following steamer at your own convenience. (The times of the next ones are affixed to the landing stages.) To speak first of the lesser, still delightful stops, both Seebruck and Chieming are little resorts devoted to sunbathing, swimming and sailing on the lake. At Seebruck the Chiemsee becomes the River Alz, which pours its waters into the River Inn. Chieming also boasts a neo-Gothic parish church (built in 1882) and a pretty former presbytery of 1530, recognizable by its octagonal tower. More fascinating historically is Seebruck, settled since Roman times. Fragments of the Roman bridge over the Alz are now in the church of St Thomas at Seebruck.

To enjoy the *Große Rundfahrt* requires at least two-and-a-half hours. If that length of time deters, the shortest trip I recommend is not simply *Zum Königschloss* but the *Kleine Rundfahrt*, to visit both the Herreninsel and the Fraueninsel. My host at the Hotel Luitpold am See, Frau Gabriele Cheema, gave me two tips which I pass on. If the day is dull, postpone your sail to a brighter one, for there are no lights in Schloß Herrenchiemsee. Second, beware that at weekends, especially around a bank or other holiday, so many visitors press on to the Herreninsel that tours around the Schloß necessarily tend to double in numbers.

Take a pullover for this picturesque sail amid elegant yachts, with beautiful peaks rising on the north side of the lake. Even in the month of June snow streaks the highest, distant ones – the Wilder Kaiser and the Loferer Steinberge – as they rise above the wooded lower slopes and the smooth green pastures below. Then to the right the thick woods of the Herreninsel momentarily part to reveal Ludwig's Schloß.

If you do not fancy the gentle woodland stroll up to the garden of statues and fountains, where Ludwig's gardeners re-created the approach to Versailles, ride there in a carriage drawn by horses. In 1874 Ludwig II had taken the trouble to visit Versailles again, to renew his ardour for the Sun King and his memory of the château he planned to re-create – only on a vaster scale – in his own kingdom. Beyond wide, low steps rises the long, pale-yellow Schloß. Armour and flaming urns top its three storeys. Once again we meet the equestrian statue of Louis XIV copied from the one set up in 1699 in the Place Vendôme, Paris. Scenes from the life of the Sun King decorate the walls of the main antechamber. 'Bullseye' windows, patterned on those which Versailles pioneered, light the palace. The Hartschier Saal, named after the king's Hartschier Halberdiers, is a copy of the Versailles Salles des Gardes. Eighteen different kinds of marble went into creating a staircase modelled on the ambassadors' staircase at Versailles. Since this staircase had been demolished in 1752, Ludwig and his architects (the principal one being Georg Dollmann) re-created it from ancient descriptions.

Louis XIV's sun-symbol shines down on Ludwig's bed, and the face of Apollo in the ceiling fresco turns out, on closer inspection, to be that of the Sun King himself. Ludwig's study, in which he hardly ever worked, pays homage to Louis XV, after whose 1760 rolltop desk Ludwig's own was crafted. Louis XV's portrait overlooks the room. Carl Schweizer, a Munich clockmaker, painstakingly re-created for this study a copy of the astronomical clock at Versailles. Above all, the Château de Versailles is honoured by Herrenchiemsee's hall of mirrors, ninety-eight metres long and lit by the candles of thirty-three chandeliers and forty-four candelabra. A stucco portrait of Louis XIV on a horse separates the hall of mirrors from the so-called hall of war.

Underneath the royal dining room you can inspect the mechanism of another of Ludwig's extraordinary *Tischlein-deck'-dich* dining tables. Over it hangs a beautiful eight-branched Meissen candelabrum, just one of the superb Meissen pieces in Schloß Herrenchiemsee. Yet although 4,000 people were employed to build the Schloß, as almost always with the fantasies of King Ludwig II, Herrenchiemsee was never finished. After more than 16.5 million gulden had been spent on the building, work was stopped in September 1885. The golden royal bedchamber alone had cost 384,000 gulden. You walk down a monumental staircase towards his huge circular bathroom, which used 50,000 litres of water heated by a couple of steam engines, and discover bare brick, still awaiting its marble cladding. The marble statue of the king here, dressed as a knight of St George, was sculpted by Elizabeth Ney in 1870.

All that remains of the former monastery of the Herreninsel is the so-called Old Palace. Happily, the monastery of the Fraueninsel is still intact and still in use. When the abbey was forcibly dissolved in 1803, the nuns were allowed to go on living there, and some were still alive when King Ludwig I of Bavaria restored the convent in 1837. In consequence the convent on the Fraueninsel ranks among Bavaria's oldest continuously occupied abbeys. There is no Schloß on this island, but its ancient Torhalle is as good as one.

As the Chiemsee steamer nears the Fraueninsel, the octagonal white tower of the monastery church, topped with its onion dome, appears first, followed as you round the island to reach the landing stage by the cool lines of the cloister itself. During the early eighteenth century the nuns over-reached themselves financially in rebuilding their living quarters, a rebuilding partly made necessary by the great influx of refugees from other convents in Bavaria during the previous century (for the Thirty Years War passed the Chiemgau by, so that this Benedictine convent flourished, while others suffered). The result, from an architectural point of view, was exceedingly fortunate. While the baroque and rococo masters were transforming other churches, the abbey church here was spared. Although I revere such men as Johann Baptist Zimmermann, to have lost the present interior of this building would, as we shall shortly see, have been extremely sad.

First, however, notice that the church tower stands apart from the church itself, and also that in spite of its elegance the lower storeys are massive. As with the tower of Erding parish church, scholars surmise that this began life not as part of a religious complex but as a defensive watchtower, probably built to guard the Fraueninsel during the Hungarian invasions in the first half of the tenth century. Only when churches began to equip themselves with sets of bells was the upper storey added. Five famous bells used to hang here, cast by the celebrated Innsbruck bell-founder Hans Christoff Löffl in 1573. Only two of these beautifully crafted Renaissance bells remain. When the abbeys of Bavaria were dissolved in 1803, the authorities foolishly confiscated the two largest of Löffl's bells and melted them down. Another had to be recast in 1874. In 1950 the present nuns commissioned a couple more to replace the confiscated ones. As for the 'imperial' onion dome, it was added only after a fire of 1572 had destroyed the belfry's wooden spire. Beside it stretches an apparently simple white church, with just one intricate Gothic pattern running along the wall below the roof of the nave.

The fearsome Carolingian door-knocker on the ancient iron door of the abbey-church is our next treat. The door dates from around 1475, its knocker from 680 or so. Both indicate the great antiquity of this three-aisled basilica, whose basic structure was already complete in the early eleventh century. Go inside to rejoice that for once the baroque and rococo geniuses were not given their heads here, for they would surely have destroyed what constitutes one of the finest examples of late-Gothic rib-vaulting in Bavaria. The first time I looked along this nave I sat down for a long time, simply adoring the architecture and (I regret to say) ignoring the Mass that was being celebrated in the church. I was brought back to earth when two rude boys walked in, both shouting to each other and eating apples. Instantly a sharp-faced young nun rose from her prayers and flung the boys out of church with the words, 'Don't come back till the service is over.'

The creator of this vaulting was Hans Lauffer of Landshut. The delicacy of his work was enhanced in 1606 when sweet ornamental foliage was diapered on it. After the Mass was finished I wandered around, looking first at the keystones, which are carved with the coats of arms of the Frauenchiemsee, as well as those of Bavaria, Saxony, Austria and Salzburg. All this cunning simplicity is set off by the contrast with the eleven baroque altars, especially the high altar. These date from the years 1688 to 1702, when the nunnery was ruled by Abbess Maria Abundantia Theresia von Grimming. The finest, I think, are those by Matthias Piechlinger. His high altar, richly carved with statues, dates from 1694. Apart from the painting of the risen Jesus appearing before his mother, which was done by Jacopo Amigoni in 1720 and brought here from Munich cathedral, the rest (including the painting of the coronation of the Virgin by the Holy Trinity) is precisely as Piechlinger left it. Piechlinger also designed and made the altar in the chapel of Our Lady of Compassion (on the south side of the church, to the left of the choir) and the altar in the chapel of the Blessed Irmengard (which you reach from the Romanesque ambulatory behind the high altar).

Irmengard was the daughter of Charlemagne's grandson King Ludwig the German, who installed her as abbess of this nunnery in the mid-ninth century. She died in 866. Soon her sanctity had spread throughout the whole of the Chiemgau, and when her corpse was exhumed in 1641 the nuns placed the venerable relic in a marble sarcophagus, which now stands in front of the main pillar of the nun's choir. Today the sarcophagus is empty, for in the 1920s Pope Pius XI finally beatified Irmengard, and now you can see her remains exhibited in a glass case incorporated in the altar of her chapel. Such are the rewards of holiness.

Much else is worth exploring in this church. Some of the pews are late-Renaissance, some of them rococo in style. The carved octagonal pulpit was made in the mid-seventeenth century, and the massive crucified Christ on the opposite wall fifty years earlier. The late-Gothic font is covered by a pretty pyramid-shaped lid, whose eight painted sides depict the Holy Trinity and the seven sacraments. Although the organ is modern, built in 1980, its rococo case dates from 1774. Some of the abundant memorial tablets and gravestones deserve more than a passing glance. Especially grisly is that against the pillar of the nave as you enter. Sculpted in 1510 in memory of an abbey bailiff, it depicts his decaying corpse.

What you cannot climb up to see are some of the most important and beautiful Romanesque frescos in the whole of Germany, since they are above the Gothic vaulting in the roof space of the church. Painted between 1130 and 1140, they were uncovered only this century. Happily, with great skill these frescos have been reproduced in the other main building on the Fraueninsel, the remarkable Torhalle. The main part of this stone gatehouse is almost as old as the door-knocker of the church. Built at the expense of Ludwig the German around 860, its lines and the placing of its round-arched windows and doorway are entirely satisfying. The entrance hall constitutes one of the oldest Carolingian barrel-vaulted halls in existence.

The Torhalle opens between 11.00 and 18.00 from May to October. Its upper storey is a chapel, dedicated to St Michael. As you climb up to the chapel you see the splendid reproductions of the frescos of the abbey-church, their features strongly delineated in brown and red. King Jereboam oversees the rebuilding of the Jerusalem Temple. I like especially the portrait of Moses, accompanied by a very stern Aaron (who carries his rod). The bearded man with neatly combed hair, his head in a nimbus, is thought to be the prophet Isaiah. They date from an era when Archbishop Konrad of Salzburg was patronising what was clearly a brilliant school of fresco-painters.

Inside the chapel itself are genuine frescos, equally dating from the 860s. Fired by their skill at reproducing the frescos of the abbey, in 1981 the scholars of the Munich Prehistoric Collection also decided to fill this chapel not only with an exhibition of archaeological findings from the region of the Chiemsee but also with exact replicas of early medieval treasures that have long since found their way to other collections. Some of these are replicas of astounding works of art. I find all of them moving. A copper-gilt chalice made around 777 for Duke Tassilo III and his wife Liutpirc, its original in the Benedictine Kremsmünster, is not only inscribed with their names but also engraved with a portrait of the duke himself. He stands above the word DVX in the inscription, identified with the letter T. The other three portraits around the chalice are John the Baptist, identified with the letters IB, the Blessed Virgin Mary, identified with the letters MT (i.e. Maria Theotokos) and an unidentified person, identified PT. Above them on the beaker are chased the figures of Jesus and his four evangelists.

Poor Tassilo, the last of the Agilulf dynasty, did not prosper. His father Odilo died in 748, five years after being disastrously defeated in battle by the Franks. Tassilo tried to win back Odilo's lost lands and was massively defeated by Charlemagne. Condemned to death, the duke was pardoned and spent the rest of his life confined to a monastery.

Other equally magical replicas in this little museum include a late-Romanesque hen with seven chickens. I can scarcely believe that this stunning creation dates from the sixth century, but that is stupidly to underestimate the skills of the craftsmen of that era. The birds peck at corn-jewels. This masterpiece had been placed in Irmengard's sarcophagus at her first exhumation. It has, some say, a religious symbolism, the hen representing the abbey of the Fraueninsel, the chickens her seven daughter foundations.

Its original is today in the cathedral treasury at Monza, as are, I notice, most of the other works of art reproduced here that I find most touching. Among such is the tiny golden diadem with a tripple row of precious stones, made for the Lombard Queen Theodelinda in 590. Another is an ivory diptych dating from the early sixth century. On one side a bald poet sits on a cushion, scroll in hand, listening to his muse, who is playing the harp. Their counterparts are King David and St Gregory, mimicking exactly the gestures of the poet and the muse. Here too is a replica of the cover of a Gospel book that Pope Gregory the Great gave to Queen Theodelinda, as well as a tiny crucifix, another of his presents to the queen. I think the pretty receptacle for her fan on display here is the original. From the bizarre wall-painting of a prophet scratching his beard to the interlaced stone carving dated around 800, every item here is a gem of Carolingian art. The museum has other rooms with changing displays of local art, none of which can match this fascinating collection of replicas and originals.

Frau Cheema had given me another tip. In the mornings the fishermen of the Fraueninsel sail on the lake. In the afternoons, if they have caught enough fish, they smoke them and sell these *geräucherte*

Fische to anyone who cares to call at their homes. 'Go past the Gasthof zur Linde,' she told me, 'and turn right at the telephone box, where a notice points you to the house of Pollfischer Febern.' She added that if the family Febern had run out of fish, I could walk further on down the little path to the next fishermen's cottages. For six Deutschmarks I bought there a couple of roast *Brachsen*, each wrapped in a paper napkin. After eating them with my bare fingers in the garden, I gave the bones to the fisherman's son who invited me to wash my hands in the family kitchen.

I did wash, yet happily licked my fingers all the way back to Prien Stock. The ship sails back from the Fraueninsel by way of Gstadt, whose simple parish church with its square tower is the first building to catch your eye, followed by houses with typical Bavarian overhanging roofs and rows of balconies, each bedecked with baskets of flowers.

Frisch geräucherte Fische are, of course, a mere snack. I remember that evening's substantial *Wienerschnitzel* in the *Weinstube* of the Hotel Luitpold am See, because someone had booked a party in one of the rooms. Through the window I could see the guests merrily bobbing up and down to the noisiest oom-pah-pah music imaginable. As I sat in the *Weinstube* drinking as a massive aperitif one of the beers which the Hofbraühaus Transtein has been brewing since 1612, I asked a fellow-imbiber whether this was a typical Bavarian band. 'More Schwabish than Bavarian!' he replied contemptuously.

As I dined, the band irresistably reminded me of Jerome K. Jerome's description of his own problems of eating in Munich in the vicinity of such music:

> If you are within a mile of a Munich military band, and are not stone deaf, you listen to it, and do not think of much else. It compels your attention by its mere noise; it dominates your whole being by its sheer strength. Your mind has to follow it as the feet of the little children followed the playing of the Pied Piper. Whatever you do, you have to do it in unison with the band. All through our meal we had to keep time with the music. We ate our soup to a slow waltz time, with the result that every spoonful was cold before we got it up to our mouth. Just as the fish came, the band started a quick polka, and the consequence of that was that we had not time to pick out the bones. We gulped down white wine to the 'Blacksmith's Galop', and if the tune had lasted much longer we should both have been blind drunk.

With the advent of their steaks, the band struck up a selection from Wagner. 'I know of no modern European composer so difficult to eat beefsteaks to as Wagner,' Jerome concluded.

Nevertheless that evening I managed to eat successfully, scanning the menu for my final indulgence and choosing one of those huge cups of chocolate ice-cream, walnuts, pistachio, sliced almonds, chocolate sauce and heaven-knows-what-else, topped with whipped cream. It was called a *Nußknacker*.

Strolling by the lakeside in the early evening of the following day (which was Saturday, 17 June 1989), I spotted just in time a notice proclaiming that at 18.30 that very evening Prien's brass band and its old comrades' association were to parade by the war memorial, in joint celebration of the 160th anniversary of the founding of the one and the 150th anniversary of the founding of the other. They were to repeat the performance the following morning, before attending a special Mass in Maria Himmelfahrt, but I had other things to do that Sunday. So I ran to the church and saw the magical sight of the old comrades in traditional gear, some of their knee-breeches made out of leather, on their venerable heads all manner of Bavarian hats, plumed and feathered and covered in badges. In the brass band the men sported green hats flamboyant with snow-white plumes, and their grey jackets were also braided in green. In honour of the illustrious dead of Prien new wreaths had been placed by the war memorial. Trees had suddenly appeared in pots around it, and two flames had been set alight. After a moment's pause at the memorial, the brass band led a procession of the old comrades through the winding heart of the town. I had expected that a couple of girls in dirndls would be playing flutes in the Blaskapelle and so they were. What amazed me was that the person leading the band, both playing and carrying a kind of massive portable Glockenspiel (the *Schellenbaum*), was also a woman. Moved to comment on this unusual phenomenon to a fellow-spectator, I was rewarded with the response, 'I know her well. She's a big girl.'

So I returned to my hotel, calling in for refreshment at a nearby restaurant whose wall was decorated with the prayer 'Gott schütze Bayern.'

South of Prien the River Prien flows by Aschau, a little health resort and winter-sports centre nestling at the foot of the 1,664-metre-high Kampenwand. You can reach the village by train from Prien and then ride by a cabin cable-car most of the way up the Kampenwand. Aschau divides itself into two. Niederaschau boasts a late-Gothic parish church dedicated to St Michael, and – as its twin onion domes make clear – remodelled several times in the seventeenth and eighteenth centuries. Hohenaschau is dominated by the Schloß we have come to see. Konrad and Arnold von Himseberg built it to control the entrance to the upper Prien valley. Although its white walls, towers and red roofs still lour over the village in a satisfactorily medieval fashion, between 1540 and 1560 Schloß Hohenaschau was considerably rebuilt and enlarged in the Renaissance style. To add to its riches, in the 1670s and 1680s the Schloß chapel was transformed into a high baroque building, with work by J. B. Zimmermann, and a contemporary Italian high altar brought here from Verona. Guided tours of the Schloß take place between 09.30 and 11.30 from May to September, and here you can also visit – in another baroque room – the Prien valley museum. For information about skiing or the many gentle rambles in this region, the tourist office in Aschau is at No. 37 Kampenwandstraße.

To explore the other castles of Bavaria you must hop from place to place, but the experience is rewarding. Almost all of them are superbly sited, and the towns and cities they guard offer other artistic, architectural and gastronomic delights. Starnberger See is surrounded by such castles. In the mid-thirteenth century the Dukes of Bavaria built a Schloß to dominate the lakeside resort of Starnberg itself, and it still does so. While you are at Starnberg make sure you cross the arched bridge near the Schloß to see the rococo church of St Joseph, whose superb high altar is the work of Ignaz Günther. If you now drive five kilometres south, by the western side of the lake, you come across a private Schloß at Pöcking near Possenhofen. Further south you pass through Feldafing, which boasts an internationally renowned golf links, to reach the sixteenth-century Schloß Garatshausen, built for the Princes of Thurn und Taxis.

Still further on at Tutzing – where, as the Brahmspromenade indicates, Johannes Brahms once lived – you find a sixteenth-century Schloß, which the Bavarian Protestants have made into a centre for study and congresses. Tutzing is impressively overshadowed by the Ilka, which rises to a height of 728 metres. Close by rises Schloß Hohenried, its corner towers quaintly topped by onion domes. Drive on to Bernried to discover a monastery that once belonged to the Augustinian canons. The monastery church offers works of art of

Gothic and rococo beauty, and Bernried boasts a second fine house of God, the town's parish church of St Maria. Almost at the southern tip of the lake you reach Seeseiten, boasting yet another Schloß.

If you drive from Starnberg down the eastern side of the lake, at Berg you can see (but not visit) the castle built in a lovely park in 1640 for the Duke of Hörwarth. Maximilian II spotted this Schloß in the 1850s and set to work re-creating it in the neo-Gothic style, adding battlements and four mighty towers. Here King Ludwig II spent his last melancholy days, as well as part of his youth. Here in 1876 he built a Gothic chapel. By the lakeside a sad cross blesses the spot where his corpse was washed up on 13 July 1886. Close by is the chapel built in 1900 in his memory, modelled on the Holy Sepulchre in Jerusalem.

All these castles are charming, though in no way do I claim that they are the greatest in Bavaria. The Schloß at Burghausen, east of Munich, might, however, lay claim to that distinction. Stretching for 1,100 metres along a terrace above the town, its varied buildings constitute the largest castle in Germany. Begun in the thirteenth century, this Schloß was undoubtedly intended as a fortress to protect its inhabitants from attack. The most vulnerable side, to the north, is defended by ditches and powerful gates. Schloß Burghausen was not finished until the fifteenth century. Today it is the home of part of the Bavarian State art collection, as well as a local history museum. I like best its Dürnitzstock, a three-storey building used both as a warehouse and as living quarters. I like second best its chapel, adorned with late fifteenth-century net vaulting.

One could spend a lifetime exploring the plethora of castles in Bavaria. Let me now, knowing that I have a final chapter in which to include a few more, make a selection of those worth cycling twenty miles against the wind to see. Near Kelheim, Burg Prunn rises above the River Altmühl. Though most of its buildings date from the sixteenth and seventeenth centuries, its keep is Romanesque, its chapel baroque. It remains noted by lovers of medieval legend for the discovery here in 1577 of a manuscript of the Lohengrin saga. In Kelheim itself Ludwig I charged Friedrich von Gärtner and Leo von Klenze to build a Befreiungshalle, over the spot where the Altmühl flows into the Danube. This massive round Liberation Hall commemorates those who died freeing Bavaria from the French during the Napoleonic wars. Built between 1842 and 1863, it can be seen from virtually every quarter of Kelheim.

Kelheim itself is walled, three towers and three city gates remaining from its thirteenth- and fourteenth-century fortifications. Its old houses are enriched with wide façades and pretty gables. The town guards part of a mid-twelfth-century Schloß built by the Wittelsbachs. Before leaving Kelheim, visit its Kapelle, in which holy house in 1231 Duke Ludwig the Kelheimer was assassinated. Then find time to take a river trip through the spectacular defile of the Danube, the Donaudurchbruch.

The Altmühl also flows by Eichstätt, where in the early seventeenth century Bishop Konrad von Gemmingen commissioned no less a genius than Elias Holl to rebuild Schloß Willibaldsburg in 1593. The castle overlooks a charming town, whose cathedral boasts an eleventh-century Romanesque tower and a baroque façade. Its stained glass was designed by Hans Holbein the Elder, its crucifix by Loy Hering. St Willibald, after whom the bishop's Schloß is named, was the first Bishop of Eichstätt, and his sculpted image (also by Loy Hering) stars in the rococo altarpiece which Matthias Seynold fashioned for this cathedral. Willibald's statue also rises above the fountain in the Marktplatz. Since we are here we should certainly look into the early seventeenth-century church of the Benedictine monastery, which was decorated by Wessobrunn masters. And since we are chiefly seeking castles, we should find the Residenz, the bishops' summer palace, which Jakob Engel began building at the end of the seventeenth century and Gabriel Gabrieli finished. The rococo brilliance of its salons is due to Maurizio Pedetti, who also designed Eichstätt's column of the Virgin Mary.

Bavarian prince-bishops were fond of summer residences. In 1680 the prince-bishops of Würzburg built themselves one at Veitshöchheim, seven kilometres away from their cathedral city. Visits take place from 09.00 to 12.00 and from 13.00 to 17.00 in summer (except on Mondays). Although parts of the Schloß are by the altogether perfect Balthasar Neumann, it is outmatched by its park, one of the finest rococo gardens in Germany. Sculpted ladies, gentlemen and horses rise from its waters. Its statues, by such eighteenth-century Franconian sculptors as F. Dietz, P. Wagner and J.-W. von der Auwera, are considered so valuable that they have been removed for safe-keeping to the Mainfränkische museum in Würzburg and replaced with replicas.

Schloß Johannisburg at Aschaffenburg, in north-western Bavaria, is as great, its corner towers and ornamented walls, its defensive wall and dormer windows rising above the river. A late-Renaissance building, built of local red sandstone in the first decade of the seventeenth century by Georg Ridinger, it was paid for by Archbishop Schweickard von Kronberg. Today it is the home of the city art gallery. Walk through its garden to reach another of Ludwig II's follies, the Pompejanum. Modelled on the villa of Castor and Pollux at Pompeii, it lies in an exotic garden which seems to have been transported to Bavaria from the Mediterranean.

Much of Aschaffenburg, including its Schloß, was burnt to the ground towards the end of World War II. Such is the German genius for restoration that today you would never guess this. Its parish church is a late-Gothic jewel with a Romanesque tympanum and a baroque interior. The former Stiftskirche, whose late-Gothic tower was added only in 1870, is in origin Romanesque, as its cloisters reveal. Its treasures include (in the chapter house) one of the rare paintings of Mathias Grünewald, dating from around 1525, a resurrection by Lukas Cranach and a Renaissance pulpit of 1602 by Hans Juncker. Statues of the church's patron saints, Peter and Alexander, adorn the Romanesque tympanum. Only Aschaffenburg's modernistic town hall spoils the ambience of the place; and to sit here as evening falls or when the Glockenspiel rings from the tower of the Schloß is a rare experience. Not far away, along Kleine Schönbuschallee to the south-west, is another castle, Schloß Schönbusch. This is a bagatelle, designed by d'Herigoyen in the late eighteenth century and set in a park landscaped in the English mode by Franz Ludwig Sckell. The information office at No. 1 Weißenburgerstraße will give you details of the concerts performed each year in these surroundings.

Mantelburg, the castle of Lauenstein (at the north-eastern tip of Bavaria), another Franconian sixteenth-century Schloß, offers a further delight. One can actually stay there, for the castle is now a hotel. To the south is the walled, medieval town of Kronach. Lukas Cranach was born here, and his works hang in the Renaissance town hall. Kronach's castle, Veste Rosenberg, dates from 1120, though its gateway is baroque.

The way initially defensive Schlösser could be later transformed into works of elegant architectural beauty is, I believe, no better illustrated than at Dingolfing, which lies in the lower Isar valley eleven kilometres north-east of Landshut. Although today no more than 14,000 citizens live here, at the time of Tassilo III it had become a major centre of the Bavarian court. In the mid-thirteenth century, because of Dingolfing's strategic importance between Landshut and the Danube, Duke Otto II decided to strengthen its defences and built here a plain, powerful brick castle. By the fifteenth century his stern, square Schloß seemed too bare for the cultivated tastes of his descendants. The Wittelsbachs added a stepped, broken gable end of such maniloquence that you gasp with pleasure every time you see its five-storeyed façade. A new playfulness had entered Bavaria.

Now a well-preserved local history museum, the Schloß rises in the upper town of Dingolfing. Before you leave Dingolfing, it is worth walking to the lower town for a glimpse of the splendid brick three-aisled church of St Johannes, which was finished around the year 1490.

By now the creation of gorgeous palaces was no longer simply the privilege of the nobility. In Augsburg, for instance, between 1765 and 1767 a wealthy banker named von Liebert commissioned Karl Albert von Lespilliez to build him the luscious Schaezlerpalais, which stands at No. 46 Maximilanstraße, opposite the Hercules fountain. Its sixty splendid rooms now belong to the State, and some of them house Augsburg's city art collection. Among the German artists represented here are Hans Holbein the Elder, Hans Burgkmair the Elder and Ulrich Apt the Younger. But this is also an international collection hanging works by such masters as Tiepolo, Rubens and Veronese. If you have time to see only a few pictures, include among them Albrecht Dürer's portrait of that other rich Augsburg banker, Jakob Fugger. As for the rooms of the Schaezlerpalais themselves, they include a gilded rococo ballroom, whose walls are hung with mirrors and whose ceiling is frescoed with a mythological painting of the four continents, as well as a magnificent staircase hall with a ceiling fresco by Gregor Guiglielmi. The Schaezlerpalais opens every day except Monday from 10.00 to 17.00 (closing an hour earlier in the winter months), and I was delighted to find that you can get in free.

This canter through the castles of Bavaria must end with four final and superb examples. Burg Traunitz at Landshut is the first. Initially it seems formidable. You climb up to its huge ditch, a moat without water. Beyond it is a wall supporting a wooden walkway. You enter by three gates. Once inside you discover the most playful castle imaginable. We have already come across Crown Prince Wilhelm's love of the

Italian Renaissance. The buffoons, revellers and jesters of the *commedia dell'arte* decorate the walls of the graceful jester's staircase of his castle. A man rides a donkey up the stairs, pursued by a pickpocket. Other painted merrymakers dance by night. Allesandro Scalzi of Padua decorated these walls, and another Paduan, Antonio Ponzano, painted similar delicately charming scenes on the walls of Wilhelm's study and bedroom. From April to September you can visit the Schloß daily, except on Monday, between 09.00 and 12.00 and between 13.00 and 17.00. It closes an hour earlier during the rest of the year.

The other three castles every tourist should see are all situated around Munich. Schloß Blutenberg in the suburb Munich-Obermenzing opens daily between 09.00 and 17.00. Lying picturesquely by the River Würm, it dates in its present late-Gothic form from 1470, the creation of Sigismund, the son of the Wittelsbach Duke Albrecht III and his wife Anna of Brunswick. Octagonal towers flank its wide white walls. Its stables are noble, its late-Gothic chapel magical. Inside this church are thirty-two fine stained-glass windows, and a lovely winged altarpiece shelters paintings by Jan Pollack.

Fifteen or so kilometres north of Munich you reach Schleißheim. Here Duke Wilhelm I built himself a hermitage which his son transformed into a palace. This is not in fact the building we are about to visit. Renaissance in style, it was demolished by the bombs of World War I, and the reconstructed Altes Schloß is not open to the public. But next door stands the Neues Schloß. Begun by Enrico Zucalli in 1693, continued by Joseph Effner after the War of the Spanish Succession, it was not finished until the nineteenth-century architect Leo von Klenze accomplished the great staircase. In between times Ignaz Günther, Johann Baptist Zimmermann and Cosmos Damian Asam added their gifts to the décor. Like the Altes Schoß at Schleißheim, the new one was smashed to pieces during World War II. The result was paradoxically a blessing, for Leo von Klenze had decided to reconstruct the whole interior in his own neo-classical style. When the Bavarians rebuilt the Schloß, they did it to the designs of Joseph Effner.

Zucalli's work is still on show here, in the garden palace, Lustheim, which Elector Maximilian II asked him to build in the 1680s for Maximilian's bride Maria Antonia. In 1968 the philanthropist Ernst Schneider donated his fabulous collection of Meissen porcelain to the state, on condition that it would be displayed in some baroque palace. You can see it here, before taking your ease in the Schloß park which was designed by Zucalli himself.

Finally, we reach Munich's Schloß Nymphenburg. The Amalien-burg pavilion in the park of Nymphenburg must rank among Germany's finest rococo buildings. Yet its inspiration is French and its architect was a foreigner. The Hainault-born François Cuvilliés the Elder was so impressed with the rococo oval salon of the Hôtel de Rohan-Soubise which Germain Boffrand had recently built in Paris that in the 1730s he virtually re-created it here (just as his mind-boggling rococo theatre in the Munich Residenz, built in 1753, architecturally acknowledges Boffrand as its godfather). The Elector Max Emanuel gave the pavilion to his wife, and the blue cabinet is where she slept. It abuts on to a glistening hall of mirrors.

Before visiting the palace itself, I like to wander in the huge garden which covers 221 hectares and which Ludwig Sckell set out in the English style in 1805. A footpath by the canal leads from the Amalienburg to the Badenburg, a bathing lodge built for Elector Maximilian II Emanuel by Joseph Effner at the corner of the great lake (the Großer See). Effner also designed the magnificent cascade at the end of this canal. From here you follow a path to the Kleiner See and the Chinese pagoda, which Effner built in 1719 and François Cuvilliés decorated in 1767. Walk back from here and you pass an absurdly pleasing hermitage, an artificial ruin of 1725, complete with a grotto chapel and a statue of St Mary Magdalen.

Now enjoy the palace itself. Agostino Barelli began it in 1664. Enrico Zucalli took over the work in 1673. In the first decade of the next century Antonio Viscardi added four pavilions. Then the stables were built, followed by a magical crescent of houses designed by François Cuvilliés in the mid-eighteenth century. Here in 1747 the Elector founded the celebrated Nymphenburg porcelain factory.

Inside the palace, the gallery of beauties always stops me in my tracks. Josef Stieler painted these ladies between 1827 and 1850. Most of the time I stare at the portrait of Lola Montez, wondering how King Ludwig I could possibly have lost his throne out of love for her. Could this prosaic woman have been the golden apple for which he turned aside from his path, and was content to do so?

Cities and lakes, food, festivals and wine

However beautiful their buildings, some towns and cities in Bavaria leave you first of all with a memory of their setting. Two seem to me especially to do so – the aspect of both immensely enhanced by water. Curiously enough they lie almost at opposite ends of the region, one on the border with Austria, the other looking over to Switzerland, and Liechtenstein as well.

In landlocked Bavaria, Lindau on the Bodensee (Lake Constance) seems a minor miracle, a genuine port that remains a gem. Once Lindau stood entirely on an island in the lake. As more and more tourists came to appreciate the beauty of its setting it burst its bounds, spreading along the lakeside too, but always it seems as if its own citizens were only extending their gardens, so to speak, instead of creating dull suburbs. Today you can walk or drive across a bridge that reaches the island, or take a train across a causeway.

Lindau has three mute guardians: the old lighthouse at the harbour (the Mangturm), a statue of the Bavarian lion, and the 'new' lighthouse which reaches up thirty-three metres from the water. The Mangturm was once part of the old town fortifications, dating from Lindau's first years of importance in the thirteenth century. As for the lion of Bavaria, he was wrought in the nineteeth century by the sculptor Johann von Halbig. You look beyond the lion and the new lighthouse towards the Voralberg and Appenzell Alps.

As for the gently impressive buildings in the picturesque streets of Lindau's Alstadt, their gables mingle happily with towers, churches, mansard roofs and fountains. The old town hall, rising between Hauptstraße and Ludwigstraße, was built between 1422 and 1436, in its early years simple and clean-cut, steeply gabled but otherwise harmoniously quiet. In later centuries it seems to have forgotten its former mild manners and exploded into a burst of colour and decoration. The interior remains late-Gothic, though here and there you can detect the Renaissance peeping through.

Stroll along Ludwigstraße to reach Lindau's new town hall, a baroque building in Bismarckplatz. Walk through little streets as far as the Marktplatz and you find two parish churches virtually rubbing shoulders in the same square. On the north side rises the Protestant church of St Stephan. Though it has stood here since the twelfth century, today its exterior is baroque, its interior eighteenth-century rococo. The Catholic church of St Maria was built opposite in the mid-eighteenth century, and next to it stands a graceful building which once housed devout ladies and is now the local government office. The Marktplatz is rendered even more pleasing by being enclosed by the best patrician house for miles around: the Haus zum Cavazzen. Built in the late 1720s, it is now Lindau's museum.

If you have time, you can find a church in Lindau that has not been transformed over the centuries but retains its original sturdiness. This is the oldest in the city, the eleventh-century St Peter, which stands in Schrannenplatz. In no other church have frescos by Hans Holbein the Elder survived. St Peter's were painted around 1490. Nearby is the turreted, round thieves' tower, the Diebsturm, whose red dumpiness is concealed by the fact that it stands on the highest point of the island.

Fish, washed down with beer, is naturally a high gastronomic treat in a Bavarian town virtually surrounded by a lake. Casino in the evening vies with yachting during the day, sunbathing or playing tennis. The tourist information office near the main railway station gladly advises on walks in the region. Since 1952 Lindau's theatre (a transformed, 700-year-old monastic church) and cultural centre have been hosting balls and operettas, farces and concerts, as well as more serious drama. The spa orchestra gives a daily concert (except on

Mondays) from May till September. Discothèques vie with evening sails with dancing on the ships.

Passau, situated on the other side of Bavaria, in spite of some fine and one superb building, is again made magical above all by water, for it stands at the confluence of three rivers, the Danube, the Ilz and the Inn. Small wonder that the Celts and Romans settled here. Then came the Christians. Their medieval bishops were no less concerned than the Romans with asserting their power, if the mighty Veste Oberhaus built by one of them in 1219 is anything to go by (he had just become a prince of the Holy Roman Empire). Today Veste Oberhaus is the city museum. It opens from 09.00 to 17.00 except on Mondays and from November to March.

As befits an episcopal city, Passau also boasts numerous impressive churches, some of them with ancient elements still worth seeking out. St Nikola, for instance, the home of Augustinian canons until the secularization of 1803, has an eleventh-century crypt. The Heiliggeist-kirche has kept its late-Gothic beauty despite later restorations. The church of St Severin has stood in Passau since the year 460, and its nave is probably Carolingian, dating back as far as the seventh century.

But lording over all these is the massive, to my mind slightly pretentious, cathedral of St Stephen, rebuilt in the Italian style by Carlo Lurago and the stuccoist J. B. Carlone after a fire of 1662 had destroyed the previous one. Everyone should tolerate a spell inside its excessive interior to listen to a half-hour concert on the largest church organ in the world – a modern work of 173,000 pipes and 231 stops. These concerts take place every weekday between May and September beginning at noon. On Thursday they also start at 19.30.

I came out of the cathedral and went for lunch. To sit alone in a *Weinstube* with one's ears pricked up can offer new insights into the human condition. At my solitary table in one of the snug inns that you can find in Passau's arched streets (or else in the nineteenth-century town hall), I listened to a married couple at the next table going so far as to award points, between one and ten, to what they had just eaten. Both agreed that they had eaten too much. The husband judged the meal worth eight points, his fierce wife nine. Meekly he upgraded his award to eight-and-a-half. Then a young couple came in to order vast goblets of ice-cream and fruit, each topped by a small parasol. The married couple's eyes opened wide with greed, before both resignedly reaffirmed that they had already eaten more than they could truly stomach. So had I, but I none the less ordered a similar goblet to those of the young couple. I chose the least fattening, which was called a Kaiser-Ludwig-Cup and consisted merely of raspberry and vanilla ice-cream, sylvan raspberries, other fruits marinated in sugar and yoghurt, the whole bristling with wafers.

After that it seemed best to take a three-river trip, rather than attempt the climb up to the pilgrimage church of Mariahilf, which Francesco Garbiano built on the other side of the Inn in 1627. When I came back I felt fit enough to wander round the back of the cathedral to explore the contrasting style of the old and the new Residenz, and to admire the thirteenth-century pharmacy in this Platz.

For nature-lovers Passau is an ideal spot to take your *Wanderkarte* and begin exploring the Bavarian forest, which (when computed along with its neighbour the Bohemian forest across the Czech border) is the largest in Europe. It includes around 1,300 square kilometres of national park, with a National Park House at Grafenau due north of Passau. What I propose to do here, however, is to begin the longest tour of my book, which sets off from Passau north-west along the motorway to Regensburg. These beautiful 140 kilometres or so of countryside take you along the glamorous left bank of the Danube, with many a pretty village and fine church *en route*. I particularly recommend two spots, Deggendorf and Straubing. The first sports a couple of baroque fountains in its Marktplatz; a town hall dating from 1605; and two fine churches, a mid-fourteenth-century Gothic basilica with a baroque tower, and the seventeenth-century Maria Himmelfahrt, with a rococo high altar.

Straubing, further west, was settled by Celts and Romans, and then refounded by Ludwig the Kelheimer in 1270. Soon it was a dukedom in its own right. In 1435 its darkest hour occurred. Agnes Bernauer, wife of Duke Albrecht, was accused of witchcraft, judged guilty and ceremonially drowned in the river.

The Stadtplatz is another Bavarian gem, graced with splendid gabled houses, a Renaissance fountain and the city tower. This white, slender monument is topped with green spires and was built between 1316 and 1393. Hans Stethaimer designed two of its magnificent churches. St Jakob, brick-built like his masterpieces in Landshut, has a tower topped by a baroque spire, which prepares you for the work of the Asam brothers inside. Most of the furnishings, however, remain as they were in the fifteenth century and include the stained glass and frescos of the Maria-Hilf-Kapelle. Stethaimer's second church at Straubing, which belonged to the Carmelites and stands in Albrecht-gasse, is less of a unity, for in the early eighteenth century W. Dientzenhofer transformed its interior (exceedingly well) from Gothic to baroque. Its high altar is overwhelming.

The Asam brothers were responsible for the Ursuline church in Burggasse. A complete contrast is the Romanesque basilica of St Peter. Built around 1200, this church retains superb contemporary west and south portals. As for Agnes Bernauer, in St Peter's graveyard you can see her tombstone in the Agnes-Bernauer-Kapelle, built by her husband to atone for her death, or you can see her tragic life re-enacted at four-yearly intervals in the courtyard of Straubing's medieval Schloß.

Straubing also boasts a fine dance of death, a baroque mural decorating the late-Gothic chapel of Our Lady in St Peter's cemetery. Its civic museum has been especially worth visiting since 1950, when a remarkable hoard of Roman gold was discovered nearby and put on display here. And each August the beer tents and funfair of the *Gäuboden* festival bring a million visitors into the little town, frightening the polar bears in the local zoo.

As Goethe rightly observed, 'Regensburg is so beautifully situated that the spot was bound to attract a city.' The Danube here has reached its northernmost point where it joins the Regen and the Naab and divides itself into two wide blue streams. Vespasian had a fortress built here in AD 77, though most of its Roman remains, such as the Porta Paetoria, date from AD 179 when Marcus Aurelius made a site already inhabited for six centuries into a stronghold named Castra Regina. The Carolingians made the city one of their capitals. Soon it boasted a bishopric, established by Boniface in the late eighth century, and from the year 1245 was the sole free imperial city in Bavaria. Between 1663 and 1806 Regensburg was the permanent seat of the imperial Diet. In 1809 the citizens put up a brave show against the French *grande armée*, and where Martin-Luther-Straße meets Hemauerstraße a plaque proudly announces that they even managed to inflict a wound on Napoleon himself. The following year Regensburg became part of Bavaria.

Regensburg boasts no fewer than 1,400 medieval buildings, for it completely survived World War II. It comes as no surprise to learn that it also boasts Germany's oldest stone bridge, built between 1135 and 1146. What continually makes one gasp is the view across this bridge, the gateway and towers, the ancient houses and dormer windows overshadowed behind by the twin Gothic towers of the cathedral.

A good place to park and begin a tour of the city is in Emmeransplatz, which you reach by finding the railway station and driving north along Maximilianstraße through the park of the palace of the princes of Thurn und Taxis. At St Petersweg, in order to reach Emmeransplatz, you turn left and arrive at their palace. It turns out to be a former Benedictine monastery which they took as their Residenz in 1812. Park in the oddly shaped Platz and admire first the Romanesque doorway of the church. Since the church has been considerably changed over the years, after fires and when its clergy and patrons amassed enough money to rebuild, you find inside a baroque interior by the Asam brothers. Yet many older tombs remain, with Saints Emmeran, Ramwold and Wolfgang in their crypts, as well as a memorial to the humanist philosopher Aventinus, who died in 1534.

To the left rises the free-standing bell tower of St Rupert, begun in 1579 and finally crowned in 1777. Some of its niches still house their statues. Gargoyles peer down at you. If you are inclined to study the history of the German postal service and also enjoy inspecting old coaches, carriages and sleighs, visit the museum in the stables. Otherwise take Manhalestraße and Waffnerstraße to see the early Gothic church of the Teutonic knights, St Agidien, created in the 1270s, with a high Gothic choir. Next to it stands the order's new home, built for them in the first half of the seventeenth century by Peter Appiani and Franz Keller.

You turn right into Schottenstraße and reach Bismarckplatz, a completely unexpected treat in this medieval town. Its graceful steps are usually peopled by the young, chattering blithely amid the fountains. The former Württemberg embassy standing in this square is a sixteenth-century palace. The palace of the crown-prince, built in 1702, is now the Thurn und Taxis bank, and as stately as ever. The two other exquisite classical buildings in this square, a theatre and a palace, were both designed by Emmanuel d'Herigoyen, respectively in 1804 and 1805. The sole reminder of medieval Regensburg here is the thirteenth-century Dominican church of St Blasius. Its façade bears a statue of the patron, St Dominic, and inside are lovely fifteenth-century choir stalls. As Bishop of Regensburg, the philosopher

Albertus Magnus lived in the convent here between 1236 and 1240, and the little square in which the church stands is named Albertus-Magnus-Platz.

From Bismarckplatz, Lothgäßchen leads west to Jakobsplatz and the marvellous Schottenkirche. The name is strange, for it was founded in 1140 not by the Scots but by an Irish Benedictine monk named Mercherdach. These Irish Benedictines were generally taken by the Germans to be Scots. To add to the confusion, the church is really dedicated to St James (Jakob). I would use the word marvellous to describe it simply because of the Romanesque north porch, alas blackened with age but depicting Jesus between Saints James and John, Adam and Eve, and the rest of the apostles. A Romanesque crucifix of 1180 hangs inside.

Gesandtenstraße leads east from Bismarckplatz, passing a little church on the right that I have never managed to penetrate, and reaching what was once the Jewish ghetto of Regensburg. It is now called Neupfarrplatz. On the site of the former synagogue now stands the New Parish Church of Regensburg. Built in 1519, it became the city's first Protestant church in 1542. Hans Leinberger painted the 'Schöne Maria' over one of its side altars in 1520. To the south-east of this church the Dresdner Bank turns out to have been built between 1731 and 1733 by Johann Prunner for a banker named Hieronymus Löschenkohl.

If you walk on to Kassianplatz you find the Romanesque church of St Kassian, with its eighteenth-century baroque interior. From here Schwarze-Bären-Straße takes you east to the south side of the picturesque Alter Kornmarkt and the Alte Kapelle. This church was begun in 1002 and continually enriched until the late eighteenth century. The Alter Kornmarkt itself is a splendid square. On its north-east side rises a Romanesque tower. On the west side stands the Herzhogshof, a palace built for the Dukes of Bavaria in the early thirteenth century. Beyond you can see the mid-thirteenth-century church of St Ulrich, and on the east side of the square rises the baroque church of the Carmelites.

In Dachauplatz, east of this church, are over fifty metres of surviving Roman wall and a former fourteenth-century Minorite friary, which now houses the city museum. In 1544 the monks handed over their priory to the city, and here was built the first Protestant press of Regensburg.

It is time we visited the cathedral, whose spires you can see rising to the north-east of Neupfarrplatz. Opposite the west façade of the cathedral is the fourteenth-century Haus an der Heuport, with a courtyard and an open staircase. Beginning life as a Romanesque church, over the centuries the Dom at Regensburg was transformed into south Germany's most important Gothic cathedral. After the old church was burnt to the ground, Bishop Leo the Thurndorfer began rebuilding a new cathedral in 1250. Simply to list its charms is to become besotted with architectural pleasure. The main choir was vaulted around 1300. The crossing and the first arch of the nave date from 1325. Although masons started on the south tower in 1341 and on the north in 1383, these 105-metre-high landmarks were not finished until 1869. A rose window of 1480, thirteen- and fourteenth-century stained glass, medieval carvings, Renaissance silver busts of Mary and Joseph and Saints Peter and Paul, plus a silver high altar created in 1785, blend into a cornucopia of religious art.

The list of gems could continue for a long time. Peter Vischer came from Nuremberg in 1521 to create the tomb of Margaretha Tucher. The stone pulpit dates from 1482, the aumbry from eleven years later. On the fifth pillars from the west end an angel greets a smiling Virgin Mary with the news of her immaculate conception. Both were carved in stone in the late thirteenth century. As for the cathedral cloisters, they contain a beautiful Romanesque chapel, built in the mid-twelfth century to house the tomb of Bishop Hartwich II and decorated with contemporary frescos. As if this were not enough to feast on, the cloisters also enclose an earlier Romanesque chapel dedicated to St Stephen.

Beware that, as the missionary centre of Germany, Regensburg has more fine and ancient churches than one can count on the fingers of both hands. At the south-east corner of the cathedral an archway leads to the thirteenth-century church of St Ulrich. Next, further east, you reach the Niedermünster, a majestic, twin-towered Romanesque church housing an early thirteenth-century bronze depicting Mary Magdalen at the cross, a crucifixion group carved in wood around 1320 and a late fourteenth-century Madonna. Its high altar was made by the Salzburg stonemason Jakob Mösl in 1763. Excavations inside this church have uncovered buildings dating as far back as the second century.

From the north side of this church Unter den Schwibogen leads you back westwards, past the former bishop's palace, which now serves as a hotel, by the cathedral cloister and by the Roman Porta Praetoria into Goliathstraße, which boasts the thirteenth-century Goliathshaus. In the 1570s it was frescoed on the outside wall with a picture of David and the giant by Melchior Bocksberger. Goliath looks suitably huge and stupid, David suitably small and lithe. South of Goliathstraße stands Regensburg's finest tower house, the seven-storeyed mid-thirteenth-century Baumburgerturm. No. 6 Goliathstraße, the Bräunelturm, is another mid-thirteenth-century Gothic house. In Kohlenmarkt at the end of this picturesque street stands the former town hall (Altes Rathaus) of Regensburg. Home of the city infor-mation office, it has stood here since 1360. The baroque east wing dates from 1661, as does the Venus fountain in the courtyard. The museum of the Imperial Diet inside, as well as the rich Reichsaal, which was decorated in 1408, alone make a tour worth while. Tours take place on weekdays between 09.30 and 16.00 and on Sundays from 10.00 to noon on the hour.

South-west of the old town hall you reach Haidplatz, whose fountain, the Justitiabrunnen, has cooled the air since 1656. No. 1 Haidplatz is the Neue Waage ('New Weigh House'), a former tavern where the Protestant Melanchthon disputed theology with the Catholic Eck in 1541. At No. 7, the early Gothic Goldene Kreuz, Emperor Charles V met his bride Barbara Blomberg in 1546.

This part of Regensburg is replete with towered, fortified mer-chants' houses, built in the Italian style between the thirteenth and sixteenth centuries. Fischmarkt, to the north, still hosts a fish market each morning, the stalls surrounding an early seventeenth-century fountain. Keplerstraße leads west from here to the Weinmarkt. The street takes its name from the astronomer Johannes Kepler, who died in 1630 at the house now numbered 5. It was built in 1540 and today is the Kepler museum. Two houses in this sweet street retain their thirteenth-century towers, and the Blaue Hecht (No. 7) is a former medieval inn.

If such a tour seems dauntingly exhaustive, you can take a twelve-kilometre sail around Regensburg. I greatly recommend this, which takes you by way of the Rhine-Main-Danube canal and the Danube itself as far as Walhalla. Rising ninety-six metres above the river, this white marble temple was built by Leo von Klenze at the bequest of Ludwig to celebrate the heroes of Bavaria.

Regensburg is a city of music, its chief attraction being the cathedral 'sparrows', an internationally renowned boys' choir. It is also a splendid centre for excursions to the neighbouring towns along the Danube. Drive north to discover two lovely towns: Amberg on the River Vils and Weiden on the River Naab. Amberg is washed not only by its river but by the beer from no fewer than ten breweries inside its late medieval walls. A double curtain wall, towers and four splendid gateways testify to the importance of this town, which from 1544 to 1810 was the seat of the government of the Upper Palatine. Its parish church, St Martin, has a tower that rises 91.5 metres from the west end of the Gothic nave. In the Marktplatz stands a town hall begun in the thirteenth century and bewilderingly altered in subsequent centuries. It boasts a Renaissance staircase and ogival windows added in the 1880s.

In Amberg too rises a church built by Wolfgang Dientzenhofer in the 1690s, a collegiate church rebuilt after a fire in 1359, dedicated to St George and stuccoed by Johann Baptist Zimmermann, and – three kilometres north-east of the town – a pilgrimage church of Mariahilf, whose late-Renaissance façade lets you through to frescos by Cosmos Damian Asam. Ask at the Kulturamt (at No. 1a Zeughausstraße) for a *Wanderkarte*, for the countryside between the Upper Palatine forest and the Jura ridge is extremely beautiful. Visit the town in mid-June to discover that the annual *Altstadtfest* is taxing all ten breweries to their uttermost. Call again at the begining of the following month to find the same thirsty guests thronging the *Bergfest* (which had its origin in the benefactions to pilgrims at the chapel of Mariahilf).

For Weiden, Hans Nopl designed in 1539 a town hall which stands in the pedestrianized Unteren Marktplatz and seems to have been sprouting green foliage ever since. It sports an open-air staircase and the coats of arms of the seven regional districts of Bavaria. Although Weiden is today a sizeable modern town, it has retained some lovely gabled houses from its past, especially around the Unteren Tor. This gateway was built in the late Romanesque era, partly knocked down during the Thirty Years War and rebuilt in 1698. Among Weiden's fine churches, such as the fifteenth-century St Sebastian and the baroque St Michael, stands a curiosity for this part of Germany. Look inside the neo-Romanesque St Joseph to surprise yourself by finding an art-nouveau interior.

And Weiden is another Bavarian town with a special musical

tradition. The composer Max Reger was born here in 1874. The young prodigy gave his first concert in Weiden fourteen years later. His former home is at No. 31 Bürgermeister-Prechtl-Straße. Inevitably his memory dominates the cultural life of the town, with annual summer concerts in the Max Reger park.

Ingolstadt stands some sixty kilometres south-west of Regensburg and, like that city, is lapped by the River Danube. To my mind one of the most charming of Bavarian cities, Ingolstadt can be strolled around in a most satisfying day. The triple walls of the early fifteenth-century fortifications still survive, as does the splendid gate in Heilig-kreuzstraße. The Spitalkirche blesses the centre of the city, Rathaus-platz, and the two town halls of Ingolstadt, one created in 1882 out of four Gothic houses, the other in 1959. The church is inscribed 'This town church was founded in the year 1319 by Duke Ludwig the Bavarian.' Inside, ten round pillars support Gothic arches, which spring across both the centre and the side-aisles. The whole was intricately patterned by later Gothic artists and picked out in gold leaf.

Behind the present town hall in Moritzstraße rises the splendidly simple Gothic church of St Moritz. It boasts the most garish stained glass imaginable in its east window, and an equally garish, but infinitely more successful, silver Madonna by Ignaz Günther. Johann Baptist Zimmermann has contributed his usual superb stucco-work. The high altar dates from 1752.

Beyond this church Ludwigstraße leads east to Ingolstadt's Schloß, but it is best first to turn west at the same little crossroads and walk along Theresienstraße to the church of Our Lady (or Lieb-frauenkirche). Theresienstraße is said to be pedestrianized, but as I walked along it a child on a bicycle ran over my heel. Children can go too far. Part way along Theresienstraße is a modern stone fountain in which bronze urchins bathe. It was so hot that real-live urchins were also bathing in its water. I looked round for the child that had run over my painful heel, but he had disappeared and thus escaped drowning in the same fountain. This street is flanked by some smashing houses, especially No. 28 with its sixteenth-century oriel window, and the inn opposite which still preserves an old crane on the corner of its warehouse.

On its south-west and north-west corners, the towers of the Lieb-frauenkirche are deliciously offset from the rest of the church. The brick church, its architectural skeleton picked out in stone, is entirely

successful. Most people try all the wrong doors before finally manag-
ing to push open the one under the flamboyant south porch. Everything inside is cool, white, plain and satisfying. This time the high altar
dates from 1572. The long, wide naves reaches up some thirty metres
to heaven. A Munich woodcarver named Wenzel contributed rich
choir stalls and an equally rich pulpit. I think the glass of the apse dates
from the sixteenth century, but cannot find a guide book to help me
out with this. In the first chapel to the south side is fine glass designed
by Hans von Krumbach in 1511. We owe the foundation of this
church in 1525 to Duke Ludwig the Bearded.

You leave the church and discover a notice pointing north around
its apse to the Asam-Kirche Maria de Viktoria. As you walk towards
the church, note on a corner (at No. 34 Kupferstraße) a plaque
declaring that here on 10 February 1542 died Dr Johann Maier. He
was known as Eck and was a great Catholic controversialist. At
Ingolstadt he energetically set about making the university (founded
here by Duke Ludwig the Rich in 1472) into a stronghold of the
Counter-Reformation. Unfortunately for the Catholics, Eck was a
wretchedly incompetent theologian, and even some of his fellow-
religionists conceded that in debate with Martin Luther their protag-
onist was demolished by the Protestant reformer.

This is a street that seems to have had mortal consequences for
Catholic champions. Further on down Konviktstraße the warm pink
stones of the rococo Asam-Kirche beckon. On the corner of Johannesstraße, just before you reach it, stands a pretty Renaissance house
where Field Marshall Tilly died in 1632. As we know, his corpse and
heart lie in Altötting, owing to his deep veneration for the Black Virgin
of that town.

Cosmos Damian Asam, so the story goes, was contracted to fresco
the Asam-Kirche for 10,000 gulden and finished the job within eight
weeks. In my view he earned his money. The sumptuous high altar is
by Johann Michael Fischer. To inspect the fifteenth-century Heilig-
kreuztor, with its stumpy round towers, its battlemented fourth storey
and its steeply sloping spire, you must take a short stroll west from this
church. Then return to Johannesstraße and walk along it (also
westwards) to reach at the end of the street the monastery of St Johann
im Gnaden Thal, whose church was built in 1487.

Here you turn right into Harderstraße, passing the monastic buildings which have stood on this spot since 1276. Across the street is a

fourteenth-century Franciscan basilica renowned for its tombs. Several of the ones on the south wall are the work of the brilliant Loy Hering of Eichstätt. Another is by Ignaz Günther. The altar of the first chapel on the south side carries the miracle-working Schutter Madonna of 1350. The stern, double-bronze doors of this church are modern, and carry the image of a stiffly seated St Francis trying to stop a pigeon from spearing his eyes with its beak.

Pass along the south side of the Franciscan church and you reach the tree-shaded Schrannenstraße, at the end of which stands the slender Lutheran church of St Matthäus. Brick, Gothic, it was built in the mid-1840s and has recently been restored. Like many Protestant churches in Bavaria it is mostly closed. Beyond the church is laid out the Jolzmarkt, from which you can go through narrow Georg-Oberhäuserstraße to Ludwigstraße and there turn right to reach the Schloß in Paradeplatz.

Despite the name Paradeplatz, this is a very peaceful spot. On the first Friday and Saturday of July, starting from here, the streets of Ingolstadt are filled with the stalls and merriment of the annual *Bürgenfest*. The moated Schloß itself is a homely affair, built of medieval brick with later additions. A round pepperpot tower is the most it attempts at pretentiousness. Ludwig the Bearded founded this castle in 1418, but its bastions date from 110 years later. I find it pleasing that the dukes made sure that its most imposing aspects are seen from the other side of the Danube.

The Schloß is now the home of the Bavarian army museum. To get back from here to Rathausplatz by a pleasing, twisting route, take Reiterkasernstraße from the south-west corner of Paradeplatz as far as Hallstraße and then follow Hieronymusgasse. On the way you pass Ingolstadt's information office, in what used to be the late seventeenth-century Kurfürstlichem-Universitäts riding school. But before taking this walk I suggest you refresh yourself in the Schloß café in Paradeplatz.

Drive north from Ingolstadt to Nuremberg. After 1945 the city fathers of Nuremberg came together to debate what should be done about the virtually complete destruction of their Altstadt, till then one of the super-best surviving ensembles of medieval building. Some of them seriously suggested leaving Nuremberg as a rubble-strewn war memorial and rebuilding from scratch on another site. You do not need great imagination to understand their dilemma, for still today are displayed and sold in the city photographs of smashed-down build-ings, narrow paths leading through the debris of what had once been beautiful houses, and grotesque blackened beams point skyward. Fortunately the majority wished to rebuild on the same spot. Today Bavaria's second largest city, with its own international airport, a modern underground railway and splendid communications, Nurem-berg is a bustling blend of carefully restored old buildings and tactfully inserted new ones, boutique and glass shopping arcades mingling with half-timbered medieval houses and Renaissance façades.

Once again, after the Allied raids, some eighty towers rise from the wide city walls, the outer ring of which dates from 1400. They surround a mostly traffic-free Altstadt through which the little River Pegnitz flows and divides itself, sometimes into three. In rebuilding the Altstadt the city fathers made the splendid decision to keep to the old, irregular pattern of streets. Wandering around them today, peered down on by the pink walls of the imperial Schloß, you could be forgiven for forgetting that Nuremberg is the home of some half a million Bavarians.

An initial taste of the Altstadt might conveniently start at the Königstor, the gate of its south-east corner, by visiting the Hand-werkerhof. The little half-timbered houses of this medieval artisans' courtyard are restorations, but the craftsmen working here are genuine enough. Opening times are on weekdays from 10.00 to 18.30, closing at noon on Saturdays. You can eat here, and you can buy the traditional handiworks of these craftsmen: dolls, works in pewter and gold, glassware.

On the way to one of Nuremberg's finest churches, the Gothic St Lorentz, which did in part manage to survive World War II, Königstraße takes you past a couple of others, first the fourteenth-century church of St Martha on your right, and then the church of St Clare, whose choir dates from 1273. From 1578 to 1620 the former housed the school of the famous mastersingers of Nuremberg.

For an extraordinary moment in cultural history Nuremberg produ-ced a cluster of Renaissance geniuses, among whom of course the poet and mastersinger Hans Sachs ranks as one of the foremost. He lived from 1494 to 1576. The woodcarver Veit Stoss was his contemporary. So were the sculptor Adam Kraft, Peter Vischer the brazier, the jurist and humanist Willibald Pirchheimer, Martin Behaim who invented the first globe, and Peter Heinlein who made the first pocket watch (which has been dubbed the 'Nuremberg egg'). All of them left their mark on Nuremberg, two of them, as we shall see, most stunningly in the church we are about to visit. For a moment here, however, I like to remember some words that a Nuremberg humanist wrote in 1512: 'When on St Katherine's day you hear the musical contests, then surely you can only wonder at finding in one place so many singers and so many harmonious voices.'

As you walk on to St Lorentz you pass on the left the Mauthalle, once the city granary. As for the spare, slender church, seen from the west side in Karolinenstraße its twin sets of symmetrical thirteenth-century spires appear to be squeezing the life out of the rest of the church. On the left stands the Nassau house, Nuremberg's oldest, begun in the thirteenth century, the upper storey dating from 1421 and now serving the citizens as a restaurant. Go inside the church to find yourself in a spacious Gothic hall, built in the fifteenth century and lit with some gleaming fifteenth-century windows. The two richest masterpieces housed by the building (and removed for safe-keeping during the war) are the tabernacle created by Adam Kraft in 1493, its spire reaching some twenty metres, and Veit Stoss's extraordinary 'Annunciation' of 1517, in which the Virgin Mary and the angel Gabriel are sublimely suspended in the air.

Nuremberg is a city of remarkable fountains. North of St Lorentz stands the majestic Renaissance fountain of virtue, designed by Benedikt Wurzelbauer in the 1580s. Water spouts fairly languidly from the trumpets of cherubs, but shoots startlingly from the breasts of powerful women. You walk on northwards to cross the river by the Museumsbrücke. Do stop halfway across to look downstream at the hospital of the Holy Ghost. Its two storeys and deep, dormered roof rise from a low, double-arched bridge, and this restrained and painterly building is usually mirrored in the river-waters below. The hospital still houses some fortunate old folks, and also makes room within its walls for a *Weinstube*. The Fleischbrücke to the west was copied in 1598 from the Rialto Bridge in Venice.

North of the bridge the Hauptmarkt is shaded by the mighty fourteenth-century church of Our Lady. Time your arrival with care, first because each weekday the Hauptmarkt is the venue of a lively farmers' market, and second because you should have begun to explore the cathedral before noon. At that moment takes place the *Männleinlaufen*. Underneath the cathedral clock models of seven

German Electors pay homage to the emperor. The Hauptmarkt houses a fountain greater than any other in the city. Nine heroes of the Old Testament, as well as seven Electors, decorate this late fourteenth-century masterpiece. Its creator was Heinrich Parler. It is twenty metres high and is known simply as the *Schöner Brunnen* or beautiful fountain.

Nuremberg's town hall stands to the north, known as the Wolfsche Rathaus after its architect Jakob Wolf. In the early seventeenth century he joined together two earlier buildings to create a Rathaus that is beginning to turn the corner architecturally from the Renaissance to the baroque. The Goosemann fountain, a peasant carrying a couple of water-spouting geese, was erected here in the mid-sixteenth century and today sweetly contrasts with the flamboyant three-tiered *Schöner Brunnen*.

Opposite the Wolfsche Rathaus stands Nuremberg's oldest church. Begun in the thirteenth century, St Sebald boasts Romanesque doorways on its west front. Its towers, reaching up for seventy-nine metres, were not finished until the fifteenth century. St Sebaldus himself lies in a tomb in the choir, a bronze and silver shrine made by Peter Vischer and his sons. The father was proud enough to add his own self-portrait to the shrine. Equally outstanding are the stained-glass windows in the choir. Almost certainly the greatest artist produced by Nuremberg, eighth after the seven I have already listed, had a hand in their design. Albrecht Dürer was born here in 1471, the son of a goldsmith who was also named Albrecht. He became a lifelong friend of his fellow-Nuremberg humanist Willibald Pirchheimer. Apprenticed to another Nuremberg master, the painter and designer of woodcuts Michael Wolgemut, Dürer became the foremost Renaissance artist in the whole of northern Europe.

Dürer worked in the Rhineland; he visited Venice and read Vitruvius to solve the problems of artistic perspective; he admired, and learned from, Italian artists of the calibre of Bellini and Mantegna; but continually he returned to his native city. In 1525, three years before his death, he published his own treatise on proportion. Its influence on other artists was outweighed by that of his drawings, which became the model for countless lesser men. In Albrecht-Dürer-Platz, west of the late seventeenth-century Fembo-Haus (which you find just north of the church), rises a huge plinth on which stands an exceedingly rugged Dürer, cast in bronze to the designs of D. Rauch in 1844.

Dürer's house by the city walls is reached along cobbled Bergstraße, which runs gently uphill from his square. By chance this home, which he bought in 1509 and lived in until his death, remains the sole totally preserved Gothic house in the city. Sandstone below, half-timbered above with a gabled roof, it now fittingly houses a museum devoted to his works (and, where necessary, containing some excellent reproductions of masterpieces now elsewhere). It opens, except on Mondays from 10.00 to 17.00, and from 10.00 to 21.00 on Saturdays.

This is now surely the time to seek out one of Nuremberg's old *Bratwürstküchen* to try some of the roasted, crispy shoulders of pork (*Schäuferle*) for which its chefs are famous. Bavarians typically eat their heartiest meals (and these are truly hearty) at lunchtime, taking merely coffee and rolls for breakfast. Lunch might start gently with *Suppentopf*, a soup created from both meat and vegetables, or pungently with the garlic-flavoured *Bayerisches Knoblauchsuppe mit Schwarzbrot-kroutons*, followed by an overwhelmingly large and tasty loin or *Pfefferlende*, often served in a powerful beef broth. The Bavarian evening meal is usually smaller, a *Brotzeit* consisting of cold cuts, sausages, cheese, radishes, meat loaf and some white or pork sausages.

Diners at Nuremberg who do not feel like a huge meal still have a treat available. Six *Nürnberger Rostbratwürste mit Kraut* (or maybe a dozen, since these grilled sausages are rarely bigger than one's little finger) offer an excellent way of staving off hunger, especially when washed down with a glass of *Hauschoppen Bauernwein*, quarter of a litre of slightly tart, very refreshing house wine served in a huge goblet with a green, coiled stem. A yet lighter snack are the famous Nuremberg gingerbread cakes (*Lebkuchen*), of which the city's bakers make 4,500 tonnes a year.

It is time to say a little more about Bavarian wine, for the *Windbeutelbaron* of Berchtesgaden misled us. 'The real Bavaria is in the Alps,' another Bavarian once told me at Inzell, adding for good measure, 'We are the true Bavarians.' When the *Windbeutelbaron* of Berchtesgaden insisted that the only real Bavarian wine is beer, he was surely betraying a similar prejudice. The wines of Franconia are justly renowned.

I did not in truth first learn about Franken wine in Nuremberg but in a tiny village called Oberlaimbach, situated between that city and Würzburg. Many of the owners of Bavarian restaurants are proud that they are also their own butchers, and Herr Erik Rückert of the Gasthof zum Adler, Oberlaimbach, actually also runs a pig farm, which ensures excellent pork. My family and I have stayed so often at this remarkably inexpensive spot that I do not really like mentioning it to others, in case it is full when we pass again. Eventually one of Herr Rückert's daughters came to stay in England for a while. Just after Christmas we drove her from Gloucestershire back to Oberlaimbach, taking the opportunity to stay a fortnight or so in the region.

Herr Rückert had given me a book on Riemenschneider in Franconia, which I wished to explore. This is a region where the ending of the religious wars left one village Protestant and the next Catholic. My host kindly told me the time of the Sunday service in the little church nearby. As I sat miserably through the incredibly lengthy sermon of the Lutheran preacher, I realized that Herr Rückert had sagely decided to stay at home. When I politely pointed this out to him later, his eyes simply twinkled.

Each evening as we came back to the Gasthof zum Adler he introduced us to yet another Franken wine, some of them bottled in the celebrated flagon-like *Bocksbeutel*, some drunk from the green-stemmed glass that is known as a *Pokal*. The only glass of wine I did not like was a *rosé*, which I had not expected to find in this region, but Herr Rückert told me that it was excellent, so I took his word for it and carried on drinking.

Although the Dürer house is everyone's favourite in Nuremberg, I find it far more thrilling to walk from it down Albrecht-Dürer-Straße to the Weinmarkt and turn right along the superb row of half-timbered medieval houses in the Weißgerbergasse. Tall and narrow, sometimes with lower storeys of sandstone, sometimes with balconies, their roofs higgledy-piggledy, dormer windows jostling against the shutters and pulleys of the upper warehouse floors, gaily painted, sometimes with flowers in their windows, these houses should be unmissable. In 1988 I continued along Am Hallertor and, to my surprise, found myself crossing the River Pegnitz by a swaying chain bridge.

I thought it time to stop and pay a visit to the Burg, realizing that I ought to have spent at least half a day there, for its main buildings range from the pentagonal tower of around 1050 through the early twelfth century as far as the fifteenth. It opens in summer from 09.00 to 17.00 and in winter from 10.00 to 12.00 and from 13.00 to 16.00.

The largest such group of buildings in Europe, part of the Burg serves fortunate young people as a youth hostel. This is by no means the only great museum in the city. Like the Burg, the eighty or so rooms of the German national museum at Nuremberg, housed in the Kornmarkt in part of what was once a Carthusian monastery, cannot be seen at a gallop. Even if you are short of time, do pause over its Dürers and look for Peter Heinlein's 'Nuremberg egg'. To add to the cultural riches of this city, because the first German railway ran between Nuremberg and Fürth, in Lessingstraße is a quite fascinating transport museum (Verkehrsmuseum), with a replica of tall-chimneyed 'Adler', the train which made the first run in 1835, in its blue and pink livery.

The annual Nuremberg festivals are astonishing in their variety. The most famous is the *Christkindlmarkt*, Germany's oldest Christmas fair. Beginning on the Friday before Advent and continuing until Christmas Eve, its origins lie in the habit, first taken up it seems by Lutheran Protestants, of giving children presents around Christmas. Not long after the mid-1550s this was certainly happening in Nuremberg. At the beginning of the next century traders were bringing toys to sell in the city from as far afield as Holland. Dutch dolls, which were called *Docken*, were particularly prized as gifts. All this took place at the normal pre-Christmas markets, and was beginning to happen elsewhere in Bavaria too. Then in 1639 Nuremberg traders decided to set up special stalls in preparation for a Christmas spending spree. Today dolls are still sold, and many reckon that the Christmas angels made of golden foil – now seen throughout Germany – originated here.

During the *Christkindlmarkt* the streets leading from Nuremberg Hauptmarkt as far as the railway station are festooned with white poles bearing garlands and lights. The Christmas crib is set in the centre of the square, surrounded by fir-clad stalls, selling Christmas decorations, little figures made of dried fruit and crêpe paper (and called *Zwetschgenmännle*), as well as the work of local craftsmen and women. People eat spicy fruitcakes, and of course *Lebkuchen* and grilled sausages. The grub is washed down with mulled *Glühwein*. The Nuremberg market begins with an elected 'Christchild' reading his proclamation from the balcony of the church of Our Lady. Then the sun sets, the lanterns on the stalls are lit, the church and *Schöner Brunnen* are floodlit and the merriment begins. Children's choirs and brass bands regale the visitors. If snow falls, all the better. During the celebrations the German railways put on fifty special trains to bring in some 50,000 visitors, who swell the total number of guests to around 2 million.

This gift for enjoyable as well as profitable festivities remains strong in Nuremberg. I was amazed to learn that the city has housed more than forty annual international toy fairs. Its toy museum, in Karlstraße, is a treat. Its international organ week at the end of June has become renowned. It holds an annual *Alstadtfest* in September. Open-air and indoor theatre, open-air and indoor concerts, opera, the zoo, motor-racing and pop festivals on the former Zeppelin fields means that the local tourist office wisely sponsors a monthly magazine, *Das aktuelle monats Magazin*, to keep visitors up to date with what is going on.

The Zeppelin arena is one of the few visible reminders of the Nazi era. It was part of a huge design by Hitler and his architect ally Albert Speer to house his chilling annual Reich party congresses each September. The Reich did not last long enough for the plans to be finished. Other parts of Speer's monumental schemes were demolished after the war. A two-kilometre-long grand avenue, down which histrionic parades to the grounds were planned, is today used for parking. Since the unfinished congress hall itself is a historical monument, I suppose it should not be demolished.

It reminds me of Dachau, the suburb of Munich which has retained parts of the concentration camp as a permanent reminder of evil. I do not think I should have gone to see this memorial had I not been writing a biography of one of Hitler's greatest opponents, Pastor Martin Niemöller, who was incarcerated there and came out alive. But had I not done so, I should never have seen Dachau's lovely parish church of St Jakob, which was built between 1584 and 1629, nor its partly ruined Schloß, whose splendid staircase and Festsaal ceiling were built by Joseph Effner around 1715. (You can view them only by going to a concert there or making an appointment with the Schloß authorities.)

Since I am momentarily making a diversion, I must add that if you do visit Dachau you should take the trouble to drive south-west to the splendid little town of Fürstenfeldbruck. As you enter the town from the south-east, flower gardens line up beside the river at the end of Hauptstraße. Just before crossing the river look inside the late-Gothic church of St Leonhard, with its contemporary frescos. It has become a memorial for the war-dead. Over the bridge the Altes Rathaus is a building of the 1660s designed by J. Marggraff. F. von Müller created the comical medallions of hook-nosed Duke Ludwig II the Severe and Emperor Ludwig the Bavarian which adorn its façade. Its open-air staircase is sweet. Nearby is another 1914–18 war memorial fountain.

Follow Kirchstraße north from the Altes Rathaus to the presbytery of 1755 and the church of St Magdalena. This was built by K. Pader in the 1670s, Thedor Jipf stuccoed the interior and the frescos are by J. Baldauf. The roof fresco of 1764 is, to my mind, superbly un-Christian, with Our Lady sitting in a chariot supervising battles. Further west along Hauptstraße you see on the left the Klosterrich-terhaus, built for Abbot Leonhard von Inchenhofen in 1621. He would have been mortified to discover that its interior has recently been transformed into a little supermarket. At the far end of the Hauptstraße rises the present town hall of Fürstenfeldbrück, a hand-some classical building of 1700, sympathetically enlarged in the mid-nineteenth century.

But none of these gems are the chief attraction of the town. A notice on the war-memorial church of St Leonhard directs you to the superb, not to say overwhelming, Fürstenried monastery church in the town park. Its convent is now Fürstenfeldbrück's art gallery. The monumental three-storeyed façade of the church grows more ornate as it rises. Inside are the *trompe-l'oeil* tricks of the eighteenth-century masters, and an altar with twisted columns that recall the baldacchino of St Peter's, Rome.

Returning to Nuremberg, you find that its monthly magazine, *Das aktuelle monats Magazin*, caters for the towns of Fürth, Schwabach and Erlangen as well. As you drive the twenty-five kilometres north-west between Nuremberg and Bamberg, try to find time for Erlangen, a spot which is as fascinating for its history as for its architecture. The Altstadt dates from the Middle Ages; but a new baroque town was added in the late seventeenth and early eighteenth centuries to house Huguenot refugees from France after 1685, when Louis XIV revoked the Edict of Nantes which had granted them toleration. The orangery and the Schloß garden, designed in 1706, are charming.

Bamberg is yet more charming, and at the same time wildly baroque. Some 70,000 Bavarians manage to live here without crowd-ing. As the citizens proudly point out, the city is built on seven lovely hills. The very heart of the city is traffic-free, but you can park near the signposted information office, which turns out to be in the former guard house (the Hauptwache) of 1774. Walk on south-west down Hauptwachstraße, which soon becomes traffic-free, to reach Maximiliansplatz. Despite its regal title, this square is the home of Bamberg's vegetable, fruit and flower market. Here in the 1730s Balthasar Neumann built a baroque seminary which today serves as Bamberg's new town hall. Here too is a fountain in honour of King Max. From Maximiliansplatz, past shops, boutiques and cafés you walk along Grüner Markt to find on your right a magnificent church. Georg and Leonhard Dientzenhofer built it for the Jesuits in the late seventeenth century. Its baroque splendour is matched by that of the Raulino house on the other side of the street and by the Neptune fountain created here in 1698 by J. K. Metzner.

Now the scene becomes breathtakingly, quaintly beautiful. We have to cross over one branch of the Regnitz by one of two bridges – I find it hard to recommend which. The upper bridge carries early eighteenth-century statues of the crucifixion and St Johann Nepomuk. The lower bridge bears a statue of the same date depicting Bamberg's patron saint, Kunigunde. The latter bridge gives you the best view of what has come to be called Bamberg's little Venice, the row of fishermen's houses on the right bank of the river. Both bridges offer the astonishing sight of the city's old town hall, floating like a ship in the middle of the water. In the mid-eighteenth century the architect Michael Küchel transformed this Gothic building into a rococo one.

On the other bank Bamberg becomes baroque again. Elegantly curving Dominikanerstraße leads from the upper bridge past a fourteenth-century church and cloister, once the home of Dominicans, now the seat of Bamberg's symphony orchestra. Then turn left to reach one of the finest squares in Germany, the Domplatz. I think its beauty is enhanced by the fact that its three major buildings, the cathedral itself, the former imperial and episcopal palace (the Alte Hofhaltung) and the massive New Residenz are in three different styles, respectively Romanesque, Renaissance and baroque.

The four slender green spires of the cathedral, seen from a distance, might persuade you that you are approaching a Gothic building, but although the Gothic style was creeping in as the cathedral was approaching completion in 1237, Romanesque is its entire thrust. Polygonal at each end, its doorways and lights are rounded. Inside, the ribbed vaults of the interior do give way to a delicious early Gothic.

They rise above a wealth of sculpture. The most famous is the Bamberg rider, an equestrian statue of a knight, set at the north side of the steps that lead into the eastern apse. His face so resembles that of a king in the cathedral at Reims that many think it was copied from the French original. Carved around 1230, the Bamberg rider idealizes knightly virtues. Behind him in the east choir is another famous piece, a Virgin Mary in swirling robes, holding a book. Elisabeth, mother of John the Baptist, is sculpted close by, as well as medieval representations of the church and the synagogue, which leave no doubt in the spectator's eye which the sculptor thought the more enlightened. Yet although I admire the technical mastery of these, and of the altarpiece of the Nativity carved by Veit Stoss in his old age for the chapel of St Peter, nothing here to my mind surpasses the tomb of King Heinrich II and his consort St Kunigunde, a virtuoso work by Tilman Riemenschneider.

Now explore the rest of Domplatz. The Reiche Tor is a beautiful gate decorated with statues of Heinrich II and Kunigunde, Saints Peter and George and, in sculpted allegory, the rivers of this region. The gabled Renaissance Ratsstube is equally attractive. The cathedral chapter house, built by Balthasar Neumann, is now the diocesan museum, and the Alte Hofhaltung Bamberg's history museum. To tour the New Residenz is to marvel at tapestries and furniture, as well as State rooms and a gallery blessed with paintings by Lucas Cranach the Elder. The opening times of all these places vary so widely that I suggest you check them first at the tourist office in Hauptwachstraße.

Sit for a while on the steps outside the cathedral before going to fetch your car. Above Bamberg tower two buildings that I prefer to visit by driving rather than by walking up to them. One is the moated Altenburg, a castle that we first hear of in 1109 and seems not to have changed since. In fact the chapel is neo-Gothic. Along with the walls, watch tower, bridge and gateway it none the less oozes the spirit of the Middle Ages. From here the views are splendid, as they are from the other Bamberg masterpiece that I would not like to miss on any visit. St Michael, Bamberg, was founded as the church of a monastery. Sumptuously rebuilt by the brothers Dientzenhofer and by Balthasar Neumann, it today serves as a comfortable home for the elderly. The cloisters remain virtually untouched by those architects and remain the largest late-Romanesque ones in Germany. Again, the view over the city from the hill is magnificent. What makes the trip a must, however, is the celebrated façade which rises above a balustraded flight of steps and was created by Leonhard Dientzenhofer in 1697. Inside, a rococo pulpit created by George Adam Reuß in 1751 bears saints who, in typical rococo fashion, seem to float in the air unsupported. In complete contrast is a suffering Jesus, with curled, bedraggled hair drooping over his poor shoulders, carved around 1350. The Gothic reticulation is said to depict no fewer than 600 medicinal herbs. Nearby is the Franconian museum of brewery, open from Monday to Friday between 13.00 and 16.00.

Music in Bamberg is also enough to entice a visit, with an organ concert every Saturday evening from the beginning of May to the end of October, as well as the performances of the city symphony orchestra and the Bamberg baroque ensemble. Those fond of lighter musical fare will enjoy the works performed by the Franconian concert orchestra in the Zentralsaal. Those who like more boisterous fun should come at the end of August to sit in the open air, quaffing and eating and watching the dancers during the Sand Church Fair. Obviously too this is a centre for walking and for boat trips.

Drive on north-west from Bamberg by the B26 along the River Main (or, if you are in a hurry, by the motorway) and after twenty-six kilometres you reach Schweinfurt. The road passes by castles and through two walled towns with half-timbered buildings, namely Zeil am Main and Haßfurt. Schweinfurt itself boasts a Gothic church of St Johannes, which incorporates some calm Romanesque elements. Although this town (which prospers on making engines and ball-bearings) was much damaged in World War II, it also possesses a lovely restored town hall of 1572.

If you go north instead of west from Bamberg, after Breiengüßbach the B4 shortly brings you to Coburg. Devotees of that threatened breed, royal families, will visit Coburg and be astonished at the way this duchy sat its sons and daughters on European thrones. The link with Britain is impressive enough. The first connection took place in 1816, when the former King of the Belgians, Prince Leopold of Saxe-Coburg, married Princess Charlotte, heir to the British throne. She died in child birth a year later. Next a widowed Coburg princess married the Duke of Kent. They called their daughter Victoria, and in 1837 she ascended the British throne. Almost incredibly, the Coburg family managed to marry Prince Albert of Saxe-Coburg to his royal cousin, and he became consort to Queen Victoria.

Memories of the prolific princes and princesses who made such politically astute matches are mostly to be found in Coburg. They hover around the splendid State rooms of the Renaissance Ehrenburg palace, whispering to the visitors on guided tours. Albert, the prince-consort, also boasts his statue in the cobbled Marktplatz, turning his back on the Stadthaus and indeed also ignoring some extremely fine gabled houses. The statue of Duke Ernst I stands in the palace square, a garden whose arcades give way to the Hofgarten, landscaped in the English style, which rises to his right. High beyond it is what the people of Coburger Land dubb the Franconian crown, the mighty Schloß that has dominated the town for nearly a thousand years.

In 1530 Martin Luther arrived with the Protestant Elector of Saxony to stay in Veste Coburg. Here he worked on what is in many respects the basis of modern German, his translation of the Bible. He preached in the church of St Moritz, a building of the fourteenth and sixteenth centuries whose lines worthily complement Coburg's half-timbered houses and its three old city gates. Do go inside St Moritz, if only to see the alabaster tomb which a Thuringian sculptor named Bergner built in 1598 for Duke Johann Frederick II. Above all, visit the triple-ringed Veste Coburg, its art collection matching its splendid halls. It opens in summer from 09.30 to 13.00 and from 14.00 to 17.00, except on Mondays. The tourist office of Coburg is at No. 4 Herrengasse.

Drive south-east from Coburg to arrive at the mecca of Wagnerites, Bayreuth. The way runs through Kronach, the birthplace of Lukas Cranach whose work hangs in Veste Coburg. Though an industrial town, Kronach's old city still preserves walls and gates, as well as – hanging in its Renaissance town hall – three original works by its most famous son. The heart of Kulmbach, the next town on the way to Bayreuth, boasts medieval fortifications, a town hall with a rococo façade and the sixteenth-century Plassenburg.

Bayreuth's musical tradition goes back much further than Wagner. It stems from the time of Margrave Friedrich I, who ruled here in the first half of the fifteenth century. When the margraves made the town their principal residence in the seventeenth century, this tradition was given an enormous boost. Once the disruptions of the Thirty Years War were over, Italian as well as Bavarian and Prussian musicians were lured here. The Bolognese architect Giuseppi Galli-Bibiena designed the Markgräfliches opera house in Bayreuth in 1764, and though the court moved to Ansbach five years later, local interest in opera persisted – though at a less well-endowed level.

It was the eighteenth-century opera house that attracted Wagner to Bayreuth in 1871, when he was looking for a concert hall large enough to stage his *Ring*. Finding after all that the existing opera house, in spite of boasting one of the largest stages in Germany, was not what he wanted, the composer determined to build one of his own in the town. Financed – though only in part – by King Ludwig II, Wagner obtained a site just outside Bayreuth, near the former Residenz of the mar-graves. He laid the foundation stone on 22 May 1872. The interior of the pink and white Festspielhaus is today like a classical amphitheatre. It is acoustically perfect (at least for the music of Wagner) and seats 1,800 spectators. The Wagner festival takes place in late-July and August.

Galli-Bibiena's rococo opera house is far more beautiful. Its façade is by the French architect Joseph de Saint-Pierre, its interior entirely of wood, save for the chandeliers, and its own acoustics perfectly adapted to the annual performances of baroque music by the Munich opera. You can visit it, except on Mondays, each day from 09.00 to 11.30 and from 13.30 to 16.00. Nearby in Maximilianstraße is the Altes Schloß, designed by Caspar Vischer in 1566. The long, elegant Neues Schloß lies south of the opera house, another work by the court architect Joseph de Saint-Pierre, and can be visited during the same times as the old Schloß.

The villa which Wagner built for himself in 1873 looks down on the garden of this castle, and nearby what is now his museum the composer and Cosima lie buried (whereas Franz Liszt had to make do with the local cemetery). Inside the museum I found touching the photographs of such of Wagner's ladies as Mathilde Wesendonck, who inspired *Tristan and Isolde*. The endless photographs of past performances of the operas wearied me. Some may prefer making use of the ice-rink or swimming pools, or even taking a guided tour of Maisels brewery and coopers' museum, which is housed at No. 40 Kulmbacher Straße in a brewery of 1887 (tours start at 10.00 from Mondays to Thursdays). Oddly enough after this rich diet of opera, Bayreuth's town symbol remains the massive twin-towers of its parish church, which is dedicated to the Holy Trinity and stands in Kanzleistraße.

Bayreuth, like Bamberg, is in splendid hiking country. Though I do not ski, looking back I still remember the pleasure of simply walking or swimming here. The Bavarians themselves frequently tell you, 'Franconia is not just famous for its wines.' True: no one should miss the delights of the Fichtel mountains, the possibility of strenuous hikes in the Franconian forest, the Altmühl valley nature park, and countless snow-bedecked Alpine-like hills, down which people breathtakingly tumble on skis. For me even more entrancing are (to borrow a phrase from Jerome K. Jerome) the 'wrinkled walls and grey towers' of this part of Bavaria.

Sometimes one's day here can be altogether ennobling. Staying once with the sage of Oberlaimbach I remember visiting in twenty-four hours two superb buildings. The first was the magical Schloß Weißenstein, which stands to the north-east of Neustadt an der Aisch at Pommersfelden and, after the Residenz at Würzburg, must surely be Bavaria's finest eighteenth-century palace (its architects were J. Dientzenhofer and the Austrian Lukas von Hildebrandt). The second was Kloster Ebrach, a magnificent Cistercian monastery, lying a few kilometres to the west. That day a young woman was practising on the organ of the monastery church, so I listened for half an hour to a free Bach concert. Then I drove back to Oberlaimbach and drank another *Pokal* of cool white wine in the company of Herr Rückert at the Gasthof zum Adler.

Index

Index